Prenatal Bonding Analysis

This book presents a novel psychoanalytic and psychotherapeutic method which enables expectant mothers to establish communication with their unborn babies.

After an exploration of the root aspects of pre- and perinatal psychology and psychoanalysis, details of the practice of prenatal bonding analysis are introduced. The volume concludes with 15 interviews where mothers who experienced the bonding analysis give first-hand accounts of their encounters.

With its theoretical, practical and testimonial threefold structure, the book aims at reaching out to both specialists and a general readership, especially prospective parents.

György Hidas, MD (1925–2012) was a psychiatrist and psychoanalyst. He specialized primarily in the work of Sándor Ferenczi and prenatal bonding analysis.

Jenő Raffai, PhD (1954–2015) was a psychologist and psychoanalyst with a main focus on pre- and perinatal psychology and bonding analysis.

Judit Vollner pursued a career as an actress and then as a science journalist. Currently, she leads communication trainings based on acting techniques.

Prenatal Bonding Analysis

The Invisible Umbilical Cord

György Hidas, Jenő Raffai and Judit Vollner

Routledge
Taylor & Francis Group

LONDON AND NEW YORK

Cover image: © Getty Images

First English edition published 2023
by Routledge
4 Park Square, Milton Park, Abingdon, Oxon OX14 4RN

and by Routledge
605 Third Avenue, New York, NY 10158

Routledge is an imprint of the Taylor & Francis Group, an informa business

© 2023 György Hidas, Jenő Raffai and Judit Vollner

First published in Hungarian in 2002 as *Lelki köldökzsinór – Beszélgetek a kisbabámmal* by Válasz könyvkiadó, Budapest

Translation by Krisztina Horváth and Anna Major

British Library Cataloguing-in-Publication Data
A catalogue record for this book is available from the British Library

Library of Congress Cataloging-in-Publication Data
Names: Hidas, György, author. | 1 Raffai, Jenő, author | 1 Vollner, Judit, author
Title: Prenatal bonding analysis : the invisible umbilical cord / György Hidas, Jenő Raffai, and Judit Vollner
Description: 1 Abingdon, Oxon ; New York, NY : Routledge, 2 | Includes bibliographical references
Identifiers: LCCN 2022032215 (print) | LCCN 202203 (ebook) | ISBN 9781032364230 (hardback) | ISBN 9781032346335 (paperback) | ISBN 9781003331865 (ebook)
Subjects.
Classification: LCC BF720.P73 H53 2023 (print) | LCC BF720.P73 (ebook) | DDC 618.2/4019--dc23/eng/20220823
LC record available at https://lccn.loc.gov/2022032215
LC ebook record available at https://lccn.loc.gov/2022032216

ISBN: 9781032364230 (hbk)
ISBN: 9781032346335 (pbk)
ISBN: 9781003331865 (ebk)

DOI: 10.4324/9781003331865

Typeset in Bembo
by Deanta Global Publishing Services, Chennai, India

Contents

Foreword

A revolution is taking place in present-day psychology, regarding the field of prenatal, intrauterine research. It has been proven that a human life, in psychological terms, begins not at birth, but conception. A new culture is blossoming at the heels of this discovery, which brings us closer to the roots of our being and prompts us to once and for all change our perception of humanity and the world. It is especially significant for us that two Hungarian psychoanalysts, György Hidas and Jenő Raffai, developed the methodology of establishing a connection between a mother and the foetus developing in her womb, the so-called mother–foetus bonding analysis, which aids the development of an invisible umbilical cord carrying signals and information between the two. Some international scientific circles deem this practice the greatest "invention" since psychoanalysis; with its help, it is not only possible to set not-yet-born infants on an optimal course of development but also to intervene with potentially life-saving results in what were thought to be purely biological processes, such as the untimely atrophy of the placenta or the rupture of the foetal membrane, which have been the cause of foetal death and premature and physically harmful births.

In 2001, the United Nations commissioned a panel of 12 scientists to, as part of its International Decade for a Culture of Peace and Non-violence for the Children of the World initiative, develop a parenting programme which it could recommend to the governments of its constituent nations. Jenő Raffai, one of the authors of this book and the president of the Hungarian Society for Pre- and Perinatal Medicine and Psychology, was also invited to join this exclusive panel – a proof of the international acclaim of the results of Hungarian research. An international training programme will soon be initiated to adopt this new technique.

The recognition of intrauterine connections may enter common knowledge as a veritable mental bomb, so we can say without exaggeration that our book uncovers thus far unknown depths of the creation of life and the human psyche, of the origin of interpersonal relationships and attempts to solve the mystery of the earliest, most profound and most intimate relationship that can ever exist between two people. Perhaps we are not using too great a word when we are of the opinion that this informative book, accessible to all, is the first in the world to report of the experiences of expectant mothers who have established an unfiltered connection with their baby still in the womb, constitutes a sensation. In the self-revealing accounts, which are shockingly powerful and sometimes filled with humour, new mothers attempt to express the intangible state in which they were connected to their baby. The honest retellings see the mothers reliving the scenes that took them aback, the coded messages, the dialogues taking place after a transfer of thoughts. From their accounts, the stories of how an unknown dimension, a new channel, where they could experience the joy of finding one another, their babies' emotions, intentions, and even their character, unfold sensitively in front of the reader. Naturally, mothers with different personalities and attitudes approached their babies through differing pathways, thus experiencing contact at various levels of intensity. However, they are unanimous when it comes to the effects of prenatal bonding analysis. Following birth, there was recognition in the locked eyes of every mother and her baby, and gained proof through thousands of tiny signs of the already established relationship they had which needed not to be created, only continued. All mothers reported of their child's psychological harmony, their happiness, trust, and the increased rate of their intellectual and motor-skill development. (The maturity and the intelligence quotient of children – well above their age level – who partook in bonding analysis have been confirmed via measurements of the latest studies.)

Prenatal Bonding Analysis is an informative book for the average reader, for the parent expecting and planning for a child, for those interested in psychology, and all who are susceptible to the changes in the spiritual perspective of our time. In the first seven chapters, Jenő Raffai and György Hidas present, via the underlying science, in a clear manner rich in turns of phrase, the roots of prenatal psychology as well as the technique of bonding analysis. The enthralling, exciting first-hand accounts, which, as the editor of the book, I myself recorded, can be read in the second half.

My co-authors, that is, the developers of the technique, György Hidas and Jenő Raffai, and I feel it important to attach an explanation to the third chapter, and thus allow the reader a glance into the inner workings of the process. Initially, our intention was to have the experts explain, in commentaries at the end of the interviews, a few potentially confounding events. However, being in possession of the transcripts, we decided that it would be a mistake to interrupt these experiences with dry, rational explanations – moreover, I should not even obstruct the flow of erupting emotions and memories with my questions; this would be overly pedantic, fastidious even. The arising questions thus do not remain open, for the reader can, to an extent, find an answer in the first chapters of the book, into which the authors have quasi pre-incorporated the commentaries.

The content-appropriate format also revealed itself during the documentation of the interviews, which, due to the informative nature of the book, is unusual. It turned out that these emotions and images surfacing from unconscious depths take shape best in a monologue format, well-known from drama and literature. I endeavoured to avoid a rounded-out, artificial text, so I strived to preserve the momentary nature, honesty and dramatic sway of the accounts by including the occasional stutter, the search for words, the wandering and sometimes dormant trains of thought, and the revealing slip of the tongue. The ideal intake method, in essence – just as that of the theatrical genre – would be audiovisual; however, this is still a purely written text. Dear Reader, please then "listen" to these intimate retellings with joy!

I would like to thank all 15 mothers, who, in the interest of our education, laid bare these so-far-secret thoughts and emotions, personal and stemming from the deepest sources.

It by all means deserves mentioning that the idea for the book presented itself in the company of Judit Révi, my friend and colleague, a year and a half ago. She, however, was unable to participate in the creation of the book due to a prolonged stay abroad. I owe her my thanks for her intellectual assistance and our inspirational brainstorming sessions.

Judit Vollner

Introduction

The first environment of the unborn child is the womb. There is a relation-ship between mother and foetus from the very first moment, and not only on a physical and biological level but also on a psychological one. They are con-nected by a spiritual umbilical cord. Every development in the mother's psy-chological world affects the body and soul of the baby. However, the stimuli and stressors of the external world reach the baby as well. The latest research shows that the mother's attitude towards her unborn baby has great bearing on the child's development, postnatal personality, relationships and integration into society. The child's experiences in the womb influence its physical and psychological development, personality and the quality of later relationships.

Pregnancy and birth encapsulate the deepest questions of human life and society, and, at the same time, are the deepest and most intimate events pos-sible between two people. Society – with its laws, regulations, prohibitions and recommendations, material conditions, security or insecurity, formal ethi-cal requisites and informal moral commands and so on – has an effect on our intimate life. Therefore, the most intimate event, the birth of a child, becomes statistical data for, and macrosocietal subject of, demographic balance, societal reproduction, labour force politics, military interests, or in the case of decreas-ing birth rates, a matter of life and death for the nation.

Human life is continuous. Our common sense tells us that it starts with con-ception and ends with death. However, our experience as psychotherapists tells us that human life starts as far back as two generations at the least, in the home of the maternal and paternal grandparents. We inherit not only our genes and chromosomal conditions, but also our epigenetics, social and cultural condi-tions, as well as psychosocial structures. They start to take effect even before conception, as seen with wanted or planned children, who get a much better chance in life compared to unwanted or unplanned ones. The prenatal period is not only just one phase in the continuity of our life, such as birth, childhood, adolescence, adulthood, menopause, old age or death. These phases are inter-dependent, while each one of them has its own specificity. Human life is con-tinuous; each developmental stage is equally important, as they are inseparable from each other and together create the wholeness of human life. The human being forms a whole on this continuum with all his or her human functions, including the physical, biochemical, immunological, endocrinological and psychological. Therefore, there is no single occurrence in human phenomenology that we can trace back to only one phase or function for an explanation.

This continuity starts in the mother's womb. What the foetus experiences in the womb is a learning process, too. As David Chamberlain puts it: "the womb is the first school of life, and we have all attended it." Learning is a necessary condition of survival because it makes the organism able to adapt to different conditions. There is no survival without adaptation, and this is not possible without previous experiences. This requires a capacity for memory and retention. The foetus swims in a river of information from the start, which it receives through different biochemical channels. These are transformed into memory traces and stored, and become the potential sources of learning processes. It is possible, therefore, to activate these prenatal memory traces and information sources in later life.

Every integrative process – whether biochemical, hormonal, immunological or psychological – starts at conception. Prenatal stress, depression, hormonal imbalances, immunological problems, infections and environmental influences, relationship disorders, as well as parental attitudes and conflicts, all affect the foetal brain and the development of personality. Therefore, the prenatal stage of life possesses great preventive potentials when it comes to psychological, mental and physical challenges.

One of the preventive methods is mother–foetus bonding analysis, which we developed in the mid-1990s, after a decade-long research process. With this method, the mother and foetus can establish a deep, unprecedented relationship with each other. They can take their fate into their own hands; they are capable of promoting the development of one another as much as the limits of possibility will allow them to.

György Hidas, Jenő Raffai

1 The intelligent foetus

We face an exceptionally difficult task in trying to define intelligence. It is no accident that no one has been able to do this perfectly so far. Too many people use the concept in too many ways for its content to be well-definable. We talk about intelligence in contexts of kinetic, affective, even social, thus associating more to the concept than merely the cognitive capacities. When talking about the intelligence of the foetus, we will attempt to outline all of these factors.

It is possible that the mere title of this chapter is provocative in and of itself in a culture which regards foetuses as vegetative beings, whose psychological development starts only after birth. Scientific research has confuted this archaic prejudice on many occasions. However, this way of thinking has been with us for over a thousand years. It is part of our evolutionary and cultural inheritance, encapsulated in an entity which is among the least changeable in the world: human consciousness.

In trying to describe the intelligence of the foetus, we must take into account the deterministic influence of both mother and father, as well as all those who are emotionally significant to the two. The continuous and active dialogue with all of these people fundamentally influences the emotional and intellectual development of the foetus. Consequently, the developmental level of newborns varies greatly at the time of birth. In consonance with the newest scientific research, we therefore seek to emphasize that environmental influences outweigh genetic factors in significance with regard to the development of intelligence. Researchers in Pittsburgh (McGue 1977) concluded that genetic predisposition is responsible for only one-third of the factors that promote intelligence, while intrauterine environmental factors are responsible for the remaining two-thirds, following a reexamination and analysis of all available data. The authors define the intrauterine environment as not only the mother's hormonal and biochemical network, but her interrelational systems and their influence on the development of the foetus as well.

Scientific research tells us that human behaviour is complex and cohesively built from the earliest stages on. For example, the human heart starts beating one month after conception, and, naturally, continues to do so through the intricate process of its own development. Similarly, the nervous system works continuously and its functioning makes its own further development

DOI: 10.4324/9781003331865-1

and differentiation possible. From the tenth week on, movements thus far spastic and irregular can be observed becoming refined and elegant in form. Further evidence shows babies engaging in motility-related games from the middle of the second trimester and onward.

Prenatal behaviour

Movement has several functions in and of itself, exploration, self-defence, self-expression and communication being a few among them. Body language expresses need, interest, ability and cognitive processes in a manner that can hardly be misunderstood. It therefore exceeds verbal communication in many respects, as it is formed earlier on, accelerates all forms of communication, recurs often, and carries the same meaning lifelong. We all speak this language. Chamberlain (1996) divided intrauterine behaviour and manners of movement into three main categories: self-induced, reactive, and interactive.

Self-induced activity

Ultrasonographic investigations tell us that foetal motility emerges from the sixth week on, and manifests itself in the following movements by the tenth week: hand to head, hand to mouth and lips, extension and contraction of limbs, spinning around its own axis, opening and closing of mouth, and swallowing. These movements suggest that the baby's repertoire of intrauterine movements is not reflex-based, or based on reactivity to external stimuli, but is instead spontaneous and self-induced. A fact of foetal life is the earlier appearance of self-induced movement than its externally induced counterparts. Interestingly, twins often exhibit entirely independent profiles of motion, which they carry with themselves postpartum. Tajani and Ianniruberto (1990) observed almost all babies between the tenth and fifteenth week already respond within moments to the mother laughing or coughing.

Babies are able to continuously move for a maximum of seven and a half minutes by the end of the first trimester, with resting periods lasting a maximum of five and a half minutes. Analysis of movements from the third trimester shows these motions to remain present until the baby simply runs out of adequate space to perform them. Babies begin travelling from one end of the uterus to the other as they grow, thrusting themselves away from the uterine wall by foot. This travel requires an elegant, lengthwise spiralling movement, consisting of the turning of the spinal column, shoulders and head, as well as the use of spinal column muscles. This artistically executed manoeuvre stays unseen for several weeks after birth. The root cause of this lies in the momentary inability of the newborn's musculoskeletal system to cope with gravitational struggles.

Immobility merits a short mention as well, which also has not avoided the interest of researchers. Milani-Comparetti (1981) presupposed three causes: pathological morphosis (death, paralysis, exposure to toxins etc.), anticipation of biological events (e.g., urination) and anticipation of an upcoming movement. We can add a fourth cause based on our own experience: the period of registration and processing of external information. Furthermore, some observations include the child becoming immobile while the mother is dreaming (as if watching the movie of her dreams), and resuming energetic activity the moment the mother's dream state ceases.

Getting back to spontaneous movement: foetuses occasionally swallow amniotic fluid even before the tenth week. Movements of the tongue and swallowing mechanisms activate before the 14th week. Some studies show that swallowing activity responds positively to sweet, and negatively to bitter, tastes. Newborn and premature babies retain this preference for sweet taste, which carries with it soothing and alleviating effects. Thumb sucking starts around the ninth week and is a preferred activity of the foetuses; as they entertain not only their fingers, but their toes as well. Some suck their thumbs with such frequency that a callus forms, which can be observed at birth.

Male foetuses start to have erections from the 16th week on, an unmistakable, but unexpected precursor of infantile sexuality.

Foetuses are very active with their hands in the womb. They touch not only their toes, but also, and perhaps more frequently, the umbilical cord. The coordination between hands and mouth, from what we can observe immediately after birth, is the result of continuous interaction between hands, cord, feet and face.

Breathing movements are performed from the 24th week onward. Initially, these happen in the form of isolated impulses. After 28 weeks, these movements become periodical, and are uniform after thirty-six weeks. In the third trimester, breathing movements are present 30–80% of the time. Researchers interpret their presence as a sign of good health. The cessation of breathing movements is a threatening sign. It tends to happen if the mother ingests narcotics, smokes cigarettes or drinks alcohol.

Research focused on sleeping has proven that premature babies are very active dreamers; the youngest ones being the most active. Those born around the 30th week dream for nearly 100% of the duration of sleep, while this number falls to 67% for those born between the 33rd and 36th week, and to a mere 50% by the 40th week. Time spent dreaming decreases to 30% by six months after birth. This data is extremely interesting, and from it we can draw some daring conclusions and build hypotheses. Dreams are accompanied by vivid and dramatic movements of the body, face and hands, as well as grimaces, whimpers and laughter. During the rapid eye movement (REM) phase of sleep which indicates dreaming, there are 10–15 second periods accompanied by convulsive movement of fingers and the extremities. This can allude to "bad" dreams. It is also possible to interpret harmonious movements, as well as smiling, as suggestive of "pleasant" dreams.

The earliest human smiles can be observed on the face of dreaming premature babies (Emde 1971). We see smiles on the faces of babies who were born on term less often, but this depends more on circumstances than on abilities or disposition. There are some cultures, such as the Thai, where most of the babies who took part in programmes focused on the development of mother–foetus relations smiled at the time of birth. I myself saw in Heidelberg, in 1995, the video recording that showed these smiling babies during their birth.

(There are different bonding development programmes in several countries with the aim of securing optimal intrauterine and extrauterine conditions for the emotional and intellectual development of the foetuses, and strengthening the bond between foetus and parents. They offer different methods and practices to expectant mothers during the various stages of pregnancy. For more information, see the tables at the end of this book.)

Most babies are able to mirror the smile of their parents from the sixth week after birth. The exceptions are babies who took part in some kind of programme for bonding development, as well as newborns who took part in a learning experiment and learned to recognize and solve problems. In these cases, they smile spontaneously, which researchers call a cognitive (knowing, related to thinking) smile, as opposed to a social one.

Reactive behaviour

There are foetal movements that are triggered by imminent danger from the external environment. These movements may be defensive, deflective or of an unsettled, rapid nature. We can interpret these movements as early expressions of organizing behaviour, or creative strategies to tackle the world. Without the mastering of these prenatal, self-organizing defensive strategies, the baby would not be able to survive, regardless of any parental support.

The first reactive behaviour was observed in the seventh gestational week (in the case of an aborted foetus). The face of the foetus was touched with a strand of hair, prompting the baby to turn its face, bending the torso and pelvis in such a way that it was able to push the hair away with its extended arm. I must emphasize once again that this baby was seven weeks old (Humphrey 1978). This tactile sensitivity (a defensive zone, which the foetus attempts to guard) expands rapidly. It includes the genital area by the tenth week; the hands, arms and legs by the 11th; and the soles by the 12th. By the 17th week, the entire skin surface is subject to this sensitivity.

Intense light can also be fear-inducing for the foetus. The direction of such light at the head of the foetus increases the heart rate, which indicates a stress reaction.

The appearance of a needle in the amniotic fluid can also be frightening for the foetus. In the case of amniocentesis, usually done between the 14th and 16th gestational week, the gynaecologist drives a needle into the amniotic fluid under ultrasonographic monitoring. The expectant mothers can thus follow on the monitor as the foetuses turn away from the needle, although their eyelids remain closed within the interim of the tenth and 26th weeks. Birnholz et al. (1978) observed a 24-week-old foetus who was accidentally touched by the needle. After turning away from it, the baby stopped the needle with one hand

and hit it several times. Some foetuses cease all movement during amniocentesis after the fluid has been taken, as if in a state of shock, and the frequency of their heart rate drops dramatically. According to some studies, this is paralleled by a drop in the frequency of breathing movements. For some foetuses, it takes days to recover to their previous frequency of breathing movements. Gynaecologists do not understand how this minimal loss of amniotic fluid can lead to such dramatic reactions, especially since the lost amount of fluid is regenerated very quickly.

Stress reactions were also observed during intrauterine blood transfusions using a needle. The levels of cortisone and endorphin hormones increased drastically, which many researchers interpreted as the first indications of pain (Giannakoulopoulos et al. 1994).

Movement and emotions are inseparably interconnected. Expectant mothers who attended a rock concert reported their babies kicking very strongly during the event, which led to a broken rib in one case (Olds 1986). The protestations in response to intense music are a good example of the babies' self-expression through means of movement.

The earliest evidence for emotional expression lies in the shocking photographs taken of 12- to 15-week-old terminated foetuses, showing ruffled eyebrows and grimaces (Humphrey 1978). Furthermore, Humphrey, by means of an analysis of available literature, found suggestions of audible, in-utero crying in the cases of foetuses terminated between the 21st and 23rd weeks. Truby (1971), the first to analyze the crying of newborns with the aid of a spectrogram, analyzed the in-utero crying of a foetus of 900 grams, aborted at the 27th week, and found many similarities among the sample and the mother's own voice. In-utero crying had thus far seemed impossible, as it requires air, at the foetus' larynx no less. Under certain, considerably rare circumstances, air can seep into this area, thus making crying audible. Thus far, 140 cases have been recorded. While we can be certain of the origin of emotions predating birth, crying indubitably becomes far more forceful after the event. The heart rate becomes changeable, with peak readings exceeding 220 beats per minute. Thus, we cannot claim to be speaking of a harmless phenomenon. Crying is an unequivocal signal, forcing attention to the suffering experienced by the baby. Crying must not be provoked under any circumstance, as if it were a healthy exercise to practice. Crying is formally qualified as the fifth behavioural condition. The first four are, in order, calm sleep, active sleep, calm awakeness and active awakeness.

Interactive-social movements

Ultrasonographic observations of twins have demonstrated interactive behaviour in the womb most convincingly. Research by Alessandra Piontelli (1992) is eminent in this field. We are going to examine her work in more detail in a separate chapter of this book. Here we will quote only one or two of her observations, regarding Luca and Alicia, whose behaviour she examined regularly for hours. It was usual for the twins to frequently and tenderly touch each other along the membrane dividing their living space. Around the 20th week, the young man was very active and alert, while the young lady was quiet and sleepy. The boy approached the membrane in regular intervals and awakened his sister who reacted to this every time. Before both of them started their own separate activities, they had rubbed their heads and faces against each other, kissed each other, stroked each other's face and connected their feet. Piontelli called them the friendly twins. The quality of their relations which formed around the 20th week remained after their birth as well. At one year of age they could walk, started to talk and spent much time together. They could often be seen playing their favourite game of using the curtain of the living room as a kind of mock dividing membrane. Luca draw the curtain, Alicia who was standing behind it popped out her head, and with loud laughing they started to stroke each other as they had done in their pre-natal past.

We do not often find such detailed and elaborate observations. Timothy Johnson, for example, recorded twins fighting in the womb. Birgit Arabin (1994), similar to Piontelli, recorded kissing twins. The facial expression of the baby who received the kiss changed to mirror happiness. These accounts are not only meant to reflect on social interactions; they are about emotions. Who would have thought earlier that this is possible around the 20th week? Twins let us know what we should have intuited quite some time ago: the womb is not only the first school of life, but the place of continuous interaction, where interactivity is more social than egocentric.

Contributions of research on premature births

The possibility of continuous observation of prematurely born babies enables us to gain a deeper understanding of behaviour before the 40th week. For example, research shows premature babies reacting favourably to gentle touches and massages. According to the research of Tiffany Field (1981, 1987), those babies who were in continuous physical contact and who were massaged reacted well: they breathed more effectively, were less frightened, did not clench their hands into a fist, were more alert and more active than their peers in the control group. Evelyn Thoman (1993) had similar results from her own tests. Babies who had continuous physical contact with their mothers purposefully chose the breathing teddy bear as opposed to the inanimate one, and thereafter formed close contact with it. It is noteworthy that they not only learned how to form attachments with the breathing bears, but they also spent more time in quiet, restful sleep compared to the control group.

Prenates also react well to music. In one premature birth ward, weight gain was attributed to increased exposure to music (Chapman 1975). According to other experiments, the oxygen intake of the babies was increased by music, and overstimulated babies became calm (Collins, Kuck 1991). In another experiment, the researchers played noises that could be heard in the womb combined with a female singing voice to excited premature babies. The result was a calm ward, which took less than ten minutes to assemble.

In a further fascinating experiment, Gatts and his colleagues (1994) tried to imitate the mother's walking with a moving bed for prenates whose weight was less than 2000 grams, alongside simulated intrauterine sounds. The babies in the experimental group gained more weight, more quickly, had fewer lapses in breathing, and exhibited greater maturity from perspectives both mental and emotional than the control group. On average, they left the hospital eight days before their partners in the control group.

We know from interactions with premature babies that they are able to imitate the mimicry and gestures of adults. This is an aptitude that was initially only observed in completely mature babies. From the 35th week on, they are able to imitate the facial expressions related to happiness, sorrow and surprise (Field et al. 1983).

Mosser (1989) has managed to prove that premature babies can register if somebody is talking directly to them, reacting with an increased heart rate, which slows back down once the speaker addresses someone else, and rises back up when the baby is addressed again.

Learning and memory

The simplest definition of learning is as behavioural change resulting from new experiences. We acquire new experiences by perceiving and processing stimuli from our environment. This is the requirement of the learning process. As we can assess from the above, foetuses answer actively to stimuli coming from the mother's body and the external environment. The scheme of this process is that stimuli coming from the environment upset the baby's equilibrium, which it can recover by accommodating to the change in the environment through perception and processing of stimuli, an equivalent behavioural change, and change in experiential patterns.

A lot of research has proven the existence of foetal learning, from the simple to the more complex. We will cite some of them here. De Casper (1994) investigated foetal learning and memory for ten years, with smart and unique equipment that he himself invented. It was a special pacifier, connected to a tape recorder. By sucking on the pacifier with different frequencies, the babies were able to activate different stories and musical motives. In one of these experiments, expectant mothers were asked to read aloud the same fairy tale to the foetus twice a day in the last six weeks of their pregnancies. The fairy tale was recorded on tape with two other unknown texts of the same length. Within several hours after their birth, the babies were able to activate the now known fairy tale with their sucking rhythm. Other experiments have proven that newborns can recognize their mother's voice among others, and even show preference to their father's voice over other male voices.

Most of the research concerned with foetal learning and memory has investigated only the simplest learning processes (that is, when during the conditioning a stimulus is followed by a response). Few studies have tried to clarify the regulational and motivational basis of learning. According to the results of new developmental research, the primary motivation is reinforced during the learning process, with the aim of elevating motivation to solve the next problem. Hypotheses are created and tested during learning. Babies create hypotheses about the connection of events, at least on a perceptual level. Naturally, the way babies think differs from the way adults think. They judge an event as true or untrue dependent on whether it has already happened. Sallenbach (1993) has investigated whether foetuses are able to create hypotheses and found the same results that newborns produced.

Auditory behaviour

Certain cross-cultural features of rhythm, melody and harmony ultimately stem from sounds produced by blood circulation and the mother's movements and speech as heard in utero by the foetus. That being said, *the emotional dimension of music originates from the connection between mother and foetus, and is not dependent on hearing capacity.*

The foetal ear begins to pick up sounds some four to five months before birth. The inner ear of the foetus reaches adult size, form and function one to two months before birth. The amniotic fluid transmits sounds to the foetal ear with little, if at all, muffling, covering over most of the audible frequency range. Only high frequencies, those above about 2 kHz, are sharply attenuated.

Foetuses respond to sounds during the last three or four months before birth by motor activity such as kicking, accompanied by an elevated heart rate and neural responses of the cerebral cortex observable through EEG.

Foetuses are repeatedly exposed to a range of audible, often quite loud sounds. These sounds may be divided into four main categories:

a. Sounds produced by the mother's cardiovascular system, especially the blood vessels in the uterine wall.
b. Sounds associated with bodily movements of the mother, especially walking.
c. The mother's voice and breathing.
d. Sounds associated with drinking, eating and digestion.

Before addressing these categories in greater detail, we must comment on music as such, in order to better understand its prenatal origins. The musical culture of our world is so colourful and diverse, that the identification of cross-cutting similarities requires an approach to research that is immensely systematic. Music theory is primarily concerned with individual musical styles and cultures, which differ to such great extents that a ubiquitous, uniform aspect may seem unlikely to exist. Even the oft-mentioned octave equivalency is lacking in some melodies, or is expressed with considerable variety in different musical cultures.

However, if we do find ourselves in search of such similarities, we can assess the following:

1. Virtually all human societies include music among their essential cultural activities. No human society has ever been discovered in which music did not play some sort of role.
2. In most societies, specific kinds of music are associated with specific kinds of emotion, and are used to arouse such emotions. Music is chosen for different social functions (e.g., entertainment, celebration, mourning, political events and so on), depending on the kind of emotions it is supposed to evoke. However, the specific relation between musical structure and emotions may differ among cultures.
3. We can categorize any acoustic structure used anywhere in the world according to the following parameters:

Rhythm: evokes an isochronous (equally spaced) beat or pulse sensation. The range and distribution of frequencies corresponds approximately to the range and distribution of human heartbeat and walking rates.

Melody: involves the rising and falling in pitch of a single voice. The range and distribution of pitches in music both instrumental and vocal is almost completely similar to the range and distribution of non-musical human vocalizations, especially speech.

Harmony: involves the blending of simultaneous voices, such that new timbres are created and the apparent number of voices is less than the actual number.

Now the question arises, how could prenatal experience explain the aforementioned similarities? Some experiments will be shown on the following pages which clearly demonstrate that an individual's prenatal experience influences that individual's perception of music. Well-known musicians such as Menuhin and Rubinstein claim that their musical careers began in the womb. That being said, for the moment we are primarily interested in auditory patterns heard repeatedly by virtually all humans before birth – the internal sounds of the mother's body.

The prenatal auditory environment includes sound patterns remarkably similar to musical structures. There, sounds are produced by the maternal cardiovascular system, movements and the voice. Infants have been found to be remarkably sensitive to elementary musical structures. According to Trehub (1987), infants can distinguish between long and short events on the basis of their tempos (basis of rhythm), perceive pitch contour (basis of melody), as well as detect harmonic pitch intervals such as the octave, fifth, and third (bases of harmony). Thus, infant sensitivity to music is a consequence of the constant exposure to the sounds produced by the mother's cardiovascular system and movements, while infants' recognition of harmony and melody goes back to the mother's voice.

Rhythm

The maternal heartbeat, as heard by the foetus, has been described by Salk (1962) as an imprinting stimulus. Imprinting stimuli are generally learned quickly during a critical period of development and strongly affect perception thereafter. Experiments show that heartbeat-like sounds played at moderate rates have a calming effect on newborn babies, causing them to cry less, sleep more, breathe more deeply, digest better and become ill less often, while sounds resembling a faster heartbeat can have the reverse effect.

Furthermore, this connectivity with the mother's heartbeat also helps explain the higher frequency of breastfeeding with the left breast, rather than the right.

A possible musical correlate of the sounds of a maternal heartbeat, at least in western music – notably, in the romantic music of nineteenth-century Europe, e.g., Chopin, Brahms, Liszt etc. – is the rubato (perceivable variations in tempo), which served to invoke various emotions in audiences. The emotion-inducing significance of the rubato may be linked to variations in the mother's heart rate, and its prenatal perceptions by the foetus.

The mother's emotional state is known to be shared by the foetus at some level, due to a hormonal identity among the two. The foetus may also pick up information about the mother's emotional state via cues such as tactile pressure (i.e., sense of touch) indicating tension, particular digestive sounds, vocal intonations typical of specific emotions, or even external sounds such as the voice of an angry partner. The foetus could thus learn to associate changes in heart rate with specific emotional qualities.

Another significant prenatal correlate of musical rhythms is the specific combination of sound and movement experienced by the foetus while its mother is walking. Bodily movements are perceptible to the foetus along with its own position in the womb due to the early maturation of the vestibular system. Prenatal experience of the mother's walking could underlie the soothing effect of cradle-rocking on babies, and could also explain why rhythm and dance are present in virtually all human cultures. Musical intuition suggests that the kind of rhythm produced by footstep sounds is qualitatively different from that produced by heartbeats. The time intervals between footfalls in walking are more regular or "metronomic" than the time intervals between heartbeats. This may be confirmed simply by watching people walk down the street and comparing the subjective impression of regularity with that of one's own pulse as it accelerates and decelerates in response to physiological functions such as inhalation and exhalation.

Prenatal conditioning by sounds associated with the mother's walking may thus underlie the experience of rhythm, as seen in African drum music and its western descendants, jazz and rock. The hypothesis of prenatal association between sound and movement when the mother walks is consistent with the strong dance-like or movement quality of non-rubato music. On the other hand, romantic music was primarily intended to be heard by a seated audience.

Another remarkable property of rhythm is how limited it is to auditory perception. Consequently, acoustic rhythms are perceived as more rhythmic or salient than those presented to other senses such as vision or touch. This is consistent with prenatal learning processes, since during this period the most salient prenatally perceptible stimuli with rhythmic properties are acoustic. If rhythm perception originated postnatally, one would expect visual rhythms to be just as strong as acoustic ones.

Musical experience shows that, in rhythmic sequences including regular alterations of low and high pitches, lower-pitched sounds are more likely than high-pitched sounds to function as musical down-beats. This observation is consistent with the generally low frequencies of prenatally audible heartbeat and footstep sounds.

Melody

The meaning of natural speech, as we know it, may be divided into at least two parts, here called the abstract and the gestural. The abstract is what is preserved when speech is written down. It includes the dictionary meaning of words and phrases, as well as grammatical constructions. The gestural part communicates important additional information such as the emotional state of the speaker, the emotional content of the utterance and the speaker's true intentions, and this does not necessarily correspond to the literal content.

The foetus is regularly exposed to its mother's speech, but of course it does not understand the abstract meaning of her words (presumptively, at least, although there is no need for a zealous adherence to this assumption). The gestural (metacommunicative) aspects are, however, far more likely to prove deterministic for the foetus. Speech research has shown that gross changes in fundamental frequency, usually referred to as prosody or speech intonation, carry a large proportion of the emotional content of speech. The prosody of the mother's speech thus may be one of the foetus' most important sources of information about the mother's emotional state – this is an important matter, given that the state of the foetus is primarily dependent on that of the mother. It is therefore plausible to suppose that foetuses are very sensitive to the intonation of their mother's speech. The speech of the mother has great importance in bonding analysis, as will be discussed later. There are many different programmes around the world aimed at developing mother–foetus bonding, but bonding analysis is the only one in which speech plays a role.

More recent studies suggest that children learn melodic contour before all else. This is not surprising given the importance of melodic contour in maternal speech. It is thus reasonable to conclude that the emotional meaning of a melody is primarily linked to its contour – a conclusion consistent with the idea that melodic perception has prenatal origins.

Harmony

One of the functions of the inner ear is to perform a frequency analysis of incoming sounds, encoding information on the frequencies and amplitudes of partial tones. The inner ear of the human foetus is fully grown and operational at least three months before birth, therefore the frequency analysis should occur in much the same way for the foetus as it does for adults. If the ability to perceive the pitch of complex tones is indeed acquired prenatally, then the newborns should have no trouble following the pitch of human voices. This is consistent with the results of a number of studies on the perceptual abilities of infants, including the ability at the age of one month to categorize speech sounds in much the same ways as adults do, as well as the ability of newborns to recognize their mother's voices.

We ought to have mentioned earlier that the balance-orienting, or vestibular, system is also responsible for musical sensitivity alongside the inner ear. This system can not only register movement and bodily position but it can sense rhythm, and analyze lower frequencies as well.

Because of the sensitivity of the vestibular apparatus, the foetus is able to perceive movements and changes of place connected to the sounds and noises created by the mother. The foetus hears not only the noises of respiration, speech, singing and walking, but also perceives the connected movements. Thus, perceptual patterns are determined by at least two perceptual modalities. That is why any of the mother's musical activity during her pregnancy influences the musical sensitivity of her baby. *The music provoking the ear and the vestibular apparatus simultaneously has much more impact on the development of musicality compared to the music perceived only through hearing.* When a mother listens to music passively during her pregnancy and does not respond to it with her body, she does not develop her baby's musicality as much. On the other hand, singing, melodic speech, "musically" rhythmical walking or dancing during pregnancy has a great impact on the development of the baby's musicality.

The musicality of the baby

The development of musical sensitivity is no less important in the first year after birth. Newborns spend a relatively long time with seemingly passive sleep during the first month (this is not the case for babies who took part in bonding analysis). Appearances, however, can be deceiving. They spend only half of this time in deep sleep, while the other half is devoted to REM sleep. During REM phases, they move a lot, smile, grimace, make sucking movements with their mouth and, naturally, dream a lot. They also perceive voices unconsciously. It is thus easy to understand how they take part in life around them with their ears, and can also enjoy music. If a baby has worrisome parents, they might, unluckily, want to guard the baby from any acoustic stimulation to ensure calm and deep sleep. This will not necessarily have a positive effect on the development of the baby's musicality and speech. Acoustic stimulation also plays a role in indirectly affecting brain activity. Ears are not only for hearing, but also an important source of energy for the brain. The brain gets its energy from the functioning of perceptual organs and 90% of this energy is produced by the ears and vestibular system.

Wakeful infants react to bodily contact first and foremost, but acoustic stimuli such as speech and music come second. After only two or three days, newborns turn their eyes to the source of acoustic stimulation and even try to turn their heads in the same direction. In an interesting experiment, newborns were able to choose between speech, music, and nonverbal, non-musical noises. They manifestly preferred speech and music to all other sounds. It is remarkable that their favourite was a combination of vocal and instrumental music.

The importance of music in the development of babies is proven by the fact that their breastfeeding proceeds more easily, better, and, importantly, more forcefully if they are listening to music.

A few words on lullabies

Newborns usually calm down quickly if we take them into our arms and cradle them. If we sing a lullaby while rocking them, the effect is even more pronounced. This is because the vestibular system perceives rocking, and it is connected to every muscle of the body through the spinal cord. Therefore, we can say that the key to bodily comfort is in the ears. The rocking also influences the auditory organ indirectly, as the auditory and vestibular systems are closely interconnected with regard to their position and function.

The significance of emotions and music

Gabrielsson (1991) investigated musical experiences as reported by hundreds of randomly-selected subjects. He found that frequent musical experiences can strengthen a person's identity and also build self-confidence by enhancing the feeling of affinity with other people. They can diminish unconscious defence mechanisms and therefore clarify feelings and thoughts. They may provide opportunities to give consolation, hope or relief from pain as well as produce feelings of freedom or the joy of simply being alive. Perhaps it is apparent by now that the roots of musical experiences go back to prenatal times, to mother–foetus bonding as the foetus experiences it. This bonding is the strongest and most intimate that can exist between two people. Until the middle of the twentieth century, scientists regarded foetuses as part of their mothers' bodies. Only prenatal psychology has definitely proven that foetuses are separate beings, with their own life and development.

2   The ultrasonographic observation of foetal life

A radical breakthrough in our understanding of foetal life came with the advent of the ultrasound, the so-called sonography, as the technology permitted the observation of the foetus within its natural environment. Ultrasonographic observations, a practice now commonplace in obstetrics, were first presented in an account by Reinold in 1971. Reinold divided foetal motility into two categories. The first category included forceful, pronounced movements, which involve the entire body of the foetus. The second category is composed of slow movements, performed by individual limbs. A newer categorization of foetal movements was assembled by David Chamberlain, which we addressed in the previous chapter.

A quintessential fact is that no neonatal pattern originates at birth, as the foetus already has the full repertoire of movements which will be found in the neonate. The only difference lies in the quality of movement, because of the increased influence of gravity after birth. Aside from movement, no other function is seen to originate at birth either. According to Prechtl (1987), "the continuum of neural functions from prenatal to postnatal life is made possible by the set of pre-adapted functions which emerge through prenatal life, mainly during the first half of gestation." Individual differences in motility can be marked from one foetus to another, composing a pattern which they retain for the entire gestational period. Respective phases of foetal life are associated with movements typical to each phase, such as the rapid movements between the 9th and 20th weeks, and the extension and crossing of legs between the 13th and 25th weeks. Breathing movements increase incrementally until the 30th week, while hiccups generally occur on the 13th, and thereafter decrease in frequency.

Normal foetuses usually show some kind of movement within ten minutes of observation. According to 24-hour observations of foetuses between 24 and 28 weeks old, foetuses are active about 14% of the time. All studies showed that mothers generally felt less movement than detected by ultrasounds. There were some mothers who seemed to be quite unaware of foetal movements. An increased heart rate accompanies certain movements following the 32nd week. The foetus can be observed swallowing, urinating, alongside the respective changes in the digestive system and bladder. Mothers cannot register breathing

DOI: 10.4324/9781003331865-2

movements, the frequency of which changes throughout the day. Eye movements can be observed starting around the 16th to 18th weeks, while rapid eye movements (REMs) appear around the 23rd or 24th week, clearly signalling that the foetus is dreaming. Foetal activity has a significant role in the development of healthy bodily, behavioural and psychological capacities. Prenatal breathing motions are indispensable preparation for the breathing necessary immediately after birth. Observations show a pronounced parallel between the wake-sleep patterns of foetuses and that of newborns. Day-night (circadian) cycles, however, were not found in foetuses.

Until the beginning of the twentieth century, the perceptual functions of foetuses were regarded as dormant, if not completely non-existent, and until the 1970s, many distinguished scientists still believed that the foetus could be stimulated only through touch. *Recent research has proven all human senses to be operative at least by sometime during the second trimester of pregnancy. The foetus reacts to tactile and vestibular stimuli, pressure, movement, taste, pain, as well as temperature changes.* The foetus has countless opportunities to register its own body and surroundings through tactile sensitivity during pregnancy. A response to sounds is common by the 20th to 22nd week, generally by means of an increased pulse. These responses were present even when the mother herself did not register the sound, ergo did not communicate her own chemical response to the foetus. The sonar world surrounding the foetus is rich, filled with noises produced by the mother's organs, her speech and sounds from the external environment. The most common sound to be heard is that of the artery in the uterus. Replaying the sounds of the intrauterine world on tape prompts unsettled postpartum babies to calm down quite quickly. The same effect can be reached by rereading stories read to the child by the mother in utero, or replaying music introduced to the baby prenatally. The heart rate of foetuses increases in response to light as well. The stimulation of the vestibular system is quite significant; this is prompted by the walking of the mother, for instance, or her sitting in a rocking chair.

The intrauterine world is subject to many changes and can show individual variations. The umbilical cord increases in length, also in response to tensile forces exerted by the foetus, and its coils are formed owing to foetal movements. Placentas themselves can vary in size and shape individually. A pause or stunt in placental growth will inevitably set back the development of the foetus. Amniotic fluid reflects the nutritional and hormonal composition of the mother's physiology. The foetus ingests and expels amniotic fluid, thus further altering its chemical composition. The taste of this fluid is changeable, and can produce a pronounced sensory effect on the foetus. Furthermore, the positioning of foetuses is just as changeable and unique to the individual as all of the above.

Dr Alessandra Piontelli, an Italian psychoanalyst and child psychotherapist, has done pioneering research after learning how to operate an ultrasound machine. She regularly observed 11 foetuses from week 16 to their birth. Her research plan also included the repeated observation of the babies' postnatal development at home, in their natural environment. She visited them weekly until the age of one, spending an hour with each, saw them monthly until the age of two, and reconnected two or three times annually up to the age of four. She even initiated psychotherapy in one case, at the age of three, at the request of the parents. Piontelli's essential realization was that of the remarkable continuity between pre- and postnatal behaviour. She further assessed something self-evident to parents worldwide: each child to be born, and born already, is an absolutely unique creature. The newborn is not a mould of nature, waiting to be imprinted by human and didactive interactions. The natural and the human interact for so long in the womb that it is practically impossible to differentiate between nature and nurture. Piontelli thus gestured to the age-old debate of whether natural predisposition, or social inputs and education is the primary influence on a child. This, however, is an oversimplification of the matter, and therefore useless for our purposes. Foetal developmental studies, ethology (behavioural science), and certain viewpoints of psychoanalysis all functioned as part of Piontelli's research. The observations of the children were conducted through the method of Esther Blick, of Tavistock Clinic, England. In the spirit of ethological research, she hypothesized a grand, yet shared, repertoire of behavioural patterns among all of humanity, present in the preverbal behaviour of infants. Her findings suggest that a child's behaviour is determined by more than prenatal experiences alone, as it is impacted by parental interactions as well. Piontelli took intellectual inspiration from Freud, Melanie Klein, Bowlby, Darwin, Konrad Lorenz, Preyer and Prechtl.

Child psychotherapists encounter a lot of vivid fantasies concerned with intrauterine life and birth in their practice. Psychoanalysts working with adults have similar experiences regarding dreams and fantasies. We know that our unconscious memories are expressed in fantasies, dreams, drawings and other creations. In her research, Piontelli endeavoured to connect the results of foetal observations with the results of infant and child observations, and interpret them with a psychoanalytic approach. It was striking to her during her ultrasonographic observations how freely foetuses move, as gravity affects them much less there. *It was also striking that each foetus has its own individuality and personality with preferred postures and reactions.* During the observations, the obstetricians (research took place in a maternity clinic) and relatives credited the foetuses with different motivations, feelings and moods. It is scientifically questionable whether this crediting has any validity at all, but we use this process nonetheless, in our everyday lives, too. As a parenthetical, I must point out the noteworthy phenomenon of Piontelli's request to be notified of the impending birth of the observed foetuses, as she would have liked to be present for the occasion. All but one forgot to call.

The story that motivated Dr Piontelli to observe twins is especially enlightening. An 18-month-old boy was brought to her by his parents for therapy. The baby was moving restlessly, almost as if obsessed with looking for something which he never seemed able to find. His parents said that he acted in a similar manner all the time. Occasionally, he also tried to shake several of the objects inside the room, as if he were trying to bring them to life. His parents told the therapist that any milestone in his development (sitting up, crawling, walking or uttering the first word) all seemed to be accompanied by intense anxiety and pain, as if he were afraid of "leaving something behind him." When the therapist simply said that he seemed to be looking for something that he had lost and could not find anywhere, the little boy stopped and looked at her very intently. The therapist also commented on his trying to shake all the objects to life as if he were afraid that their stillness meant death. At this, his parents almost burst into tears, and proceeded to tell the therapist that the boy had been, in fact, a twin, but that his twin sibling had died two weeks before birth. This boy therefore had spent almost two weeks in utero with his dead and unresponsive twin. The simple realization of this, as well as the verbalization of his fears that each step forward in development, starting from the first warning signs of his imminent birth, might have been accompanied by the death of a loved one for whom he felt responsible, brought about an almost incredible change in his behaviour. All this, in turn, facilitated an intense process of mourning in his parents, who up to that point had been unable to express the pain, anxiety and guilt that the event had stirred in them. This episode always remained on Piontelli's mind, together with a desire to know more about the mysterious link which often unites twins. Such a link, as well as the awareness of the aforementioned terrible loss, lead her back to experiences before birth.

There are debates within the psychoanalytic movement on the psychological birth of the human infant, from which point in time it possesses a psyche. In the sixteenth century, Rabelais, a doctor and a priest, pondered at what age it would be possible to baptize a foetus. There are psychoanalysts who considered that the infant is not psychologically born until the fifth month of its postnatal life. Others considered mental life to be operative from birth. Only very few supposed that foetuses have mental life, ego functioning or even the possible bearing of foetal life on the future development of the individual and the mental functioning of the baby. Even those specialists who accept that maternal emotions and fantasies can have a strong impact on the foetus, tend to consider the psyche of the foetus as a "tabula rasa" (empty page) and do not presuppose any mutuality between foetus and mother. Based on our accumulating knowledge, now many are certain that there is a mutual relationship between them.

The prenatal observation of twins may provide answers to questions concerning the strictly postnatal possibility of a mental or psychological birth due to exposure to human interactivity, as these circumstances translate into an in utero context for twins. As per the established theory, the foetus is immature by all means, and its mental and emotional development should be unaffected by the presence of another being. Or, could this intrauterine cohabitation catalyze an earlier psychological birth? Is the connection between twins even tangibly observable in utero? The influence of maternal fantasies, emotions and states of mind and psyche on not one, but two foetuses are also drawn into question. The effect of maternal emotions should be uniform on the two foetuses, if we attribute a considerable significance to such maternal influence. The following observations of Piontelli may prove intriguing in this context: Marisa and Beatrice had a habit of hitting each other in utero, and carried on much the same postnatally, to the extents made possible by the development of their motor functioning. Alicia and Luca, on the other hand, caressed each other through the membrane separating the two in utero. Their favourite game at the age of one was caressing one another through a curtain in between them. Marco, who buried his face in the uterus as if it were a pillow, insisted on a pillow-shaped pencil case four years following his experience. Pina was the most daring of the foetuses, until she came frightfully close to miscarriage. Her explorative behaviour carried into her postnatal life, as she stayed ever active and bold, although she was haunted by considerable fears of enclosed spaces, decreased appetite, and a fear of being "washed away."

According to Piontelli's observations, not only does the prenatal environment influence the behaviour and personality of the child, but also the interactions with the parents. All her psychoanalytic and observational data prove that *there is a fine behavioural and psychological continuity extending from foetus to infant to child.* Giulia was one of the least active of the observed foetuses. Her main activity was licking the placenta, pulling it closer at times, and holding her hands between her legs. She was in a peaceful state of oneness with the rhythm of her mother's breathing. Her mother said, "[S]he was very comfortable in there," and indeed, her birth was slightly overdue and quite traumatic for her mother, but Giulia looked unperturbed by it in spite of all the commotion around her. Once out, she initially licked rather than sucked her mother's breast as she had licked the placenta. Later, with the assistance of her mother and grandmother, she acted as if her postnatal world were a womb, too, in which all she had to do was relish her food and other sources of sensual gratification. The breakdown of this paradigm was precipitated by the birth of her brother, which served as undeniable proof that someone else occupied her pre- and postnatal space. In her psychotherapy, Piontelli mainly devoted her efforts to help Giulia achieve a psychological birth and a somewhat less wholehearted devotion to sensuality as the centre of her life.

While in the womb, Gianni clung to the cord almost constantly, was rigidly immobile and had to be delivered by Caesarean section, with the obstetrician commenting on his tight immobility. Gianni continued to be obsessively rigid, clinging to routine and people in much the same way as he clung to the cord. It is as if he were holding himself together in the womb by what Bick (1964) described as a "second skin formation" and continued to do so. The dizygotic twins showed markedly unique behavioural differences. Their characteristic patterns of relating to each other in the womb were continued after birth, too. Sharing the same womb did not seem to affect the basic temperament of each individual child very much, although each child showed, after birth, clear signs of being powerfully affected by sharing their space with another being. As a foetus, Marco was much less active and friendly than his twin sister, Delia, and this difference continued in infancy and childhood in spite of the parents' preference for Marco. Marco was bigger than Delia and was born first, but after birth Delia progressed more quickly. Delia continued to be an alert and interested child, while Marco, according to his mother, wanted nothing more in life than to sleep. As small children, they often collided when going through doorways and Delia, smaller and quicker, usually slipped through first. In utero, Marco most often buried his face in the placental pillow (see above), while Delia was active, and kept performing new movements. She tried to reach out to Marco but he withdrew and sometimes even pushed Delia back to her place. Luca and Alicia were temperamentally different before and after birth; still, they were gentle and affectionate with each other in both periods. Luca was smaller, more active and the first to be born. At four years, Luca progressed more than Alicia in his kindergarten tasks and social contacts. Luca played with cars and made the little car win the race. Alicia made her teddy bears hug and caress each other as she and Luca used to do in utero.

The most striking pre- and postnatal continuity occurred in the case of Marisa and Beatrice. As mentioned before, they constantly hit each other when in the womb and continued to do so throughout their infancy and early childhood, with the loving amusement by their mother and grandmother of the naturalness of their jealousy and mutual dislike.

Giorgio and Fabrizio had a very unusual experience in utero because they shared not only the same genome but also the same amniotic sac, and were thus intertwined with each other all the time. Fabrizio was always the first to move, followed a moment or two later by Giorgio, a pattern that was still noticeable at four years of age. Both suffered a strange and neglectful postnatal experience in which they were left alone in a dark room for much of their waking life. After initial underdevelopment of speech and other behaviour, they improved notably once they went to nursery school, but each one had a cruel expression and terrible experiences as twins. They hate each other but cannot manage without each other.

These research findings about the continuity between pre- and postnatal life are obvious, still, many people think of the infant's mental life as starting at birth. Some speak of "psychological birth" as occurring sometime later, when the infant shows signs of differentiating self from object, namely anyone else. Piontelli observed that there were links between the children's behaviour in the consulting room and their significant birth traumas. One little boy, for example, repeatedly pointed his head at the doctor's stomach, and said "inside, inside." He then turned the tap on and soon the room was flooded with water. He noticed a picture of a swimming pool and just wanted to plunge into it, as he equated the swimming pool with a watery interior. It became clear at the sessions that separation was unbearable for him. In his fury, he tried to destroy the world all around him. He seemed to experience the end of the session like a violent birth, and tried to resist it by sitting down. On the basis of her research, Piontelli supposes that children are unlikely to remember their experiences in the womb and their birth consciously, but they repeat them, act them out and try to work through them as they grow and develop. This was especially striking in the relationship of twins, who were complaining about congestion and lack of space. They preferred to play games connected with pairs and couples. They seemed to be forever linked by the fact of having once been together as a pair inside too narrow a space.

While we are on the subject of twin pregnancies, we have to mention the process of a fertilized ovum's, a zygote's, embedding in the uterine wall. This is a very important and sensitive phase of embryological development. Patients in deep regression, when recalling their intrauterine experiences in an altered state of consciousness, reported that they felt deadly terror during this embedding phase. They felt that they were unwanted children, that they belonged nowhere, that there was no place for them to go, and they "decided" that the world was not safe but hostile. They sometimes felt deep hopelessness, but other times they were angry and exacted revenge. They oscillated between these extreme mental states or had strong rescue fantasies. In these fantasies, either they rescued others or were rescued by others. A lot of patients who have problems in controlling their aggression report that they lost a twin in their prenatal life. The problems with their aggression are connected with their masochism and their neurotic self-devaluation. Recent embryological research indicates that losing a twin sibling in utero is far more frequent than previously thought. According to embryologists, the estimations of twin pregnancies compared to all conceptions oscillate between 30% and 80%. As the number of twins born is much less than this, it is supposed that many pregnancies involve the death of one or more twins in utero. This event may occur before the embedding of the zygote, during that phase or occasionally even later in gestation. People who lost a twin share common psychodynamic features. They live through deep, unspeakable feelings of loss, despair and anger. They usually do not express these feelings, but sometimes take them out on others. They have chronic, unvoiced anxiety and permanent feelings of insecurity. They are afraid that the loss could be repeated. They try to defend themselves against the loss, so they avoid forming relationships with other people or, on the other end of the spectrum, live in utterly dependent relationships. Some are unable or neurotic to bond with others because they do not trust human relationships. They do not believe that a relationship can last. They accommodate to other people immoderately, because they are driven by their unconscious feelings of guilt. They unconsciously fear that if they do not accommodate to the expectations of others, they would die. This exaggerated conformity leads to hostility and aggression, as this constant conforming to others comes with a neglection of the self. These feelings of loss and mortal fears can eventually turn one against himself or others, expressed by sadistic or masochistic behaviour or criminal aggression. If we want to comprehend the psychological consequences of such a loss, consider the case of Piontelli's 18-month-old boy patient who directed her attention to twin pregnancies. The prenatal loss of a twin is a traumatic event and the effects are far-reaching. The trauma arrests the bonding process of the foetus and newborn child. We know that there is a critical period after traumatic events when people need empathy, acceptance and understanding, which can abate the effects of the trauma and start the process of healing. *Babies who have suffered intrauterine or perinatal traumas usually do not get any understanding or empathy, because nobody believes or accepts that they could have suffered from trauma. This lack of acknowledgement makes such babies mistrustful and hinders the bonding process.* Babies who have not suffered trauma, or whose trauma was accepted and understood, can bond more deeply. From a preventive point of view, it is very important to diagnose and treat pre- and perinatal traumas as early as possible. This point is also illustrated by the little boy's case, in which the trauma of the child and parents could be jointly treated. *These early traumas form the frame of reference in which we evaluate later events in life.*

If we are able to diagnose and treat these early traumas during pregnancy or in the first year of life, then the developmental process can be freed from the effects of pre- or perinatal traumas, and children can live and develop without the weight of their prenatal past. Unresolved, untreated traumas stunt the process of psychological and intellectual development. *Once again, we must emphasize that children who have not suffered traumas, or whose traumas were successfully treated, develop more quickly. They have more self-confidence, more empathy, are more creative, more cooperative, more mature emotionally and are also able to feel deeper love for others.* That is one of the reasons why prenatal care of expectant mothers, foetuses and expectant families, as well as the early psychotherapeutic treatment of pre- and perinatally traumatized infants, is so important.

3 The effect of maternal stress and anxiety on the foetus and child

János Selye, a Hungarian-born Canadian endocrinologist, discovered in the 1940s that the human body does not react in a specific way to any sort of stress. Stress is a nonspecific response of the body. What does that mean? All stimuli and external stress are unique in a sense, that is to say, specific. We are cold in low temperatures in order to produce more heat. Our veins contract in order to reduce the amount of heat that leaves through the surface of our bodies. We sweat in hot weather so that the evaporation of sweat can cool our bodies through the skin. If we consume too much sugar and our blood-sugar levels rise above what is normal, the body secretes a part of the sugar and burns the rest until the blood-sugar gets back to its normal (secure) level. All medicine and hormones, once administered, have a specific impact. Diuretics help to secrete urine, adrenaline quickens the heart rate, blood pressure and blood-sugar levels, while insulin decreases blood-sugar levels. Independent of the nature of their effect on the body, they all share a common feature: they require that the body adapt and rearrange itself. This is the nonspecific requirement. From a different angle, the aforementioned effects, beyond their specific consequences, increase the need for adaptation reactions in a nonspecific way, and, as a corollary, the reimplementation of equilibrium. From the point of view of what initiated the stress-response, only the scale of the need for required adaptation matters.

The first description of the set of symptoms arising from various pathological external influences (syndromes) was published in 1936 and became well-known as general adaptation syndrome or GAS. GAS has three phases:

1. The alarm reaction. The body develops the symptom response characteristic of each stressor: initially the level of the body's resistivity decreases and death may occur if the stressor is very dangerous.
2. Resistivity. If it is possible to adapt under continuous stress, resistivity develops in the body. The signs of alarm reaction seemingly disappear and the level of resistance increases above the norm.
3. Depletion. The energy reserved for adaptation may be depleted if the organism is exposed to the same stresses for a long time after adaptation has occurred. The signs of alarm reaction appear, now permanently, and death sets in.

DOI: 10.4324/9781003331865-3

Perhaps the most important aspect of this process is that, when under prolonged stress, the body's ability to adapt, in other words, its adaptation energy, is finite and can be depleted.

Selye correlates the three phases of GAS with the three phases of human life: childhood, when the level of resistance is low and the body reacts vividly to all stimuli; adulthood, when the body has already adapted to the impact of the most commonly repeated stresses and resistivity is high; old age, when resistivity decreases irreversibly until death, the final depletion, sets in.

The true advances in stress research was the discovery of the objective characteristics of stress, the most important of which are the enlargement of the adrenal glands, stomach and bowel ulcers, hypertension and some heart diseases.

It is possible to experimentally demonstrate the phenomenon of stress syndrome in pre- and perinatal psychology and medicine. That is to say that the simple and at the same time complex fact that the stress of the mother is the stress of the developing child and that a mother under stress will bring into the world a child under stress can be quantitatively measured by the objective experimental methods applied to stress syndrome.

If we list the most obvious, universal stress factors which are free of any cultural or civilizational circumstances, then we have to begin first and foremost with the biology of human birth, which has become riddled with trauma due to forces acting during phylogenesis. Another stressor is the relative lack of oxygen at the end of pregnancy. At this point, the placenta is on the verge of surpassing its oxygen-processing capacity. Prechtl (1987), for example, is of the opinion that it is this lack of oxygen that induces birth. We can then find various stress factors related to the phenomenon of birth.

A third such stress affecting humans is premature birth. Portmann (1969) writes that apes are born already as small children, whereas human infants are born in foetal state. According to phylogenetics and the nature of biological functions, a pregnancy should be 20 months long. In this case, the newborn would be able to adapt to its social environment with its own biological provisions and may behave according to its own needs. The phylogenetic transformation following the increase in the volume of the human brain first presents itself in infancy, which has taken up more and more time during human evolution. It lasted three to five months in homo erectus, but it is longer than a year for homo sapiens. This change evoked the pro-social behaviour of the parents and promoted the stabilization of their relationship. It is possible that without this factor, the relationship between men and women would be even more problematic and lacking in perspective.

Infancy – the first year of life outside the womb – is a uniquely human period of time, which is unrestrained by any instinctual functions. Caring for infants is a specifically human task and is very much culture-oriented. Therefore, infancy may be humane or inhumane. The basic values of the given culture are continuously present in this year-long passage of life.

It is important to note that it is possible to work through the pre- and perinatal stresses during infancy if favourable conditions are given. But unfavourable conditions can intensify the impact of these stresses and it becomes impossible to integrate them. *The lack of instinctual programmes and the fact that the infant is at the mercy of the adult's behaviour make the human infant very vulnerable. Whether or not the infant is able to work through the trauma of birth or he/she would suffer psychosomatic illnesses during later development depends on the quality of care.*

Research on prenatal stresses was initially directed toward simply uncovering a connection between maternal stress and the child. Sontag (1966) was the pioneer of this area. He considered the father/husband's military service to be a stress factor. He compared the children of mothers with soldiers as husbands with the children and foetuses of families untouched in this respect. The foetuses and children of soldiers produced a higher pulse which remained until adulthood. This prompted the experts to conduct further research. Hau (1973) reached the following conclusion: babies who were born from stressed pregnancies sleep less, are more restless and irritable, their body weight is lower and their mood oscillates between crying and apathy. Stott (1963) showed that frequent illnesses following birth are a consequence of stress during pregnancy. Stott considered the mother's social and cultural hindrances as a stressor. Ferreira (1960) confirmed Stott's results. He also found that where social and cultural hindrances obstruct the blossoming and subsistence of the motherhood of the expectant mother, the child's development will also be hindered.

Researchers first probed the physical and biological impacts of stress through experiments conducted on animals. The offspring of experimentally stressed female rats were irritable and prone to illnesses, and they expressed disturbed social behaviour even in adulthood and transmitted it to the next generation. The offspring of prenatally stressed Rhesus monkeys had difficulties adapting to new situations.

The male offspring of stressed female rats tended to exhibit feminine behaviour, while the female offspring were more aggressive than their mother and showed less interest toward their environment. Deviances in sexual behaviour were perceptible in all experiments – male offspring were more vulnerable in this respect.

The problem of unwanted children is especially peculiar. Sexually mature animals are ready to fulfil their function as mothers and fathers. For humans – due to biological and cultural reasons – this is not the case. Biological maturity stands a long way away from parental suitability. Many other factors attach themselves to this that may result in an unwanted pregnancy. The authors have dedicated a chapter to the psychological constellation of being unwanted. However, it will do well to list here the most prominent indicators: being unwanted turns into the rejection of one's own person, which in turn becomes self-destructive behaviour.

There are three different categories of modern human stress research. The first category of research looks for connections between maternal emotions during pregnancy and complications during pregnancy and birth. The results exhibit a significant deviance. The only statistically significant connection proved to be in the body weight of unwanted infants, which was 250 grams lower on average. Retardations during intrauterine growth, abortion and pre-eclampsia (a type of epilepsy) occur with a greater frequency, but not in a significant way. A much more remarkable correlation is that low birth weight is a risk factor of perinatal illnesses and death, and, in later life, of coronary illnesses, which contains in it the possible hazard of a heart attack.

Correlations between low birth weight and slower development, behavioural issues and mental illnesses have also been found. Several studies unanimously support the findings that the infants of mothers who are supported by their environment during pregnancy have a greater birth weight. Of course, the nature of the psychosocial assistance the expectant mother receives needs to be considered. It appears that properly acquainting expectant mothers with the appropriate information regarding their pregnancy can in itself reduce the level of psychological stress during pregnancy.

The second category of research is concerned with the connection between developmental anomalies and maternal emotions during pregnancy. The results are quite surprising. These connect the psychological stress experienced by the expectant mother with severe morphological anomalies such as Down syndrome, hare lip, cleft palate and with less severe morphological anomalies such as infantile pyloric stenosis (a condition in which the opening between the stomach and small intestine thickens, causing the muscles to block food from entering the small intestine), ulcers and various psychiatric illnesses in childhood. Most recently, two investigations of great volume found that severe yet unexpected traumas, for example the death of a child during the first trimester of pregnancy, are serious risk factors in such congenital illnesses as spina bifida (a birth defect in which a developing baby's spinal cord fails to develop properly), cleft palate, or diseases of the heart and liver (Hansen et al. 2000, Nimby 1999).

Lou (1994) uncovered a connection between prenatal stress and a decrease in the volume of the baby's skull as well as neurological problems in infancy. This finding makes it more probable that *prenatal stress hinders the development of the foetal brain*. There are also studies of prenatal stress and later schizophrenia (Hultman 1997, van Os, Selten 1998).

Van der Bergh (1990, 1992) discovered in his long-term studies that there is a link between prenatal stress and the infant's motor activity and behaviour, such as more frequent crying and hyperactivity. When the study was repeated at the children's ages of eight and nine, boys were found to be hyperactive, have problems with self-control and an increased level of aggression, whereas girls prominently exhibited problematic behaviour in social relationships.

The third category deals with the impact of prenatal emotional stress on the behaviour of foetuses. *Maternal anxiety affects the motor activity, pulse frequency and behavioural patterns of the foetus.* Foetuses of depressed mothers move more in utero, but their motor development lags behind that of foetuses of mothers who are not depressed. This contradiction is purely virtual. The reason behind the greater motility is increased endorphin secretion. Endorphins have natural pain-reducing effects and cause euphoria. At the same time, their secretion, that is to say, the securing of a pleasant disposition inside the womb requires more and more stimulation, which the foetus provides via vestibular stimuli stemming from its own movement (DiPietro et al. 1999).

4 Later effects of unwanted pregnancies

Why this chapter on unwanted children? If we're here, alive, then, in some way, we are or were wanted. Or is this not necessarily the case? It appears that it is not. Statistical data and the harsh realities of life say otherwise: many of us came into this world literally as children who were never expected nor wanted. However, not much is said about this topic as it is a taboo even in our modern society.

In the 1960s, the latest medicinal invention was of pragmatic use to a great cross-section of society: the appearance of contraceptive pills made calculated family planning possible. Up until that point, sexuality, conception and pregnancy were all essentially left up to fate, and couples simply followed the tide. What remains of this today? According to the most conservative estimates, even today, every third child is born into this world an unwanted one. Neither theological, nor moral, nor rational restraints were able to tame humanity's reproductive habits throughout history. Just as the unspeakable things – the death and disease of mothers and newborns, the constant danger of their exposure to hunger and famine, poverty and war – looming over the eventuality of childbirth, these possibilities were regarded as outcomes of chance, above all influence. On the other hand, it is difficult for us to stomach the practices of early societies and even our western ancestors until the eighteenth century, where the occasional murder of infants was a sometimes hidden, sometimes overt method of birth control and regulation. In this day and age, the autonomy of a child as a human being is self-evident, and many of us nurture connections with the children we once were.

At the same time, we are also aware of how fresh this cultural achievement is, which may be regarded as one of the conquests of the French Revolution. Though the notion of equality is older than 200 years, it only became a part of the democratization of our society at a fairly slow pace.

In the same vein, the fact that we are more receptive to, and aware of, the specific needs and conditions unique to each child's development is attributable to the effects and influence of findings in the field of depth psychology (and especially psychoanalysis) – these results are the fruit of a lengthy and to this day unfinished developmental process in this area of the profession. It is

DOI: 10.4324/9781003331865-4

worthy to note that, to our parents (and in some cases, sadly, even today), beating children was an acceptable practice, alongside ignoring crying babies, who are, after all, sending distress signals and pleading for help in putting an end to their agony. The "beating, which has yet to harm anyone" and the "cry, which strengthens the lungs" were a part of the consensus on how to raise a child. It is only today that these slanted values are being reexamined and erased. Violence against children is regarded in a worse and worse light, and, more and more, there is light shone on the many crimes committed against children, among them sexual abuse.

Meanwhile, the conditions necessary for the development of a child, as well as those necessary to establish healthy parent–child and other relationships, have become more and more ingrained into public conscience. This process is intertwined with the advent of "gentle birth" movements, the emergence and expansion of the notion of the "rooming-in" system, which is yet more evidence of the slow humanization of society. Modern research with infants has produced scientific fundamentals to support the changes that took place in the attitudes and practices towards the treatment of newborns that are acceptable to the zeitgeist. *Psychotherapists are experiencing more and more often with their patients that trauma and feelings of pain and suffering during the foetal, newborn, and infant stages of life can have lifelong effects, and, on a societal scope, can darken the lens through which we view the world.*

In recent years, the world of a child before birth has entered into the limelight. Today, we can safely estimate some ten thousand psychotherapeutic cases where a substantial amount of decisive "life" experiences were recorded during the prenatal life and birth of patients. A new culture is developing, one that is bringing us closer to the roots of our existence. The blossoming of this culture is aided by the technological and scientific advancements of our day, with whose help the prenatal environment (the womb) can be monitored well before they come into this world. *We are the first generation who gets a front-row seat to all 266 days of a pregnancy. This provides us with unique opportunities to empathically identify and get acquainted with the world of experiences of the baby in the womb, with whom we can thus begin, earlier than ever before, to forge a bond and construct a healthy relationship.* Previously, the child was only perceptible to the mother via its movements – perhaps not even as a baby, but only as a large belly. Today, through the use of intrauterine photography and ultrasound technology, the child can be seen, becomes "tangible" for the father as well, and, what is perhaps more important, he/she becomes identifiable by the public conscience as a being existing in our reality.

With this greater awareness, however, *comes also a necessary acknowledgement of the side of prenatal existence that is often painful and tragic, which, since it also becomes visible in the eye of the public, loses its traditionally idealized status.* This utopian construction of life in the womb was part of nearly a thousand years' tradition, which was centred on a mother who creates conditions akin to paradise for her unborn child. Today, we can monitor through cameras the frightened reaction of a child when, for example, the placenta is sampled for diagnostic purposes by inserting a needle into the uterus. We can follow the child with empathy as he/she is either paralyzed in the womb, and freezes up at the time of the mother's fright, or, as a reaction to the mother's anxiety, becomes anxious as well and holes up in the corner of the womb. Especially unsettling are the ultrasonic inspections of twins in the womb, during which one can witness such complex emotional-relational movement patterns as were previously unthought of even in our fantasies. TV movies of today bring the tormented and vulnerable lives of premature babies to us; we can participate in their dearth and in the fragility of their "semi-existence."

The reality of prenatal life is given even more precise contours thanks to modern science and medicine taking such issues as the behaviour of unborn children, the mechanics of their sensory systems and not least those of their learning patterns under a microscope. It has been found *that even before birth, babies exhibit complex movement and behavioural patterns, some of which can be perceived even after birth, and their relationary significance can be analyzed. The sensory system is as developed around the middle of pregnancy as it is at the time of birth.* For example, reactions to pain can be shown from the sixth week, and there is evidence of the existence of complex sensory abilities found during the first trimester. The ability to process tactile sensations is especially significant during this period, since the baby gathers the first experiences of touch and of connection with another entity through these channels. We are slowly beginning to understand the ways in which a baby forms his/her own world of experiences through internal sensations. In adult patients – for example, during therapeutic regression – we can perceive the resurgence of these uterine emotions, and, albeit in a transfigured form, we can get in touch with the patient's world inside the womb. This sharpens our perceptions as well, just as children re-experience events that took place before, during and immediately after pregnancy through playing games. For example, the multiplying numbers of waterslides and regular slides indicate an increase in the number of traumatic births, since the purpose these newer and newer tools serve is for children to replay their traumatic birth experience and thus process it.

The memory and apprehension-retention capabilities of intrauterine and newborn babies is also amazing. Noises, rattles, stories, and songs heard before birth remain in a child's recollection following the event, and he/she will recognize it just as the heartbeat of the mother as well as the voices of both mother and father. The same is the case with prenatal speech. The newborn of a Hungarian mother will prefer Hungarian, that of a Chinese mother will prefer Chinese dialects.

Our newfound knowledge of the experiences of a child during the time before birth makes it possible for us to vicariously experience the psychological state of unwanted children, which is an incredibly special and tragic psychological constellation, as we will see later on. This is, of course, not easy, since our view has been – and is – distorted by popular consensus and perception. Before, the idealized image of the benevolent and omnipotent parent couple made us blind to their child's immeasurable suffering; now it is the image of the mother, creating a paradise in her womb for her child, that is making the appreciation of reality more difficult. This maternal idealization, which has its roots first and foremost in religion and pedagogy, is one of the reasons why the great discovery, our acquaintance with and charting of the world of the womb and the intrauterine baby, was postponed until the end of the twentieth century. The delay, for which, from generation to generation, we are still paying our dues, has several other causes, them being, among others, positivism in the natural sciences, which simplifies pregnancy and foetal and childhood development into a biological-medicinal process. This viewpoint self-evidently omits any consideration of the spiritual activity of the child as well as his/her relational origin and nature.

If we return for a moment to the idealization stemming from religious preconceptions, we can see that, in the case of an unwanted child coming onto the scene, the mother's guilt and accountability take centre stage, while the fate of the child remains without reflection.

According to these two viewpoints rooted in our cultural reality, not being wanted or expected as a child has no bearing whatsoever on the remainder of the child's life. We are now going to attempt to shine a light on a new psychic and social area of consideration by describing exactly the effects that being unwanted has on a child's life. The first deep-therapy descriptions came to be between 1984 and 1986, and they were primarily concerned with patients who experienced an attempted abortion as foetuses (Janus 1994). Since then, we have been and are therapeutically processing many cases of attempted suicide in which it came to light that the date of the act of trying to destroy one's self coincided with the date of the attempted foetus removal.

The knowledge we have ascertained in the last two centuries regarding the developmental needs of children and youngsters – and not least our latest findings on unborn children and infants – point us to the fact that parents seriously lack the ability to satisfy these needs. The American psychohistorian, Lloyd DeMause writes: "The history of childhood is a nightmare from which we have only recently begun to awaken" (DeMause 1974: 1). Only the power of religious images – which render spiritual this traumatic reality to console us – makes it possible for us to bear this pain and suffering.

The gumption of an unwanted child to live a life is not a closed case, nor a job well done. The time has come, however, for us to write about it. We know that the greater part of society – and here, the estimates hover around one and two-thirds of the population – is suffering from such tormenting symptoms as a diminution of self-worth, feelings of worthlessness, of emptiness, diffuse anxieties, depressive moods and many psychosomatic illnesses. Add to this group alcoholics, drug addicts and last, but not at all least, those with antisocial, criminal personality disorders. In light of the research to be presented, we can confidently say that the backdrop to their symptoms is predominantly made up of the dearth and miseries of their prenatal life. *The awareness of the prenatal significance of being unwanted can help us understand the later trials and tribulations of such children, and for us to be more effective in helping remedy these issues.*

Let us not forget that those children who are born from unwanted pregnancies are more at risk of being neglected and abused by their parents. All societal problems whose symptoms are manifested in violence, deficiencies in the ability to make human bonds, drugs, alcohol, or mental illnesses, are fundamentally formed in the womb. Therefore, we should focus both the human and financial resources at hand for prevention during this time period, if we want to stop chasing illusions and hope and work towards positive societal change.

The groundwork for this change can be laid by the scientific revolution taking place at the end of the twentieth century, thanks to which the definitive role of life before and around birth has entered into the forefront of our individual and social consciousness, in our personality development, relationships, culture and civilization. While pregnancy is one of the most intimate and internal affairs in the lives of only two people, some of the greatest questions concerning our society accumulate in this process. *In other words, the most dramatic and expansive societal issues are rooted in the quality of a pregnancy.*

Many signs point to a sometimes overt, sometimes hidden, anti-child attitude in today's Hungarian society. Adults do not, or do not know how to love their children enough. There are multiple reasons for this incompetence. In society's insensitivity and disinterestedness towards children and childhood are reflected the childhood miseries of parents. The adult who is raised, and later becomes a parent, as an unwanted child is essentially riddled with emotional deficiencies, living in unhappiness and lacking perspective in relationships. There are varied reasons for his or her having a child or children; often, the person can be forced to do so by circumstances, but, in the process of raising them, the parental pattern is unconsciously repeated, and the parent neglects the child the same way the parent himself/herself was neglected by his/her parent. In this case, the parent cannot avoid neglecting the child, since his/her adult life is preoccupied by searching for a way to alleviate the feelings of want accrued during childhood, and feel relatively good in the world. Torments and traumas thus live on and are deflected from generation to generation.

Empirical analyses

If we want to professionally gauge the effects of a psychological problem such as the feeling of being unwanted, then we have to record behaviours and reactions that can be measured objectively. Even if we are successful in finding such a concrete factor, it is still possible for an unsolvable question to appear: does the psychological problem actually reflect itself in the aforementioned measurable behaviour? The following study from Prague may serve as an example, in which the fact that the mothers represented in the study appeared twice before the committee for abortions to get rid of their children was used as the measure of the extent of being unwanted. However, the only conclusion apparent from this fact is that these mothers consciously rejected their children. Their unconscious predispositions are entirely unknown to us, not to mention the fact that, from the perspective of the foetus, the reactions of the mother's partner also need to be taken into account.

We are well acquainted, from our general knowledge of mankind and our experiences with psychotherapy, with the duality of man's world of experiences and his world of desires. It is easily possible for a child to be rejected consciously, but desired for unconsciously. This fact, of course, makes relative the possibility of objective measurements in such cases as the lifelong effects of being unwanted. The clarity and expressive power of the evidence gathered in this study is thus especially unexpected. Nevertheless, due to the reasons detailed above, it is always necessary to reflect on the limits and possibilities of these methods. There are studies which seek to directly study rejected pregnancies and the phenomenon of being unwanted.

Especially significant in this area is the study of Rottmann. The researcher from Salzburg was able to show that the more conflicted, ambivalent and rejecting a mother is towards her unborn child, the more distressed the newborn will be. The so-called Kipp syndrome has been noted as appearing during the first 48 hours after birth in rejected newborns, be their rejection conscious or unconscious – these symptoms being alternating apathetic behaviour and constant crying. The most drawn-out births, as well as the greatest number of complications arising during birth was also highest in this subset. The converse of the correlation was also verified: children accepted either consciously or unconsciously by their mothers were the most balanced, experienced the quickest births and the lowest number of complications during delivery. These data are exceptionally important – a birth is a serious psychological and bodily shock delivered due to evolutionary-biological reasons. (Human evolution suffered a fracture due to, on the one hand, adopting a straightened posture, which caused a decrease in volume of the pelvis, while the volume of the skull increased due to the progressive growth of the brain. Evolution resolved these contradictory tendencies by essentially halving the duration of a pregnancy, and thus we are born in nine months instead of 22. The human race is, then, entirely composed of premature births, and as such – and is unique in this aspect in nature – falls back upon the need for protection and nurture. There are anthropological movements which regard this evolutionary fracture as the reason for the prosocialization and familialization of the human race.) The investigation of Rottmann and others all lead to the conclusion that *accepted, loved, expected and planned babies were statistically verified to have developed better both intellectually and emotionally, than those children who were rejected or not planned.*

Rejection becomes directly clear in those cases in which an unwanted child rejects establishing a relationship with the mother following birth. We have encountered more than one such tragic case, which can often be a vital indicator (a suggestion related to the phenomenon of life), where the newborn child is preparing, based on his psychological circumstances and predispositions, to fulfil his mother's woes and negative feelings towards him.

The Prague experiment

Abortions, either due to medical or social reasons, were introduced in the former Czechoslovakia in 1957. At the outset, the law was so liberal that abortions were a legal form of avoiding an unwanted pregnancy. There were about 45 abortions for every 100 live births. However, the law did not secure a wholly free path for abortions – the committee responsible rejected about eight percent of petitions for abortions the first time around. However, if the mother found a job after the first rejection, this was usually enough for the second request to be accepted. Thus, after two rounds, the number of overall rejections fell from 8% to 2%. Matejček and Dytrych formed a group of children whose mothers turned twice to the committee to get an abortion, and were twice rejected (David et al. 1988, Matejček 1994). From these cases we can safely assume that these children were rejected by their mothers in at least the first few months of pregnancy. The study utilized 220 boys and girls born in Prague between 1961 and 1963. The same number of children constituted the control group, who were planned or at least accepted. The fundamental hypothesis of the study was this: there are differences between children who were rejected and those who were planned or at least accepted by their parents. The differences are negative in the point of view of the rejected – they experienced a hindrance in the development of their personality, and, as opposed to children who were desired for, lived mostly in problematic domestic situations.

Initial results

The following data were recorded from each child between 1970 and 1974: information and statistics regarding the birth of the child, physical development, illnesses, documentation pertaining to schooling, an interview with the parents, and a questionnaire filled out by both parents and teachers. The children were approximately nine years old at the time of recording the data. Regarding genetics, the developmental path of unwanted children seemed to be normal. In any case, it was noted that the mothers seeking abortions twice were much later in seeking out consultation for their pregnancy. They neglected regular check-ups, and participated in mandatory prenatal care very rarely. It is interesting, then, that they experienced less difficulties during pregnancy, giving birth and puerperium. It, of course, does not follow that mothers who did not want to be pregnant had pregnancies that came to completion without any complications. The researchers set out with the assumption that in this group the conflict – wanting a child or not wanting one – takes place on a conscious level in the brain. The mother who appeared twice before the committee showed directly and without remorse her attitude towards having a child. From this, it can be deduced that those expectant mothers who openly accept and do not try to hide the fact that they do not wish to be pregnant are less likely to respond psychosomatically to the conflict. In their case, there is little to no amount of repression, which is the fundamental mechanism of developing psychosomatic symptoms and, in general, all other complications with a psychological background. After a long fight, they accept the unchangeable on a rational level. The mothers who made up the control group, who were eager to have children or at least accepted them, confessed that they had doubts during their pregnancy, and came into conflict with themselves because their pregnancies were not traceless, proceeding without physical or psychological complications.

The start in life

The structured conversations were conducted by a psychiatrist who posed the following questions to the new mothers: what effects did having a child have on the financial situation of her family, what effects does it have on her health, both mental and physical, on her relationship with her partner and other family members? It is significant that the mothers from the control group voiced their concerns for the negative effects of having a child on their health more often. The group of rejecting mothers reached a higher score in regards to every other factor. Based on these results, the starting point of wanted versus unwanted children is roughly the same. Still, the first significant sociobiological factor, breastfeeding, places unwanted children at a great disadvantage as unwanted children were breastfed either for a much shorter time or not at all.

Development from a health and societal standpoint

There were no discernible differences between the two groups concerning serious illnesses, accidents, operations and hospitalizations. However, unwanted children required more medical attention in the cases of common diseases and illnesses.

Performance in schools was, aside from a truly minuscule number of exceptions, noticeably worse in the case of unwanted children. Their attitudes and predispositions towards schooling was also problematic, according to their parents and teachers. Compared to children who were wanted, more unwanted children voiced a strong dislike for attending school. It is thought-provoking that unwanted children were more likely to be rejected by their peers in a classroom setting. They were regarded as "smart-mouthed," "hostile," "zero" and "deviant." In their social conduct, unwanted children gave little evidence of moral behaviour, were prone to outbursts of rage and easily provoked. The difference between the two groups was significant from a statistical perspective despite the fact that these differences are often hidden and are difficult to grasp.

It manifests itself in many small, seemingly insignificant, deviances which nevertheless add up under scrutiny and reveal their importance.

Second and third phases of research

Following the first round of results from the study, researchers went after the question of whether or not the differences between the two groups remained six years after the first study. This was the starting point of the second round of inquisition, which took place when the children were 14 to 16 years old. Of the unwanted children, 212 out of 220 were successfully contacted, and 215 of the desired for children were also reached. In summary, they were able to assess that the differences were as strong after 15 years of family life as before, and, what is more, the antisocial and deviant tendencies of unwanted children showed even more prominently.

The assessments of the second stage of the study provided inspiration for the third phase, which took place during the original group's adult life, reaching 161 unwanted and 152 desired for children.

Experimental results

Unwanted children were treated for alcoholism nearly twice as much as those desired for. The number of criminals was also nearly twice as high in the group of unwanted children as the control group. This result was based on minor criminal offences. More serious crimes were committed nearly three times as much by unwanted children than those who were accepted.

Of the control group, 31.5% said their life leading up to that point could be described as positive, while only 8.7% of those who were unwanted as children thought so. Of this latter group, 39.3% were of the opinion that they were overrun by their worries and problems, while only 17.4% of the control group thought this way.

Unwanted children reported significantly more often that their parents were dissatisfied with them, and that this is valid for the present day as well.

There was no significant difference between the two groups in the type of vocation or in the competence for completing their tasks. However, unwanted children reported a greater dissatisfaction with their current workplace and their relationship with their co-workers and superiors.

Repeated disappointment in intimate relationships proved vastly more common in the case of unwanted children. A significant majority were of the opinion that love causes more difficulties than provides happiness. The first sexual relationships in this group usually came not as a result of a personal connection or love affair, but of superficial connections. They were less consistent with regards to their sexual partners, varying them more often than the control group.

The researchers posed four further questions to those married (50–50 persons in each group). They were looking to find out the degree of satisfaction those asked were experiencing with their marriage and their relationship with their partners. Unwanted children reported significantly more often that they deemed their marriage unhappy. If they could turn back time, many of them would not opt to marry their current partner a second time around.

Conclusions

The experimental results verified the hypothesis that being unwanted means being more threatened even in early adulthood. However, "being threatened" is a complex notion. *The digressing psychosocial development and malaise of the unwanted child can be seen as a complex intermarriage of adverse circumstances present in our culture whose origin, in any case, is the rejected pregnancy, the prenatal life.*

Help is available for unwanted children as well as for mothers who reject their pregnancies. Parents who deem that, for some reason, their child is at risk of emotional hardships since his or her birth, should turn to a psychologist. Because children at this age still possess the ability for vast developmental advancements, help can be especially effective.

The decisive step for the parents as well as those adults who were unwanted as children is to have the courage to look their internal and external experiences in the eye, no matter how traumatic they may be. Only after this has been achieved can the later effects of earlier impairments be recognized, and only then does it become possible that the person in question comes to be at peace with their fate and identity as caused by their being undesired, and only after that is it possible to lay the necessary foundations for a changed life.

If, for us professionals, the notion of therapy seems wise, it is the first sign of the resurgence of our self-healing powers. With this, there appears an opportunity for identifying with one's self and opening up the perspective of a different life.

Therapy, however, is always struggling to keep up with the events of one's life; it cannot prevent them, though the emphasis lays on prevention. The future of our society – in my opinion – hinges upon an educated and responsible approach to becoming a parent, which is a multi-generational process, which requires present and future parents to be aware of their past, since there is scarcely an event in human life as daunting and challenging as pregnancy and childbirth. Accepting our parenthood also means to rediscover and accept the child living in us with all its problems, anxieties, fears, wishes and needs. It is only this way that we can guide the smallest and weakest creature in our world on its own path.

5 The psyche of the foetus in the mirror of psychoanalytic theories

Rabelais, the sixteenth-century French monk and physician, took for granted that foetuses already have a soul while in the womb. In his famous book, *Pantagruel*, he raised the question of what gestational age the foetus in the womb could be baptized. The notable Hindu physician and doctor of embryology, Charaka wrote in 1000 BCE that the expectant mother has a strong internal psychological relationship with her foetus (Gupte, D., Batta, B. in Fedor-Freybergh and Vogel 1988). However, modern European medicine supposed for a long time that psychological life only starts after birth. Misconceptions about the life of the foetus still exist today, spawning from various reasons. Embryology, as far back as mediaeval times and beyond, was interested first and foremost in anatomy and the mechanics of pregnancy and birth instead of the foetus itself. As a consequence of this perspective, embryologists view foetuses, from the fifth month of the pregnancy and apart from a few aimless kicks, as "peaceful and vulnerable creatures, who are quietly preparing themselves for life after birth." This mentality is the reason that soon-to-be-borns and new-borns are regarded as inadequately functioning adults and not as competent foetuses and infants. Obstetrics and paediatrics paint an image of a baby that does not have any personal thoughts, feelings or memories. For a long time, medicine lacked the tools to record voices or pictures in the womb, nor could they perform tonal analysis, EEGs and other tests.

Sigmund Freud's theoretical hypotheses that human personality and development are determined by early-life experiences and that infantile sexuality does exist caused outrage for a long time. The practice of psychoanalytic therapy and the theory that developed in parallel with it began a new chapter in the world of psychology, but the findings of this new approach were only accepted slowly by the scientific community, and are, to this day, surrounded by doubts and animosity. The branch of psychoanalysis developed by Freud investigates the psychological life of humans, the origins of neurotic and psychosomatic illnesses, neurosis and psychosis, and attempts to remedy them. The famous methods of this branch of psychoanalysis are the interpretation of dreams and free association. The essence of this latter practice is that the patient, in an analytic setting, voices his/her thoughts and ideas – anything that comes into his/her mind – without criticism or censorship. The analytic setting is already

DOI: 10.4324/9781003331865-5

well-known thanks also to caricatures: the patient is lying down; the analyst is seated behind him/her. The basic hypothesis is that in this way it is possible to reach the patient's hidden network of psychic links, and the power of internal phrasing and verbalizing through expression makes the thus far concealed connections visible to the conscious, and the apperception of this newly conscious material changes the mental and psychological state of the patient. The recounting of dreams plays an important role in this process, as well as uncovering their hidden meaning with the help of the patient's free association.

Psychoanalysis, as a method, is a dynamic organization of the psyche, which can guide us towards uncovering the unconscious. *Making the unconscious conscious – this is a main thesis of psychoanalysis.* While being a therapeutic method, psychoanalysis has also become a tool for the scientific research of the human psyche.

Until the beginning of the twentieth century, even psychoanalysts thought that psychic functions begin to take place only after birth, up to which point, the child-to-be is simply a creature without perception, emotion or a consciousness – it is not yet a person. Freud wrote, in the 1909 edition of his book, *Interpretation of Dreams*, which was published ten years after the first edition, that he had been late in recognizing the significance of fantasies and unconscious thoughts, which were concerned with life in the womb. These fantasies and thoughts can shed light on the meaning of a peculiar yet common anxiety, namely the fear of being buried alive, and the deepest basis of the belief of a life after death, which, according to Freud, is only the projection of a mysterious prenatal life into the future. "Birth is the first anxiety-provoking event in the child's life, and it is the source and model for all subsequent anxieties" (Freud 1972). It is interesting that, some years before, Freud had referred to a conversation with a midwife who told him that the presence of meconium in the amniotic fluid is a sign of fear on the part of the foetus – therefore, the foetus has emotions.

The realization that life is continuous, that it does not start at birth but at conception, and that the act of birth is only a caesura in this continuous process, was slow to enter the minds of psychoanalysts. *The consequence of this interruption is that we do not remember our life in the womb, but, unconsciously, we are constantly striving to re-establish our lost continuity and live in denial of the trauma of birth.*

The months of our prenatal life appear in our dreams, fantasies and unconsciously motivated deeds in a symbolic form. Psychological functioning exists from the moment of conception and cellular memory stores the impressions that reach us. Nándor Fodor (Fodor 1949), a Hungarian psychoanalyst who lived in the USA, supposed that this memory of the body, as he called it, is a deeper layer of our consciousness, perhaps the genuine basis of the unconscious. This organismic memory is generally psychologically incomprehensible, but is still an ever-present fundament. Our unconscious memories from our embryonic time remain with us and are active throughout our lifetime and continuously determine our actions.

Our dreams of birth enlighten the chain that connects generations. We have anxious dreams when we traverse narrow spaces or are submerged in water. The basis of these dreams consists of our fantasies of life in the womb and of birth. Today, we claim that these may not only be fantasies, but real-life memories. A good example is the dream of one of Freud's female patients: "During a lakeside vacation, she falls into dark water, where the pale moon is reflected in the lake" (1909). These dreams are birth-dreams. We interpret the dream by reversing its manifest content, that is to say, replace falling into the water with coming out of it, in other words, birth. We can also recognize the place where human infants are born if we consider the meaning of the French word "la lune" (moon). The pale moon then gains the meaning of pale buttocks, from which infants are born. And what is the meaning of the patient's wish to be "born" during her summer vacation? "I asked her this," writes Freud,

> and she answered without hesitation: Was not I reborn in therapy? The dream is an invitation to continue the therapy at the summer resort, for me to visit her there. It might also contain a timorous ambition to become a mother.

The relation between analyst and patient is very important in psychoanalysis, so the dream might allude to the unconscious wish of the patient to conceive a child with Freud. (This dream is from 1909, the year the concept of countertransference in psychoanalysis first appeared in the literature. The catalyst of the creation of the concept was the relationship between C.G. Jung and his female patient, Sabina Spielrein, who later became a remarkable psychoanalyst as well.)

Birth, as a significant psychologically and physically traumatic event, whose nature is as such due to evolutionary circumstances, sparked important theoretical debates in the field of psychoanalysis (this has been previously mentioned in the antecedent chapter on the later effects of unwanted pregnancies).

Sándor Ferenczi, a Hungarian psychoanalyst, in the *Stages in the Development of the Sense of Reality* (Ferenczi 1913) decidedly commits himself to the notion that in the same way that the marks of phylogeny are inherited by individuals, prenatal psychological processes influence psychic development after birth. The behaviour of newborns shows the continuity of psychological functioning. Circumstances after birth can indeed be very unpleasant for newborns as Leboyer (1975) has described in his work on gentle births. Ferenczi is of the opinion that the distress of the newborn stems from its wish to return to the security of the womb. The famous Hungarian psychoanalyst presumes an even earlier root to this ubiquitous yearning. According to him, humans are a descendant of creatures that made their way to dry ground from the primaeval ocean, and brought with them the longing to return to the ancient sea. The womb with its amniotic fluid is the primaeval ocean projected into the woman's body, and this is where we all wish to return. We find three hypotheses at work here: (1) Psychological functioning is present in the foetus continuously throughout life. (2) Birth is physically and also psychologically traumatic. (3) There lives within human beings a wish to restore their prenatal, intrauterine state. These movements are not linear nor are they exclusive.

The psychological reactions of the expectant mother contribute to the perception of the foetus about itself and its intrauterine environment, and these perceptions remain through adulthood. The foetus has knowledge about itself and about the expectant mother's emotions towards it. The foetus perceives both itself and the mother as well as their interactions. The British psychoanalyst J. Sadger wrote that "the fetus senses correctly whether or not her mother loves her fetus, whether she gives her fetus plenty of love, only a little, or none at all, or, as in many cases, she simply feels pure hatred towards it" (Sadger 1941). Body language is a direct method of communication that develops in humans long before speech forms; it is a continuous function that has fundamental significance throughout human life. Contemporary technical tools make it possible to observe the movements, detections and emotional expression of the foetus during pregnancy. On the basis of these observations, we are able to create hypotheses about the personality of the foetus. The research of foetal behaviour increases the depth and scope of prenatal psychology; it is an important addition to developmental psychology and neonatology, as well as a positive contribution to the success of primary-trauma psychotherapy and our understanding of human consciousness.

Foetal movement is the first sign of a functioning nervous system. The expectant mother usually feels her child's movements from around the 18–20th week of her pregnancy, but, with the help of modern technology, these foetal movements can be detected from the sixth week. (We have already written in detail about the development of foetal movement in our chapter on the intelligent foetus.) We can learn a lot about the interactive and social movements of the child from Alessandra Piontelli's ultrasound observations of single-child pregnancies as well as those with twins. (See the chapter on ultrasonographic observations in the present book.) These investigations show that the womb is an interactive environment, where relationships are more often involving two people rather than being egocentric. Mother and foetus eat, sleep, do sport, smoke cigarettes, take medicine and suffer accidents together. If the father has a fit of anger, both mother and foetus suffer. The effects of such an event on the foetus were demonstrated with ultrasound scans in 2002 at the prenatal world congress held in the Netherlands. The sexual encounter and orgasm of the expectant parents causes changes – increase and decrease – in foetal heart frequency. The response-movements to the foetus's kicks can create a sort of interactive game of "mutual knocking" between parent and child.

The ability of newborns to recognize the songs and tales they perceived in the womb, the voices of their mother and father as well as their mother tongue demonstrates prenatal social interactions, as well as the development of recollection, memory and the ability to learn. Human touch improves the breathing functions and general activity level of premature babies while curbing anxiety.

The reaction of foetuses and neonates to music can be miraculous. In an interesting study, foetuses were conditioned to a Prokofiev melody. Following their birth, this melody had the effect of calming the children down. Brahms' Lullaby was played for premature babies in another experiment, and they gained weight without increasing their calorie intake. Irritable premature babies calmed down when intrauterine sounds (maternal heartbeat and a female singing voice) were played to them. Many experimental results prove that the memory of foetuses is accurate and stores the various experiences imprinted on it. Spectrographic tests show that foetuses are able to recognize their mother's voice as early as the 26th gestational week. Prenatal memory imprints – even if they only exist on a cellular level – and those of birth are preserved, and their effects extend over all of one's life. It is possible to recall these memory-traces and imprints and can be used as sources of information in various psychotherapeutic settings.

There are different prenatal infant stimulation programmes in several countries aiming to enhance parental attachment and strengthen the bond between parent and foetus. Increased levels of awareness, and an acute perception of sounds, music and touch have been noted in the babies who took part in one of these programmes. After birth, their speech, fine and gross motor performance, emotional regulation and cognitive processing abilities were significantly more advanced compared to the performance of children in the control group. Intrauterine dialogue between foetus and parent as well as prenatal infant stimulation have unique preventative capabilities that make them a once-in-a-lifetime opportunity as a primary remedy for later psychological, emotional and physical ailments. This dialogue also prepares both parties for the optimal birth position, birth and its healthy procession, and defines the child's later interactions and emotional attitudes towards life.

Birth is a significant interruption in the procedure of human life. The psychological consequences of this event were recognized by psychoanalyst Otto Rank in his 1924 book *The Trauma of Birth*, in which he developed a complete psychological and psychotherapeutic theory (Rank 1924). His intention was to give the book to his mentor, Sigmund Freud, explorer of the unconscious, as a birthday present. Freud considered Rank's theory era-defining at first, but changed his opinion in a few years, regarding Rank's work as essentially implausible. Freud resolutely held that the traumatic nature of birth stems from the fact that the event itself – that is, the experience of birth rendered traumatic during the process of evolution – is the cause and the mould of anxiety. Rank, however, believed – having examined the unconscious from every angle and revealing the complex pathways through which its contents entered the conscious – that he had reached the ultimate source of the unconscious: biologically comprehensible psychosomatic symptoms and illnesses.

> In attempting to reconstruct from the first time from analytic experiences the to all appearances purely physical birth trauma with its prodigious psychical consequences for the whole development of mankind, we are led to recognize in the birth trauma the ultimate biological basis of the psychical.

Rank supposed that the trauma of birth is the basis of human unconsciousness. The essence of treating neurosis is that the patient relives the trauma of birth in the hands of the analyst, whose task is to help the patient process, work through and understand the trauma – finally, the urge to repeat this primal trauma can be eliminated. In Rank's opinion, this technique, as well as the philosophy accompanying it, has the power to significantly shorten the time necessary for psychoanalytic treatments to be successful. Time has not proven the effectiveness of this Rankian method; however, by placing birth trauma as an evolutionary consequence at the centre of his thesis, he has drawn attention to the psychological importance of perinatal events and fixations (bonds) created with the mother. The theories of Rank and Ferenczi – who, in 1924, wrote a book together on the future goals of developing psychoanalysis – have fundamentally changed the father-centred, patriarchal psychoanalytic theory, shifting the focus to the mother. The bonding between mother and foetus, mother and child, has become a basic axis of psychoanalytic thought.

It has become generally accepted today that *parents contribute to their children's intrauterine development not only with their genes, but their behaviour also severely affects this process*. These influences also have evolutionary consequences. Research shows that positive influences from the mother can enhance her child's survival chances and adaptive capabilities. It is a well-known fact that the mother sends biochemical contents to her foetus, but the fact that she also sends mental information is not so well-known. Our perceptions about the world and accompanying emotions – fear, anger, love, hope – evoke physiological responses in the human body. The foetus does not "know" the details that caused the mother to respond in a certain way, but through "umbilical affects," it perceives the physiological consequences and emotional effects. Long-standing negative emotions from the expectant mother will impair the foetus. Such feelings are, for example, the rejection of the child, anxiety for the child or for her own survival, and suffering stemming from physical or emotional abuse. The consequences of negative or destructive attitudes and emotions can be repaired during pregnancy through psychotherapy if they are diagnosed in time. The attitudes and perceptions of the parents help the baby to adapt to his/her new environment. *Parental anger and fear received in utero impairs the development and health of the foetus as it senses the biochemical effects of these emotional stresses*. We know from tests conducted using large sample sizes that the intelligence of the newborn is defined much more by the intrauterine environment than by genes.

Having said all the above, for the physical and psychological health of future generations, we have to engage with consciously undertaken and planned conception as well as the pre- and perinatal care of mothers and children who are still to be born. Italian researchers have reported that the relationship between mother and foetus is bilateral, not only on a psychological but also on a cellular level. Prof. Mancuso (Mancuso 2000) found that the "person" of the foetus and, indirectly, also the person of the father cause enduring changes in the mother. Beginning with the fifth gestational week, when a woman realizes she is pregnant, the foetus frequently sends messages to the mother via chemical substances such as hormones, neurotransmitters and other molecules. These chemical materials help the mother's organism to adapt to the presence of the new entity in her body. The embryo, it was found, also sends stem cells which, by the grace of the maternal immune system, settle in the mother's bone marrow and produce white blood cells. In this way, expectant mothers also inherit marks from their children.

Aside from its physical corollaries, the bond established between mother and foetus is also important from a psychological perspective. It possesses functions ensuring the survival of both parties. Winnicott (in Davis 1981), a British paediatrician and psychoanalyst, recognized and recorded the concept of primary maternal preoccupation, which is a special case of these two personalities tuning to each other's frequencies. This infatuation is a special psychological state of the mother in the weeks preceding and following the child's birth. We know that birth is initiated by signals from the foetus, and that giving birth is the consequence of the harmonic actions of the two parties. The mother builds this preoccupation through perceptions about her bodily functions which are frequently imaginary and take place mainly in her unconscious. This state has the following signifiers:

- Its development is incremental, and, especially towards the end of the pregnancy, it reaches an increasingly emotional state.
- It lingers for a few weeks following birth. Recollection of themselves during this period becomes more and more difficult once they return to their regular state. Winnicott thinks that the mothers repress the memory of this state.
- This is a state that is accompanied by reserved behaviour and feelings of doubt (if it did not take place during pregnancy, it would be characterized as an illness), or, on a deeper level, may appear as a schizoid episode, in which a part of the mother's personality takes control of the whole.

After birth, the actions of the mother can be explained by this emotionally acute state. While in this state, the mother is increasingly capable of identifying with her child and senses its needs. This synchronizing reaches its peaks before and after birth, yet it is present throughout all of the pregnancy. This process of the mother identifying with her baby is one of the factors that ensure a maternal psychological presence for the psyche of the foetus. Mother and foetus share a tight biological and psychological bond, and the harmonic or disturbed existence of this bond has extensive effects on the development of the child in utero and beyond. With the knowledge we possess today, we have the ability to optimally assist the intrauterine development of our children.

6   Approaches to the unconscious

The theory of the unconscious is one of Freud's most original contributions to psychology (Freud 1946). His theory has ancient and prestigious antecedents. Plato theorized that the human soul consists of two strong, winged horses. One of them is noble and beautiful, while the other is uncouth and shameless. They pull in exactly juxtapose directions, and the coachman can barely control them. According to another tradition, Christian theology, following the original sin of Adam and Eve, the two were both subject to opposing drives, one being a duty to their divine creator, the other their mortal, carnal needs. Several sensitive explorers of human nature recognized unconscious mental functioning during the Enlightenment. Georg Christoph Lichtenberg, a German philosopher, wrote in the eighteenth century that one can acquire exceptional self-knowledge through the study of dreams. Goethe and Schiller considered the roots of poetical creativity to lie in the unconscious. Romantic poets paid attention to the obscure spheres of the mind, and Schopenhauer and Nietzsche had similar opinions.

Freud had translated these poetical thoughts into the language of science in a precise way, and these became the foundation of his psychology. He defined the origin and the content of the unconscious, as well as the ways that human unconsciousness strives to express itself. "Psychoanalysis is faced with the necessity of handling the unconscious with the utmost gravity, following a study of pathological repression." *Acknowledging and incorporating the unconscious is equally crucial in pre- and perinatal psychology. Unconscious psychological processes play deterministic roles in mother–foetus bonding, understanding prenatal experiences, and interpersonal relations in general.* With some training, we can recognize the functioning of the unconscious, and understand its messages. We can thus influence ourselves and our unborn child. Our unconscious psychic processes affect our everyday lives in several ways, they influence us, communicate to us. The influences of our unconscious psychological processes are manifold in everyday life; they continuously send messages and can either enrich or disturb our behaviour.

At the beginning of the twentieth century, Freud pointed out that the human psyche is guided by strict laws, and that it is therefore necessary to assume the existence of a hidden mental space. Such would provide explanations for

DOI: 10.4324/9781003331865-6

phenomena from hypnosis, dreams, parapraxes, as well as neurotic symptoms and contradictory, seemingly illogical actions. Simultaneously, Freud distinguished the truly unconscious material from those that are merely temporarily not in the realm of consciousness, but can be recalled. He differentiated the preconscious from the unconscious proper. The latter is full of explosive old and new materials, which guard suppressed thoughts and truculence, as well as instinctual urges and desires.

Later, in the 1920s, Freud inserted the domain of the unconscious into the structural model of the psyche, finding considerable overlap with the structure's lowest rung, otherwise known as the id. The id is accompanied by the ego and the superego within the structure. An open connectivity between body and unconscious is of great importance to mother–foetus bonding analysts, as bodily functions can be swayed by information and emotions communicated by the unconscious, while the inverse is also true, with information flowing into our unconscious from our body, manifest, among other things, in dreams. Furthermore, the psychological contents and conflicts of the self are prone to materialize somatically. Thus occurs the "mysterious leap" from the psyche to the body, and thus develop hysterical and psychosomatic symptoms. On the other hand, one may access the psyche from the body through prenatal experiences, which make their presence known through dreams, acting out (unexpected or incongruous behaviour), or symptoms. Our unconscious is composed in part of suppressed experiences of our own, their associated, re-attainable emotional responses and the ur-fantasies from the time of phylogenesis. What may manifest as fantasies during analysis today was once a concrete reality in human development. For example, children complete their individual perceptions and truths with those of prehistoric times. In other words, what was factual reality in prehistoric times is now psychical reality. The human unconscious harbours ur-fantasies, ranging from temptation through castration to the primal scene (the copulation of parents). All are concerned with origins. The primal scene is of the origin of the self and conceiving, castration fantasies are fixated with the differences between the sexes, while temptation is the dramatization of sexuality. We are addressing a collective unconscious after C.G. Jung, which discerns the possibilities of inherited psychological functioning, specifically inherited brain structure. These can be parallels in mythologies, motifs and images, which present themselves at any time and in any place, without any historical precedent or migration. The earliest, deepest layers of the individual unconscious are formed by the cellular memory (Nándor Fodor calls this organismic memory). Psychoanalytic evidence suggests that this layer holds cellular experience pre- and post-conception, which can be evoked and appear in dreams, as well as in psychoanalytic settings. Barbara Findeisen, a subject of psychoanalysis, gave an account of one such dramatic experience in an interview (Mendizza 1996). Barbara entered a regressive state and suddenly felt overwhelming panic. She uttered the words "[D]o not stab me, do not throw me away!" adding that cognitively, I did not understand any of it. I was lost in the past, in a regressive state, and was terrified. In subsequent episodes, I pleaded "do not kill me, and I will make you happy." This had become the mantra of my life. I devoted my entire childhood to pleasing my mother. My basest defense mechanism and means of connecting with others was the pleasing of others, at my own expense.

The memories of early traumas are sustained, below the surface. They are present in our dreams, dispositions, even our vocabulary. We carry them with ourselves day and night, yet we are wholly unaware of their origins. These levels of the unconscious can be reached through various means. Some use hypnosis. Occasionally, emotions, words or memories erupt from the unconscious during psychotherapy or in deeply regressed states that have no pertinence to, or reason in, our present. These memories reverberate through our everyday experiences. Pre- and perinatal experiences do in fact define the first dispositions one may take on, such as "the world is an unsafe place" or "I am not good enough." The foundation of trust or distrust is formed in the womb, during birth and immediately after birth. These early messages set the tone for the rest of one's life. Furthermore, the mother's emotions also affect the biochemical environment of the foetus. Some researchers point to umbilical affects, the effect of emotions on the physiology of the unborn child in a sort of mirroring, however, our current models cannot discern what leads a foetus to feel wanted, or unwanted. Sándor Ferenczi suggested that motherly love – oversimplified in scientific jargon as oxytocin – is a counterbalance to the child's death drive (Ferenczi 1939). Freud's theory supposes living beings as harbouring parallel life and death instincts, the latter of which is the motivation to ultimately return to one's original, inorganic state. Biologists, however, question the existence of such a death drive. Our own birth traumas, bodily and emotional alike, is part and parcel of us. Childbirth may evoke such memories of one's own. It is therefore quintessential that the expectant mother work through her own birth trauma. If she does not, she may fall back into this initial emotional state while giving birth, which can prove detrimental to herself and her child as well.

I would now like to return to the origin of the unconscious. There are several hypotheses about this, which are not mutually exclusive. Initially, the creator of the unconscious was held to be the psychical mechanism of repression. Freud supposed an original, in other words, primal repression, which pulls all later repressions to itself and holds them in the unconscious. Other psychoanalysts supposed that the trauma of birth can create such a primal repression, however, contemporary researchers believe that any major trauma, even social ones, at any time in life can lead to such primal repression. The astronomical black hole can therefore be a proper metaphor for the unconscious and primal repression, as it is not possible to perceive it directly, and only through its effect can we know of its existence.

According to other theories, the basis of the unconscious consists of primal fantasies and phylogenetic contents. Lipót Szondi, a Hungarian researcher, discovered yet another stratum of the unconscious. His theory was that this stratum consisted of the familial network of genes and this network influences our character, choices and psychological constitution.

Dreams, along with the psychoanalytic method of interpreting them, create the "royal road" to the unconscious. The thoughts encoded into our dreams, as well as their essential content, can be reached by performing association with their imagery and manifest (evident) content. In these dreams, our wishes, memories of early – and even our first – experiences may be expressed in a visual, dramatized form. *The symbols present in our dreams are universal, and, as such, appear in identical scenarios across different cultures.* Some typical symbols of birth-induced trauma are: crawling through narrow openings, standing riveted to the earth, sinking into sand or mud, feeling crushed or squashed, drowning in water, being pulled underwater by crabs or vortices, a state of fear of being eaten by wild animals or monsters, nightmares and sudden onset of feelings of suffocation, of being buried alive, of being mutilated or falling to our death. In many cases, the trauma of birth can be the root of fears of madness, rape, pregnancy and the supernatural. Many birth-related dreams are recurrent; they repeat from time to time in the same or slightly altered form, while expressing the same essential content. The recurrence of a dream reliably indicates that there is substantial shock underlying its manifest content. Nándor Fodor delineated many types of dreams about birth, we quote here one typical example:

> I am walking through a very big house. There is a huge stove inside. Whenever I enter the room where the stove is, the door closes behind me and I am not able to leave. I can get to my mother only if I crawl through the narrow cambered opening of the stove. It looks too narrow for me to get through it. I am frightened.

The symbol of the arch is self-evident; it alludes to the cambered part of the os pubis. There is no escape from dreams concerned with traumatic birth experience other than waking. "The characteristic inescapability of these dreams is crucial from a diagnostic standpoint," writes Fodor. Freud discovered the existence of the unconscious during the psychoanalytic examination and treatment of neurotic patients. Experiments with hypnotism at the end of the nineteenth century concluded with similar findings. In an interesting experiment, the subject, under hypnosis, was told to open up his umbrella outside the office, in the corridor, after the experiment. The subject did as he was told once conscious and leaving, but could not explain why he did so. It is possible to find sensible stories in the backdrop of neurotic symptoms with the method of free association. Unconscious mental content forms a group separate from other creations of the mind. The symptoms themselves are conscious, their psychic preconditions, however, are not. The connections into whose context we place the symptoms are also part of the unconscious until the analyst renders them conscious through interpretation. The fact that psychoanalytic interpretations can give meaning to neurotic symptoms undeniably proves the existence of unconscious psychological functions. Whenever we uncover a symptom during psychoanalysis, we may conclude that the underlying unconscious processes hold the content necessary for proper interpretation. The precondition of symptom formation is that this content must be unconscious.

The discovery of the unconscious caused a new crisis in the complacency of mankind. The first crisis of this kind is attributable to Copernicus, who proved that the earth is not the centre of the universe, but an infinitesimally small component of a system barely fathomable in its excessive size. The second crisis reached humankind when biological studies shattered our conception of man's alleged privilege by creation, and called attention to our roots in the animal world and the indestructibility of our animalistic nature.

The third and perhaps most damaging insult human grandiosity was received from twentieth century psychology, which proved to the self that it is not even the master of its own house, but a slave to scant messages concerning the unconscious events of his psychological life. When we talk about the psychological functions of the unconscious, and connect this with the id in the structural model of the psyche, we picture these structures and layers in space, more precisely, in space-time, since they consist of dynamic processes. This space-time system cannot be localized with the actual structure of the brain, but the well-oiled functioning of the latter is a prerequisite to that of the superstructure. Our brains' conscious, preconscious and unconscious systems are all part of this superstructure. When researchers explore the unconscious and perhaps attempt to alter its functioning through psychotherapeutic interventions, we say we are bringing into consciousness an unconscious image or an experience-complex living in our memory. Experiences prove that *the untamed effects of memory imprints on our unconscious behaviour becomes processible and regulatable as soon as we are able to summon them into our conscious and express them.* Repressed mental content can be freed from repression only if we successfully unify it with the unconscious memory trace. This is only possible once the resistance is dissolved. Resistance is a psychological force which seeks to obstruct confrontation with embarrassing, repressed content.

András Feldmár (Feldmár 1997), a psychiatrist of Hungarian origin but based in Canada, conducted a revealing experiment when he questioned the mothers of his younger suicidal patients about the histories of their pregnancies. The mothers told him that they had tried to abort their foetuses or remove them in some way. A surprising bit of data presented itself in the calendar dates of the suicidal attempts, which coincided with the calendar dates plus 18–20 years of their mothers' abortion attempts. The assumptions placed in the network of connections are that the foetuses were able to process the abortion attempt on an experiential level, and created a psychological formula in which they identify with the violence committed against them, and attack themselves – doing so without being aware of their own motivations. In this case, the mothers attested to the original trauma whose flames were fanned in the children's unconscious memory. If this is not the case, it is possible to evoke the forgotten unconscious experience and, integrating it into the conscious memory system, to defuse and neutralize it.

At its core, the unconscious consists of instinctual motivations and reverberations of desires. All other content that, for whatever reason, is introduced to this system, revolve around this kernel. There is no negation, doubt or different levels of certitude in this system. The energetic charge of an idea transfers easily to other ideas (for example, a person insignificant in reality may receive a great emotional charge from an important person) and this energy can be condensed into one central idea (in dreams, for example, it is possible for a certain face to be composed of the characteristics of several different faces). This process is called the primary process and it also plays an important role in the creation of dreams. In the unconscious, it is impossible to categorize based on time – time does not pass; our childhood wishes do not change. *Unconscious processes hold no regard for reality* – the dead are alive, old people are young and so on. There is no contradiction, fathers and sons are interchangeable. This fact is recognizable only given the conditions and circumstances of dreams and neuroses. Experiences preserved in the unconscious can come to life in the form of fantasies, bodily sensations, auditory hallucinations or visual perception. One pregnant patient in a relaxed state during mother–foetus bonding analysis hears the clashing of dishes and cutlery in the background while in contact with her baby. On a following occasion, she shares that she relayed her experience of this sensation to her mother, who remembered that she had been working in a kitchen during her pregnancy with the patient. The expectant woman is now recalling the noises she heard in the belly of her mother. Her pregnancy brings alive her own prenatal memories and experience. *The unconscious is able to react directly with the unconscious of another person.* The fantasies and emotions triggered in the other person are transferred by virtue of this property.

Our hypothesis is that one of the connecting pathways between the bonding mother and foetus is direct communication between their respective unconscious. The feelings and thoughts of the foetus appear on the mother's dream-screen (the psychological surface onto which our dreams are projected). According to Freud's theory, images and constructs of our unconscious become conscious if they are connected to corresponding verbal constructs, and therefore gain expression on a higher level of psychological functioning – speech. We are able to reach the unconscious through meditation, different relaxation techniques, psychedelic substances and psychoanalysis. Unconscious contents manifest themselves spontaneously in dreams, slips of the tongue or parapraxis, jokes and neurotic symptoms. These flares of the psyche may broadcast messages from our prenatal time and birth, and provide the remarkable opportunity of the psychotherapeutic correction of attitudes, incorrect self-evaluation and problematic relations to the world stemming from this period. Our early experiences may be mirrored in anxious dreams in which, for example, we are plummeting but wake up before hitting the ground. We would not survive such a fall in reality. People who frequently experience dreams of this nature often also have a fear of closed spaces. The experience of birth may be the origin of the fear of falling. Dreams about falling out of a window are also typical birth-dreams. A female patient recalled having a recurrent dream of falling off a swing which revived her birth trauma. Similarly, trauma experienced during birth may lurk behind the fear of riding the underground; the tunnel evokes the journey through the birth canal. Jacob's dream from the Bible may be the oldest written record of the ladder-dream. This dream symbolizes the fall of mankind from heaven to earth, and illustrates the loss of our spiritual eminence thanks to the phenomenon of birth and humans becoming corporeal beings. Nándor Fodor wrote in his book, *The Search for the Beloved* (1949), that life on earth started long ago in the lukewarm waters of the primaeval ocean. It is written in the Bible that "the spirit of God was floating above the waters." One crucial step forward in evolution was the adaptation of ancient creatures from marine circumstances to living on land. In our lives, whenever a baby is born, this significant act is repeated, at least in symbolic form. Human life begins in the warm amniotic (ancient) fluid. From birth, the child lives on land, as our ancestors were drifted onto land by the warm ebbs of the primaeval sea. Therefore, it is not surprising that many pathological fears of neurotic people are centred on water. This kind of fear is quite widespread and manifests itself in multiple distinct ways; it can be connected to seas, rivers, lakes or even bathtubs. Children often fear that they will be swept away by the tiny swirl of water flowing out of the bathtub; they fear it will swallow them whole. The unconscious identifies water with amniotic fluid and imminent birth. We know that amniotic fluid can flow around the baby when the membranes rupture and its flow may wrap the umbilical cord around its neck. It is possible that blurred memories stemming purely from the body create the basis of this anxiety. It is not important on what basis the patient transfers his sufferings from birth onto water while this shift or displacement exists. If we can show this displacement to the anxious patient and he/she is able to recognize the misunderstanding, he/she is able to conquer the fear.

A hydrophobic female patient dreamt that she was in an orchard surrounded by hedges. Both the garden and shrubbery were "unkempt." She crawled through a hole in the shrubbery and fell into a canal. There was a hole under the water and that pulled her further down, to a place of serenity where all was peaceful. She was aware that she was surrounded by water and somebody was calling her name but it was as if she had no feeling in any part of her body – she wasn't feeling anything of herself. The dream's symbolism is so evidently related to birth that, without a doubt, there is a connection between the patient's hydrophobia and her entrance to this world. Her dream expresses this substance as a mirror would. In orchards, fruit grows from seeds. The symbol of the garden of life – into which she was lead through a shrubbery – is a "denseness" which has corporeal significance. Her fear of swirls embodies her fear that she will be "swallowed back" into her mother's body. The canal represents the cervix. The peacefulness refers to the peace of the womb before birth. Her being called by her name is the first sign of her new destiny, but fear does not accompany the message because the exit into this other environment, the ordeals of birth, are so far unknown to her. This woman recalled another dream in which she was falling into water from a dam, only to be rescued by her mother. Her mother then fell into the water and the patient rescued her in turn. The latter movement of the dream symbolizes the childhood fantasy in which there occurs a generational swap. Young girls say "when I grow up, I will be big like you are, mom, and you will be small like I am, and I will carry you around." In this dream, her child-soul is crying for freedom from her hydrophobia. The water is the symbol of life, but also the symbol of death. Symbolic death is the price we have to pay for a new life, as our dreams concerned with water can testify.

We were all living in another world before birth. Every utopian vision stems from our nostalgia after the lost serenity of the womb. It rarely happens that a patient is able to relive the ordeals of birth on the psychoanalytic couch. A great amount of proof needs to be collected about an event as emotionally charged as birth for us to accept the patient's accounts as accounts about the real event of birth and not about a fantasy. However, these fantasies can also be interesting in and of themselves. We will now quote from a dream of one of Nándor Fodor's patients: "My head hangs down and I am going downward. I feel that I will be born. It is not easy, so I try to help with my legs. This is a peculiar situation. My head is on its side." The patient's head was tipped to one side, hanging partially from the couch. He shook himself and sighed: "it was a terrible event – being born." Suddenly, he remembered that his mother had told him that the obstetrician had to use his instruments to help the birth. His head was in the wrong direction and was hurt. He showed a wound on his forehead. Then he recalled a detail from another dream: he was frightened by a repulsive man bending over above him. The man lifted up a briefcase and closed it. He thought that the man in his dream was the obstetrician. Fodor conceives that a newborn is not able to form such exact memories about his surroundings immediately after birth. But sensory perception is not necessarily the only channel open to us for mapping our world at the time of birth. At birth, our unconscious is not yet flooded with perceptual stimuli, but it can function in an identical manner to archaic experiences as we are able to see when investigating telepathic phenomena. If such mental capacities do exist at all, we may assume that they take part in cognition and turn to the new world in the interest of survival. The unconscious –- with the characteristic sensitivity of a photograph – records the events. Whether this unconscious storing happens through maternal mental functioning – since her soon-to-be-born child is connected to her through the psychological umbilical cord – or is independent of it is not an imperative question. One expectant mother had the opinion that it is a very different experience for her foetus if it hears music as passed through her psyche or simply her abdominal wall.

Careful study of pregnancy can provide valuable data about the real basis of fantasies apparently concerned with prenatal life experiences. We need criteria to be able to distinguish the memory traces of actual prenatal experiences. We can come to know the psyche of foetuses by investigating postnatal dreams, with ultrasound observations of foetal gestures and facial expressions, or by mother–foetus bonding analysis, where the self-expression of the foetus is reflected in the mother's psyche.

Let us think of the previously mentioned research of Dr Mancuso from Milan, which proved that the stem cells of the foetus make their way into the mother's internal systems as messengers and that these stem cells also contain the genes of the father. These stem cells demonstrate the needs of the foetus for the mother; they inhibit the functioning of her immune system, so that her body can accept the newcomer. We can also suppose that the foetus is in some ways being mentally prepared for its birth and perhaps has premonitions about the transition it will have to face. Experiences we have gained during mother–foetus bonding analysis have shown that the mothers and children who are coached via this method usually experience a less traumatic and stressful birth.

In prenatal dreams, the element of time is often present. Fodor is convinced that every dream has a hidden date. Said date is most easily concealed beneath numbers, but different activities may also contain time definitions within themselves. An expectant mother would have preferred if – contrary to the obstetrician's prediction – her child were not to be born on Christmas Day, since she then would not be able to celebrate the holiday with her family. We were of the opinion that it would be wise for her to ask the baby in a relaxed state – during analysis – to instead arrive two days earlier, and it indeed happened as she requested. This example shows us that in every unborn child – perhaps transmitted by the mother – there exists some kind of timekeeping or calendar. To quote the poet Attila József: "my organs are clocks, which run as the stars" (from the poem "It will be good to remember"). Indeed, there is a biological clock working in every living organism which follows the motion of the planets, day and night. Let us simply think of the correspondence of the times of birth with the full moon and with dawn. We know the localization of this clock in human anatomy: Joanna Wilheim (Wilheim 1995), a psychoanalyst from Brazil, supposes that, stored in the nucleus above the crossing of the optic nerve located in the brain, cellular memory functions from the moment of conception, or even before that, in sperms and eggs. She supposes that this cellular memory also plays a role in creating the foundation of the human unconscious and is definitive with regards to our later life. Fodor supposes the existence of a purely organismic memory system; besides that, prenatal experiences affecting the unborn are also stored in the brain along with the function of adapting to these effects. An organismic psyche or the assumption of an organismic consciousness follows from embryonic development, which controls the relationship of the developing human with the womb. The relationship between the human unconscious and this organismic consciousness is unclear. From a structural perspective, we can imagine this organismic psyche as a deeper stratum, perhaps as the real foundation of the human unconscious. This foundation is usually unreachable by psychological means, but it is present and without this foundation, it is impossible to construct any human edifice. The unconscious psyche "thinks" via the conscious mind. Fodor's research on telepathy in 1949 supplied him with facts that showed the unconscious has its own perceptual channels. Telepathy is one of these channels, but it is impossible for the conscious mind to understand its exact nature. It is possible that telepathy functions between mother and child and can play important roles, for example in separating the neonate from its mother's body. I would here like to remind the readers of Winnicott's concept of the primary maternal preoccupation. The loving expectations and reassuring thoughts of the mother may exert a highly positive influence on the foetus – the opposite, of course, is also true. The loneliness of an unwanted child is more than just a post-birth psychological construct; it goes back to the psychic isolation inside the womb. D.H. Lawrence, in his book titled *Sons and Lovers*, writes of a mother with her unwanted child in her arms:

> Its clear, knowing eyes gave her pain and fear. Did it know all about her? When it lay under her heart, had it been listening then? Was there a reproach in the look? She felt the marrow melt in her bones, with fear and pain.

In the novel, Lawrence writes about his own mother and the questions stem from his intuitive questioning of his own prenatal soul.

The psychoanalytic integration of personality cannot be completed until the prenatal levels are reached, because the psychic foundations of our existence are formed before our birth.

The trauma of birth is the introduction to prenatal integration. In the most important phase, prenatal concussions must be dealt with. The first step in working through such shock is that the conscious mind must obtain knowledge of their existence and their nature. Since words were not at its disposal at the time, the prerequisite to their catharsis is the intellectual comprehension of their nature. *Fostering comprehension opens a mental channel through which early reactions born of fear may enter the conscious and relinquish their hold.*

Falling in our dreams: always a recollection of birth, a child's first fall. A dream where the dreamer falls into the open mouth of a tiger evokes the ordeals of birth. The tiger can be the symbol of death in the unconscious, but it can also symbolize the absorbing mother, who swallows the child back into her womb – this is a common infantile fear. The image reminds one of a story of Ferenczi, who illustrated identification with the aggressor via a small bird, who, in his fear of being swallowed by a bigger bird, flies directly into its throat.

The unconscious stores memory traces from the time of conception; it also guards the collective configurations of humankind's ancient, shared experiences. Our unconscious is a storage of veritable events, while also being a highly dynamic psychological domain which exerts its influence on our everyday life. Most of the time, we only recognize its existence after its manifestations have already taken place. There are several methods which can help us to reach the layers of the unconscious and make its contents – psychological motivations, past traumas and wishes – conscious and integrate them into our personality.

7 The method of mother–foetus bonding analysis

We started to work out the method of mother–foetus bonding analysis together with my training analyst György Hidas in the mid-1990s. Now, when this book is published, it is 2002, and, as follows from the natural order of things, thanks to the accumulation of data and experiences, the technique is still developing, and, hopefully for quite some time, will continue to be. We can therefore safely say that the mothers and babies who thus far took part in and completed bonding analysis (their number exceeding 200) did not do so with equal conditions and opportunities. For example, the third expectant mother enhanced the quality and odds of success of the 15th, the 120th of the 152nd and so on. With each case, we gained more experience and honed our technique, our wisdom grew, as did our knowledge, and we were able to progressively help expectant mothers more and more. We are therefore grateful to each and every one of them. We can safely say that we took care to aid each patient with the maximum of our momentary knowledge in extracting as much gain from the hidden benefits and opportunities provided by the mother–foetus relationship as possible. We were not successful every time. Although we established a technique and a craft, thanks to which we – let me stress again, with the help of the participating mothers – gained knowledge which is entirely new and original, we cannot say that we possess the philosopher's stone. It is possible that what we do not know outnumbers what we do, and it is likely to stay that way.

In the meantime, the method of mother–foetus bonding analysis has been accepted in international circles of scientists working in the areas of pre- and perinatal life as a blueprint. We first introduced our method in Heidelberg in 1995, at the 12th world congress of the International Society for Prenatal and Perinatal Psychology and Medicine, in a lecture titled "Intrauterine Mother Representation," where we delineated the psychoanalytic-theoretical foundations of mother–foetus bonding analysis. Much water has since flown down the Danube. The demand for training in the method has since increased in Hungary as well as among the international scientific community as a whole, which indicates that we are at the outset of a foundation of a new school of psychology.

There are two ways of establishing such a new school of thought. Either the existing literature is synthesized, that is to say, someone interprets the content

DOI: 10.4324/9781003331865-7

in a new, original way; alternatively, clinical practice may serve as the foundation. Someone discovers a new symptom or occurrence, and utilizes a new, original approach both in treatment and in the theoretical reasoning behind it. Our method belongs to the second category. The antecedents go back about 10–12 years. In the mid-1980s, I was working in a psychiatric ward for children and adolescents. A child's suffering is especially hard to bear – adults ought to defend, not turn against, children and leave them at the mercy of the power and impulses of themselves or others. With a bit of simplification and hyperbole we can say that we see the child's behaviour, in whose reflection we in turn see the origins of the behaviour, the parents, their mental problems and relationship issues.

Adolescence is an especially problematic, vulnerable phase of life, where practically all emotional equilibria are upset and the adolescent is suddenly confronted with a different parental image than the one constructed earlier. Crises are unavoidable in this critical period; their absence is more disquieting and dangerous than their occurrence. But this crisis-period may come to last. The adolescent may be unable to solve the problems of this transitional phase and the crisis may lead to a psychotic state. So, I started treating psychotic adolescents. The method of treatment was psychoanalysis. After a while, the therapeutic relationship between my patients and I started to expand beyond the scope of the usual psychopathological and interpretational frame of reference we know from psychoanalytic literature and clinical practice. In these cases, the psychology of prenatal life came to the forefront – a "terra incognita"; a field in which we had no experience nor any literature. Now I would like to lead the reader to the roots of bonding analysis via a case summary.

One time a new patient, a 16-year-old young man, was brought to our ward in a serious condition. He had not eaten any food made by his mother at home for the past few days. He lay on the floor of the ward, crying that his mother wanted to kill him by poisoning his food. Psychiatrists call this phenomenon delusion. After a short while, he started to suspect that each member of staff wanted to destroy him. It was only possible to feed him through intravenous therapy. He was decrepit and exhausted and lay in bed for days. I visited him in the mornings, sat down next to him and asked how he was doing. One day, I asked him what he was feeling instead of my usual question. "I feel cramps in my whole body," he answered. Some days later, he felt strain inside his body directed from within to without to counteract the pressure. We call these sensations bodily sensations. In normal states – that is, in healthy, balanced individuals – they do not occur, only in deep regression, when the patient reverts to a developmental level that has since been far surpassed. The presence of bodily sensations means that the person falls back to a visceral, vegetative level, which is the dominant way of functioning in prenatal life. We were left with no option but to analyze his bodily sensations. This is a particularly unconventional approach in psychoanalysis. If we stick to the principles of psychoanalytic treatment, we are asking our patients to broadcast their thoughts and associations freely and without censorship, which is bound to a very high level of organization; we are treading in the domain of symbolic thinking, underlying which is verbalization, itself anchored in speech – therefore, free association covers a postnatal lifespan, taking place long after birth.

After starting to analyze the bodily sensations of the young man, he started to feel that he was inside my body. A therapeutic relationship was established between us, and in his connection to me he started to repeat his own developmental history. His perception of himself in my body was first of all a quite unusual and thus far unheard of occurrence. Second, it was an evident mapping of one's first relationship, which is created in the womb between mother and foetus. He felt himself in my body as he had once felt himself in the body of his mother. The fact that such a developmental period appears and becomes activated in a therapeutic relationship signified that some problem had not been resolved at that stage; something was blocking the developmental process – it was stuck, and if some serious psychological stress or strain afflicted the patient in later life, it was possible for him to fall back to the developmental level where the obstruction occurred. One of the most therapeutic effects of psychoanalysis is that in the relationship with the analyst, if the patient is fortunate, he will relive his relationship-developmental history and, after the fact, resolve through this process the so-far unresolved problems that hold him prisoner, expose him, tie him to his past, and, as a consequence, "rewrite" his present. In psychoanalysis, we call this process transference. The patient recreates his parents, the most important people of his life, in his analyst and furnishes the analyst with their characteristics, intentions, drives, etc., then reliving those real or fantasized events which he experienced at some point with those emotionally significant persons.

Anyway, I was saying that the boy felt he was inside my body. However, after a while, my young patient started to feel that I was the source of pressure from outside (this is transference), that I wanted to kill him and that he must strain his body constantly to balance my deadly embrace. These bodily sensations increased with every session. Parallel to this, though, the grasp of his delusions of being poisoned loosened and he started to eat, albeit reluctantly and suspiciously. We did not have to feed him intravenously any longer. We had passed the stalemate.

In the transference, then, I appeared to be a destructive mother to him, who perceived himself inside my body. This already is appreciable as a message from his prenatal lifetime, only we are as yet unable to exactly decipher its meaning, what it is composed of, what experience or sensation it covers. I would like to stress here that we are talking about the conception of bodily sensations and not verbal memories. From the fact that his delusions of being poisoned weakened as his bodily sensations strengthened and he began to eat once more, we can conclude that he had relived some prenatal experience involving his mother in his adolescent crisis. He regressed to his prenatal phase but because he had no memories, only bodily sensations, he projected these onto his mother and relived them in the present in the form of a delusion about poisoning. In this sense, he became the captive of his past in his present life.

The therapeutic process and relationship between us became complicated in such a way that he began to "incorporate" himself into me. This meant he did not perceive himself as an independent, distinct individual inside my body but an organ in my body, and this perception only strengthened. He then did not understand at all why I wanted to get rid of him, one of my own organs. Why was I thinking that he was a foreign body? If I would not have considered him a foreign body, I would not have wanted to expel him. His feeling that he was just a foreign body within me stayed with us for a long time. This boy was able to voice not only the foetus, but also the mother inside him. When he verbalized these maternal feelings, it turned out that his mother had long feared him as a foreign entity. She had been afraid that he would proliferate and devour her. He would become a cancerous tumour. This immunological war had raged between them for months. I have to mention here that multiple expectant and new mothers report anxiety-spawned fantasies similar to the ones my young patient expressed in this state. It is probable that real physio-immunological reactions that take place at the time of the embedding of the fertilized egg create the foundation of fantasies where expectant mothers either consciously or unconsciously identify their growing foetus with a cancerous tumour and therefore want to – even involuntarily – expel it: the immune system of the mother identifies the fertilized egg as a foreign body because of paternal genes and attempts to expel it. The baby, however, wants to be embedded. A life-and-death struggle commences between them. It is perhaps not a coincidence that a great number of spontaneous abortions take place in the first three months of pregnancy.

In this phase of the analysis, it became clear that this young man was stuck in the intrauterine developmental phase. For whatever reason, the boundaries of his body were not mentally established, through which he would have been able to identify himself as an entity separate from his mother. He instead experienced himself as an organ, a part of his mother's body. This is what can be deduced from our transference relationship where he repeated his prenatal experiences with his mother and where it became clear that his own personality had not been established. He therefore experienced himself as part of my body, one of its organs. This "incorporation" experience paradoxically evoked another fearful thought, namely that he must exit from my body sometime: bondage and release. As this thought took shape – which is simply the exchange of the desire for immortality with feelings of mortality – his annihilation anxieties worsened. I believe this is an understandable consequence. The feeling of immortality in the foetus is given too great an emphasis if only for the reason that it acquired the maternal body as a life-sustaining resource after a life-and-death struggle. I hold the gradual recognition of mortality by the foetus as one of, if not the, biggest psychological fracture in a human life.

Continuing my patient's story – when his annihilation anxieties started to increase again, he began to make serious accusations towards me for wanting to expel him from our shared body. This way, I was to take away his body. Therefore, he was to become God, who has no body, only a soul. His anxieties became so severe that he found a unique way to tame them. On one occasion, he told me that he was not himself anymore. He was János, one of his classmates. For a long while, he interchanged persons in this manner until I happened to say to him that the reason he has lately been embodying various persons and adopting their forms is because he knew very well that they will not give birth to him, and thus he will not be destroyed, but live forever. He then returned to my body once again. He gave up on attempting to becoming another person in substance. He confronted his unbearable anxieties once more and I again became unbearable for him.

He had an incredibly memorable attachment to his heart. From his perspective, since the both of us had one shared body, we also had only one heart. If I were to give birth to him, one of us must necessarily lose his heart. On an occasion where I was pondering how we could acquire two different hearts, he suddenly started to feel a double heartbeat. I was flabbergasted and hopeful. This perception meant that he had started to form representations of his organs, therefore acknowledging his existence on a psychological level, to be more precise, of an important, central part of himself. So I was hopeful.

It happened as I had theorized. The perception of his own heartbeat repeated, which in turn led to the formation of his heart's mental representation; in other words, he became aware that he had his own distinct heart, different from my own. However, possessing this knowledge resulted in him playing out his birth experience for the first time in our relationship, repeatedly, for many hours, admittedly on a purely physical level at first: motion patterns that accompany the birth process can be seen at epileptic seizures. Through countless repetitions, the incident was completely transformed into a mental representation: the birth experience that had been moulded from physical sensations was transfigured into thought. His psyche was forming almost exactly as models predict, as physical events began to be transformed into psychological ones.

However, he did not become a new man as a result of the rebirth as I had hoped, and I was thoroughly disappointed. He felt like a skeleton stripped of flesh. He existed for quite some time as a skeleton. Then he shrank and became a dwarf. I happened to tell him that he was a skeleton and dwarf because he had lost his mother's body and had thus become less, smaller. He reacted to this statement in an unexpected but quite fruitful manner: expanding his boundaries, he enveloped his environment. Whereas earlier he was in his mother's body, his mother's body was now in turn within him. He started to perceive and use as a reference frame his own corporeal boundaries rather than those of his mother. As the mental representation of his mother was established and solidified in his psyche, so did his boundaries, and he started to perceive himself as a separate human being, distinct from his mother and my body (Raffai 1988, 1991, 1994–95, 1995b).

If, thinking through the case, we ask ourselves what exactly took place in this analysis, and what conclusions we may be able to draw from it, we may say the following: something happened to my young patient within our relationship that should have happened to him in his relation to his mother in the womb – he needed to feel that his body has separated from that of his mother, and he therefore has his own identity and his own constellation of experiences. This included the establishment of the mental representation of his organs and body as well as the representation of his mother. We may call this collective the foetal self-consciousness. Self-awareness and self-perception cannot be established without the subjective mirroring of another person; therefore, it requires bonding. "The unacknowledged fetus is neither a separate object nor a separate subject in and of itself, but is one with its mother, so at birth it loses its mother's body which it perceives as its own" (Vas 2001).

There we have it – our case, and many others like it, which, at least in the statistically deterministic sense, cannot be said to be representative, more so ontologically. From these cases, it can be concluded that the roots of psychoses go back to the prenatal phase of life and points of vulnerability can be found in the mother–foetus relationship. In this case, however, it would be useful to think about prevention and to work out a method with whose help "accidents" such as the one that surfaced in the case study could be averted.

Nevertheless, we have no clue as to the cause of the incident, that is, why the young man failed to develop corporeal boundaries and separate himself from his mother during the first nine months of his life. Our rough, general answer was that the cause was the deficiency or absence of mother–foetus bonding. The only way one gains knowledge of himself is through the reflection in another person, through an interpersonal relationship. As expressed by the beautiful words of the poet, Attila József: "no matter how you bathe it in yourself, you can only wash your face in someone else." It is not a coincidence that the reflective role of the mother in the development of foetuses and infants has today become a standard and fashionable heading for developmental psychology. The new millennium is not about genes; it is about the psyche blossoming within and as a result of interpersonal connections and relationships.

At that time, we did not ascribe any special significance to such data as deaths happening around or during the pregnancy and grief in identifying the preludes and catalysts to illnesses until we stumbled onto a particularly interesting study. Finnish researchers performed studies in which they tracked and compared groups of babies whose mothers lost their husbands during pregnancy, and those who lost their husbands after the birth, respectively. It was later revealed that psychotic illnesses were significantly more common in the group which contained mothers who lost their husbands during pregnancy than in the group where the deaths occurred after the birth of the child (Huttunen and Niskanen 1978). The expectant mothers thus transmitted the trauma to their foetuses in the womb. But how does arrested development ensue from this? How can the mother's trauma hinder the establishment of the foetus's body boundaries? I believe this is the decisive question. It seems that we will be able to answer this with the help of mother–foetus bonding analysis, but let us not get ahead of ourselves.

The aforementioned cases drove in us a strong interest towards prenatal psychology. It was already under assumption that there are complex psychological reactions and processes taking place in the womb between the baby and its mother, or even, with the mother providing a transmission channel, between the baby and the father. It was surprising how rich the psychological literature was in readily available research, investigations and observations. Of course, we were also surprised this data had escaped our notice. Why are we conditioned by society to consider only the postnatal phase of life as human existence?

We read surprising things which only served to further emphasize the impact of the intrauterine period on the later development of personality. At the same time, the literature drew our attention to the startling degree to which the foetus is vulnerable and exposed to various relational and circumstantial effects.

We quote here some more interesting research results. It has been found from comparative studies of desired and unwanted children that the rate of infant mortality, brain injuries, mental retardation, and severe social problems appear in a significantly greater number among unwanted children (Blomberg 1980). Other studies concerning unwanted children have found infant mortality in the first month of life to be twice as high compared to desired children (Bustan and Coker 1994).

Yet another investigation showed that babies whose parents had ended their relationships during pregnancy were born with lower birth weight than babies whose parents' relationships were harmonious or whose mothers were single (McIntosh et al. 1995). It can be plainly seen from this research that the development of the foetus depends not only on the mother but also on a larger social system of which the mother is only a single component, albeit a decisive one.

For example, the role of fathers in the development of foetuses has lately become a forefront issue. Hormonal research from saliva samples proved that the concentration of oestradiol, a female sexual hormone, increased in the blood of expectant fathers while the level of male sexual hormones decreased during the wives' pregnancies (Blazy 2001). This indicates a regress to the prenatal phase on a psychological level. The foetus inside them becomes activated and they communicate with their foetuses on an unconscious level just as the mother does. From this perspective, we cannot think that it is all the same what fathers think or feel about the baby or what they transmit to it.

Thus the father also has the power to be destructive. This is proven in a case in which the mother held on to the child against the father's will. The family in question already had a child. The father threatened his wife with divorce if she were to keep the baby. The mother miscarried in the second month of the pregnancy. The mother later commented that the baby did not want to stand in the crosshairs between them, so it gave itself up instead. The father's will was stronger; he won the battle for the child's perishing; the foetus obeyed its father's internalized wish.

In another case, where the parents' conflicts increased in frequency towards the end of the pregnancy, the foetus froze up when the mother projected the father's image before it. Earlier, the baby responded to its father's gentle caresses through the mother's belly, but never once during tense times.

These episodes show that we must not mystify the dual-union of mother and child. We must open our minds to the concept that *the intrauterine child lives in a complicated interpersonal network and if one member in this system does not function optimally, it is primarily the foetus who suffers the consequences.*

A study conducted by Austrian researchers also calls attention to the significance of intrauterine relationships. The study observed 27 pregnant women who were not aware of their own pregnancy until – quite surprisingly – the onset of labour. The researchers recorded four instances of foetal mortality, one developmental retardation, three premature births and one neonatal death (Brezinka et al. 1994).

Let us now mention two other surveys which provide a direct connection between the personality of the mother and the behaviour of the foetus. In total, 1,312 mothers who had suffered depression during their pregnancies, and their babies immediately after birth, participated in the study. The newborns were crying uncontrollably in the first few days and their score on the depression scale was in line with that of their mothers (Zuckerman et al. 1990).

In yet another investigation, researchers observed that babies of mothers who were rejecting their babies on both conscious and unconscious levels showed the symptoms of Kipp syndrome in the first 48 hours after birth in the form of alternating apathetic behaviour and hyperactive crying (Rottmann 1974). The number of complications at birth and premature births was the highest in this group. Other studies also prove that extremely negative maternal attitude manifests itself in the higher number of spontaneous abortions and premature births, as well as in longer, more complicated deliveries.

To go even further into the research, let us quote the results of Roe and Drivas (1993). They compared a group of unplanned babies with a group of babies who were expected and planned for at three months old. The group of planned babies performed significantly better in measurements of cognitive development and bonding capability.

Our therapeutic experiences and research data prove that there is a penetrable prenatal relational space which is filled with events of positive and negative qualities, which, if neglected, may produce tragic, and, if utilized, positive consequences influencing mother-baby bonding after birth and later personality development. As Brezinka's results show, some foetuses that live in an intrauterine relational vacuum due to a denial of pregnancy will not even start physical development; others either die or suffer severe developmental impairment. In other cases, where the baby is only an abstract idea to the mother, and thus is not present in her consciousness as a distinct personality developing in the force field of interactions, severe developmental handicaps will occur.

We cannot pass by mothers, whose attitude towards pregnancy, stemming from their various anxieties, prompt them to be of the belief that a baby should be left alone in order not to harm it, without a few criticisms, for the reverse of this opinion is true. *The most harm we can do to foetuses is by not taking any notice of them.* This is also what the above studies show. Let us ask the question: how would any of us feel if they had their share of being ignored by others? Would not we feel like non-existent beings, without personality or identity?

On the basis of our therapeutic experiences and scientific literature, György Hidas and I began to think of creating a preventive method. At the outset, our aim was to prevent psychoses that may occur later in life. The main question is, of course, how and with what modifications it would be possible to apply the therapeutic method we were using in curing psychoses to expectant mothers. It was clear then that the analysis of bodily sensations lead us back to the prenatal time of life. How can expectant mothers reach the bodily sensations of their foetuses, the communicational channel through which the most essential unconscious information travels? Other channels for communication are naturally at her disposal, such as the movements of the baby, the mother's inner voice, music, the mother's movements, stroking the baby through the abdominal wall, etc.

The crux of our discussion is not that mothers do not have a natural connection to their baby, rather, it is the depth of the relationship that is the question, as well as the different ways the mother's mental state, social past, her own foetal experiences, parental projections, and not least the tensions of her psychosocial environment may distort or otherwise influence this relationship.

It is evident that foetuses are capable of psychic functioning. How, then, can we make these functions understandable and reflective to the mother to foster a productive dialogue between the two? After lengthy experimentation, we decided not to change the psychoanalytic frame of the situation, so the expectant mother lies on the couch in a relaxed state and the analyst sits behind her, as if at the periphery of their relational space. The main goal is not the development of a therapeutic connection between the mother and the analyst but the establishment of a deep bonding between mother and foetus that cannot be reached during a normal pregnancy. We were aware that the substantive events which determine the fate and developmental opportunities of the baby take place on an unconscious level and are often in need of correcting. This is one consideration. The other was attempting to help the establishment of an emotional and cognitive bonding space between mother and foetus which each could penetrate and understand, in which emotions could be shared and thus the regulation and differentiation of the relationship, as well as rendering it harmonious, would become possible. We were able to make foetal emotions accessible for the mother by tuning her attention to the wave of emotions from the baby towards the mother instead of to that of free association. Regarding the frequency of the sessions, meeting twice, and, on rare occasion, three times per week proved to be ideal.

Mother–foetus bonding analysis always starts with a "first interview." This is a structured conversation in whose framework we assess the mother's personality, her relational system and her relationship with people who are emotionally important to her. We also estimate the maturity of her personality, her bonding capacities, tolerance of psychological stress. We assess her attitudes towards her baby as well as the accompanying fears and anxieties. We collect data about her own prenatal experiences – had she been a desired or unwanted child, what was her birth experience like, etc. We then inform her about the essence of the method, the structure of the sessions and make a contract. During the elaboration we emphasize that the two of them are the primary authors of the story of their relationship. Accurate, absorbed, steady and hard work is necessary. There is no trickery, no smoke or mirrors. It is in this relationship that the personality development of the baby is determined as well as just how good of a mother the mother can be. The task of the analyst is, first and foremost, to assist the mother in constructing the bonding space. The analyst does not, however, interfere with the spontaneous process of bonding. There are certain mental techniques in the bond-establishing repertoire which we recommend during the sessions. Such a technique, for example, is the regular massaging of the baby with the inner (mental) hand.

Another task of the analyst is to interpret, and thus put an end to, unconscious processes that may harm the baby and topple the relationship itself. The analyst, having a knowledge of the actual events, may suggest that the mother give great emphasis to the reflection of certain relational events. It is necessary for the analyst to interfere directly – of course, on a psychological level – if the baby's life is in danger due to a negative change in its vitals and provided that the danger can be averted by psychological means. We give examples of such interventions below.

A special process begins to take its course from the 36th week. By analyzing the birth experiences as well as several thousand therapeutic hours of more than a hundred expectant mothers, we have created a script in the form of a written text that optimally helps the mutual separation of the parties and, most carefully, prepares them both for birth. There are seven structured sessions, followed by a full rehearsal, at the outcome of which we ascertain whether more sessions are needed or the bonding analysis may be considered completed. The process ends with the birth. We meet the baby and parents on one occasion after birth and discuss the birth experience as well as the experiences of their first period of time.

Let us stay for a while at the framework, at the foundations. Together, the analyst's office, the two-person setting, the silence, the spatial configuration, the mother's reclined position, the distinguished behaviour of the analyst also symbolize the receptive, protective womb. As a consequence, the mother herself can get in touch with her own prenatal and birth experiences. The former helps her to form a deep bond with her baby, the latter to be able to process her own birth trauma and stopping it from impairing the birth of her child. The analyst works to tune in to the mother's feelings, who in turn identifies with the analyst, and thus becomes able to more easily establish a relationship with her baby. This process explains why many expectant mothers struggle to maintain their relationship with their foetuses with the same depth and efficiency as if they were to get help in relationship maintenance from an analyst. Transference also develops in mother–foetus bonding analysis between the analyst and the mother. Expectant mothers enter into an emotional relationship with the analyst and unconsciously identify the analyst as a parent or as some significant aspect of a parent. This secure emotional relationship has powerful facilitating capabilities.

Part of the setting is also that mothers- and fathers-to-be get some home-work. We recommend for the mother to sit in a rocking chair ten minutes a day and listen to music, and for the fathers to establish a connection with the baby on a daily basis in the second half of the pregnancy. Fathers can get in touch by first stroking the baby through the abdominal wall; later, we encourage them to talk to the baby, tell a brief story or sing songs – all on a daily basis. We have already written about the role of the vestibular system in personality development in the chapter on the intelligent foetus. The immaturity of the vestibular system impairs the child's ability to concentrate which leads first to difficulties in learning and behavioural problems, and consequently, to a nega-tive self-image, and, finally, depressive symptoms. The rocking chair provides the most effective stimulation for the vestibular system we know of today.

By establishing a connection with her baby, the expectant mother creates a psychological space so that the child can acquire emotional and cognitive experiences.

We use the mother's ego as the foundation for bonding and dialogue. The mother becomes able to perceive and to enter the psychological space of the baby using her ego. The messages originating from this space appear on her inner screen, the same place where dreams and fantasies show (Hidas 1999). These sensations may transform into images and thoughts inside the mother and mobilize fantasies and emotions. This method of communication works both ways. The baby is able to decode the mother's messages which arrive as images, thoughts, fantasies, and to provide a corresponding answer. They natu-rally share each other's mental contents in the common bonding space. This means that *the initially common contents become private as the baby processes them. The nature of this processing provides the experience and the mental contents with indi-viduality. When what was once common becomes internalized.* Therefore, it does not matter much whether or not what goes on between them is merely projected by the mother. If the readers ask how it is possible that the baby understands the mother's messages, I am only able to give a partial answer. In my opinion, the foundations of understanding lay in the ability of experiences to be shared. What we can share with others, others can also relive and thus understand it. But we are, by the way, mostly in the dark concerning this field. For example, do we know how many layers of meaning a given word may take on? Consider its affective, cognitive, semantic layers and so on.

The establishment of the mutual bonding space is the necessary precondi-tion in order to start this communication process and the mother's ability to receive the baby's messages and translate them onto her inner screen in the form of some pictures or thoughts, like when a television transforms incoming electronic signals into images on its screen. We are not of the opinion that in this procedure the baby sends a symbolic, that is, a visually complex message to the mother and this image appears in every detail; rather, we think the mother synthesizes the end product from the raw material using her psychic apparatus. I would like to emphasize that the raw material defines the end product; it is possible to produce only what the raw material permits. We are probably talking here about the mechanism of human psyche formation: *the party possessing the higher level of psychological organization and more complex psychic apparatus analyzes the simpler signal, then deconstructs it into its basic elements, lifts it into the symbolic sphere and mirrors it back to the sender. This way, the baby's feelings are, on a complex level, reflected and become identifiable.* This is the fundamental process of psychic construction in bonding analysis. We suspect that this is the reason why babies of bonding analysis possess a superior ability to abstract and can navigate the world with a playful fluency.

However, we must be careful with the above assertions. We do not want to make the mistake of underestimating the proficiencies of foetuses. We have had a lot of surprises during mother–foetus bonding analyses. I will allow myself to mention only one dilemma: with regard to visual thinking and communication, it will not hurt to mention that foetuses dream the most. And in dreams, images are formed. It often happens in bonding analyses that babies react not to the mother's inner voice, only to her visual messages.

Let us return to the frame of reference. Bonding analysis oversteps the boundary where mother and foetus play only passive and unmindful roles among the psychic factors determining the nature of their relationship. The mother, with the help of the analyst, is able to further develop the natural relationship and so-far unconscious dimensions become accessible (Hidas 2000). Our experience showed that the mother's unconscious affects the development of her baby much more than their conscious relationship, for example, when she talks to the baby or caresses it through the abdominal wall. Let us view a few examples.

In one case of bonding analysis, the baby was still in a breech presentation near the end of pregnancy. The mother was afraid of birth complications. Despite my suggesting to her many times that she ask the baby to turn around, she did not follow my advice. During a later session, an important motive that, though she had already mentioned, I had somehow forgotten, resurfaced, namely that she herself and also her mother had been born in this same position. I suggested that the mother tell the baby the following: "I might be telling you involuntarily that I was born in this position and made you think this would also be good for you. This, however, does not mean that you need to do as I did." My assumptions were founded on the possibility of identifying with the mother's unconscious information. The baby turned around that day and changed its position frequently. It was in a breech position again at birth. We could only guess at the reasons at the time; in light of recent events, however, we now are aware of them, three years later. We will also talk of this later.

Another expectant mother fell into panic from time to time that she would not be able to carry her foetus to term and that she would give birth to a premature baby. It turned out from the anamnesis that her own mother was very impatient with her pregnancy because she felt it hindered her scientific career.

It was not difficult to connect the two factors. The mother of the patient was talking through her whenever she felt panic about her ability to carry her child to birth.

One important technical element of bonding analysis is the mother's fusion with the womb which makes it easier to get in touch with the foetus on the top of several other benefits. In some cases, the mother-to-be becomes able to close the open cervix in a purely mental way, eliminating the need for cervical cerclage. She is able to expand it if necessary during birth. She is also able to soften her cervix if it hardens. The babies are very grateful on those occasions. When they are too small to make their presence perceptible by kicks, during relating, they cling to the wall of the womb to which their mother is fused. But they never do this if the womb has, for some reason, hardened.

The following contents of the mother's different developmental periods can be manifested in the transference in the interpersonal space of bonding analysis (Hidas 2000):

1. The feelings and attitudes of the mother's mother, primarily towards her foetus during her pregnancy, their effects and memory traces which were stored in the foetus at the time. We call this the foetus's intrauterine maternal representative (Raffai 1995a, 1996, 1997, 1998).
2. The mother's experiences and sensations before, during and after birth.
3. The expectant mother's feelings, attitudes, fantasies and thoughts, even those from before conception, the transmitted representation of the child's father and not least the mother's pre-formed mental representation of the foetus. This representation has a strong influence on the development of the foetus's self-image. If the foetus sees in the mirror of the mother that he/she is a vegetative being without consciousness, he/she will react accordingly. If he/she sees that he/she is an equal partner who can influence the relationship and the personality of the mother with his/her responses and actions, he/she will develop a stable and strong self-representation as well as self-confidence. We witness this phenomenon in the majority of children who were born having partaken in bonding analyses. Many babies develop with such intensity after birth that the parents find themselves unable to keep up with their child's mental growth.

The sway of the mother's emotional attitudes influences not only the baby's emotional development and bonding capacities but also the functioning of the baby's entire psychosomatic system. In fact, to an extent, lifespan and quality of life may be determined during a baby's prenatal time. Here I reference more recent research concerned with maternal stress that concluded that the mother's emotional attitude towards her foetus may lead to coronary disease, possibly increasing the chance of stroke in later life (Van der Bergh 2001). Unwanted children as well as those who were conceived unexpectedly, if it has taken more time from either the maternal or paternal side to be accepted, are primarily exposed to such emotional stress. Let us illustrate this point with a case vignette.

The baby was conceived by chance. This conception crossed plans the parents had had for many years. Still, the thought of abortion never even occurred to them. The mother needed a great deal of time to accept the newcomer. Several months passed by before she could accept and love the baby. On the 36th week, the gynaecologist began examining the functioning of the foetus's heart and found that the pulse frequency was 180–200 beats per minute and increased above 200 if the baby moved. The situation was life-threatening so the possibility of an immediate Caesarean section emerged. In the end, the doctors decided to have the mother attend daily heart frequency measurements of the foetus.

I first suggested that the mother massage the baby with her inner mental hand several times a day from head to toe. After two days, the lower bound of the pulse frequency decreased to 160 and reached 200 only when the baby moved; this was enough to decrease the frequency of examinations. Since the readings were still too high and could be expected to restrict the baby's life course and have a negative influence on his/her quality of life, I suggested that the mother use her inner voice to tell the baby the following:

> You have arrived unexpectedly. We were not prepared to have a child. It has taken us some time to accept and love you. You must have felt that we did not want you, did not need you, that you were unnecessary. This must have been heartbreaking for you. But now you know that we have accepted you and love you. You are important to us!

This message evoked dramatic reactions on both sides: the mother wept for ten minutes and the baby reacted with tempestuous movements and extreme excitement that outlasted the mother's emotional shock. I was afraid that the baby would be born there, on the spot. They both got rid of this crushing emotional burden that had held them prisoner up until that point. At the next measurement the baby's pulse frequency stabilized between 140 and 160. Their relationship, and within it, they themselves were healed. We succeeded in averting the danger of a later heart attack in the intrauterine context where it had been formed.

At the beginning of mother–foetus bonding analyses, we dealt with mothers for whom it was easy to get in contact with their babies. They taught us that the inner voice of the mother and the act of emanating love have great power in establishing such connections – this fact has since been proven by other studies (Busnel et al. 1998). Later, we experienced an influx of mothers who, though able to fuse with their womb, when met with the baby, became helpless.

One of them was clueless after having made contact with her baby. After a brief hesitation, she started to tell the baby about her day. The baby did not move or react to this message. The mother was worried that the baby was ill or had some unknown problem. I told the mother that the foetus will react to messages that pertain to or involve it. This information established the mental framework of their cooperation. The mother then told the baby she loved it and that she was very happy they had found each other. The little one started to move, and so the bonding process began. It happened on several later occasions that the process of mutual empathy got stuck and the mother did not understand the baby's messages. In such cases, we usually suggest the mother signal to her baby that she has difficulty understanding and ask the baby to let her fuse with him/her to be able to think and feel through the child's mind. This minor technical measure always helps the parties to get in touch. The foundation of this technique lay in considerations concerned with empathy. Nothing less than the nature of the content the mother is able to transmit from the private world of inner experiences, and what she is not, depends on her capacities for empathy. The former is human to human psychological union, and the latter is mental isolation (Stern 1985). If the mother is unable to understand some of the baby's messages, he/she assumes that his/her experiences cannot be shared. Therefore, the experiences do not connect people but separate and isolate them.

If the emotional-cognitive bonding space is established between mother and foetus, nearly all relational events can be communicated. We have to stress here once more that the establishing of the bonding space starts with the mirroring of relational events. One mother described this phenomenon aptly:

> it is as if the thoughts formulating within you were not your own. To me, the message appears first as some kind of feeling or sensation and I decipher its meaning only gradually and I myself convert it into intellectualized thoughts.

This same mother, when having trouble perceiving her baby, told it, on my suggestion, that she would like to better feel and understand it, and, if it would not be a problem, she would prefer it move closer to her heart. The little one always obeyed. It occurred once that the mother could not feel the exact position of the baby's head. So, she asked the baby to signal using its head, and it nodded. Afterwards, she could find the head with ease. It has happened that the delivery date could be negotiated with the baby. In another case, a baby turned upside down during labour at the request of the mother. Often, curious mothers ask their babies to turn towards the detector during ultrasound observations because they would like to know their sex. The babies obey many times to the great surprise of the examiner. In other cases, the mothers succeeded in spectacularly decreasing their babies' pulse frequency during medical examinations by emanating love to the baby. The possibilities therefore move between truly distant boundaries.

When we suggest to expectant mothers that they communicate their own difficulties regarding establishing the bond, understanding and mutual relationships, we are further expanding the bonding space to accommodate not only the baby's shared feelings which form a conglomerate of experiences but also the mother's mental state so that it can be reflected in the babies' consciousness, thus the babies are able to attune themselves and produce adequate responses.

The road from establishing a connection to building the bond is a long one. It requires systematic, enduring work. The relationship that the mother does not represent mentally, and thus does not accommodate it in her conscious, cannot transform into bonding because the emotional substance is not differentiated from the body; neither does it become the other person's distinguishing characteristic. No babies in bonding analysis react to the caresses of strangers – only to people represented in bonding.

Though we learned a lot from mothers who could not get in touch easily with their babies and forced us to be creative in difficult moments and lead them to the path to establish the bonding space, we gained at least as much knowledge from those who proved gifted in developing the bond. I quote two examples from the research material of the Mannheim University Clinic, where the effectiveness of mother–foetus bonding analysis has now been studied for several years. In the research programme, we conducted mother–foetus bonding analysis in the clinic's maternity ward. Both episodes are taken from the respective second sessions.

Gudrun is in the 22nd week of her pregnancy. She successfully managed to get through to her baby at the very beginning of the session. The baby moved towards the mother's heart with lightning speed, landed just under it and tapped thrice. The mother felt that the baby wanted to play with her. However, no action followed. The little one waited a few seconds and then withdrew to its original position in the corner of the womb and became still. I told the mother it seems the baby was hurt then because she did not play with it. The mother was able to identify with this statement and the baby immediately got going again so that they could begin to play with each other.

What could have happened in the bonding space during these minutes? With my help, the mother comprehended and was able to mirror the baby's feelings, who, as a consequence, ascertained from this experience that he/she was able to share his/her mental states because there was someone who understood the way he/she felt. With this, the baby freed itself from its paralyzing captivity. Instead of psychological isolation, it created a mental union with the mother. This proves once again that if a baby shares a mental state with a human being who is different from his/her self, then it is possible to share subjective experiences on this basis. This includes the sharing of emotions and mutual recognition as the basic elements of bonding space. Acknowledging someone else's inner world of experiences is equivalent to entering it and sharing its contents, thereby reinforcing said other person (Borstad 1988).

It was a pleasant surprise when, a year later, at a conference in Mannheim where the first partial results of the study were presented, Gudrun and her son appeared at our bonding analysis workshop. They sat next to me on the podium. The young man scanned the crowd with pride and confidence. The public dubbed him a power-baby.

In the second example, Dagmar was in the 20th week of pregnancy. At the establishment of the connection her baby also started moving towards her heart. In its joy, the baby got so close that it hindered Dagmar's breathing, which she voiced to me. I suggested her to tell the baby that it was causing an inconvenience for her and to ask the baby to move down a little bit. The baby drew down and, just as it reached the bottom, up again, settling under the mother's heart. Dagmar was taken aback. I asked her why she was surprised. "When I asked the baby to move down a bit he/she went down so deeply that my lower abdomen started to hurt. I was thinking that it would be much better if he/she came up a bit and the baby did so immediately," she answered. We can see here how empathy bridges the space between two separate consciousnesses. This episode promptly reminded me of Busnel's experiment which proved that babies react to their mothers thinking about them by changing their heart frequency. Busnel's results, it seems, are merely the tip of the iceberg.

The possibilities of establishing bonding thus move between distant boundaries. Until recently we had been working only in the common psychological domain when some dramatic changes in the biological system of a few mothers-to-be forced us to apply the method of bonding analysis to correct the errors of systems we had assumed were purely biological.

One pregnant patient who had a very good relationship with her baby was diagnosed by ultrasound in the 36th week of her pregnancy with superannuated placenta, a decreased amount of amniotic fluid and low foetal weight. The gynaecologist called an immediate conference of doctors. They were debating whether to perform a Caesarean section. In the end, they ordered two daily CTG examinations as well as the daily measurement of bloodstream through the placenta (flowmetry). The mother was of course in a panic. Already, she had started to massage the placenta with her inner mental hand during the session. The following sensations were felt: increased pulsation and breakthrough. She was also directed to continue this practice at home due to the dangers of the acute intervention. Her test results improved so much by the next day that the gynaecologist thought the daily tests unnecessary. The beneficial effects of continuous massaging were stable for a week and a half when flowmetry (placenta bloodstream measurement) signalled anew the deterioration of the placenta's state. Again a conference, again the daily examinations. I developed an interpretation during the night and asked the mother during the next session to tell her placenta:

> you can feel as much that you are the mother of my baby as I do. Perhaps you also wish for him/her to live as long as possible. Since you are linked, you might feel that you have the same life source so you are using up each other's lifetime. Based on you making yourself wither before it is time, I suppose that you think that your normal functioning takes time away from the baby's life. That is to say, the longer you live, the shorter the baby's life will be. You are wrong. The sense of guilt that withers you is unnecessary. The nature of the connection between the two of you is quite the

opposite. The longer you function, the longer the baby's life will be. This means that you must not wither but renew yourself.

After the message, the mother registered the following bodily sensations from her placenta: breakthrough, churning, discharging and cleaning. To the shock of the doctor, the next day's ultrasound and the results of the flowmetry signalled placenta regeneration. The baby was born one and a half weeks later on the 39th week but not because of the state of the placenta.

The message that regenerated the placenta would require a complicated explanation. Therefore, allow me to note simply that behind the interpretation lay the mother's deepest, unconscious fantasy of self-reproduction and immortality where she reproduces herself from her own cells. This may induce feelings of remorse in the baby because by not becoming the mother, the foetus may feel that he/she took the mother's life and deprived her of the possibility of eternity.

We can identify this fantasy of eternity realized in the fashionable concept of cloning. As if there were a moment in evolution (I do not know if this is the case) when it had to be decided whether the individual would be immortal or the species. We know that the decision favoured the species. The wish of the individual to be immortal, however, has remained, and directs the development of civilization to reaching the level where such a thing becomes possible. This is cloning.

Let us return, after this brief detour, to the baby whom we rescued from premature birth. The baby was still in breech presentation towards the 39th week. We did not understand the reason for it. In such cases, we first ask the mother if she has any feelings that prevent her from letting the baby go. Most expectant mothers' feelings are ambivalent: they would like to give birth to the child, but at the same time, they feel attached to it and it is hard for them to let go. We found no such reservations in the mother. We asked the same question from the baby who communicated to our surprise through her mother that if he/she were to back away from the mother's heart, to which he/she is closest in breech presentation, he/she would shrink, lose his/her body and die. The baby had a fear of death induced by backing away from the mother's heart.

I was stunned. What did this mean? Well, it communicates the very same thing as the case of the psychotic patient I quoted at the beginning of this chapter; the differentiation of the corporeal boundaries was not completed. Consequently, the baby felt in his/her experiential identity that his/her heart and that of his/her mother were one and the same and thus their body was as well. If the baby backs away from their common heart, he/she starts to feel annihilation anxiety. I did not understand the reasons. Many questions arose in me when, just like lightning, my memory suddenly struck and I remembered that the patient had lost her mother in the third month of her pregnancy. Naturally, I recalled the results of the Finnish research project, the connection between losses during pregnancy and later psychoses of the child, the transmission of trauma. I understood only then how losses during pregnancy may cause differentiation problems in the formation of the foetus's body boundaries. The expectant mother unknowingly substituted the baby for her lost loved one. She unconsciously made the foetus part of her body to prevent further loss.

I believe the connection between the loss during pregnancy, the breech presentation of the baby and the risk of later psychotic illness of the child is evident from this perspective. It seems that the heart has a central role in the differentiation of body boundaries, as well as in the development of identity and individuality in the history of ontogenesis: it is the central organ through which the process of becoming unique, of becoming an individual, begins in a psychological sense.

Following its declaration, we still had a few sessions left to help the baby establish corporeal boundaries.

Now we possess the answer as to why the baby in the case excerpt quoted earlier did not turn before birth when it had been in the breech position. The baby's mother also suffered a great loss: she lost her own mother shortly after conception.

To end this chapter, I would like to illustrate the opening up of bonding analysis towards the biological systems with a difficult story. I had a psycho-analytic patient, a sensitive young lady with depressive symptoms. Her relationship with her psychotic mother lay behind her symptoms; my patient had continually fought her mother in an attempt to decrease her influence. After around three-quarters of a year of treatment, she became pregnant through artificial insemination. We started bonding analysis. Christmas was coming, so we had a three-week break. The baby was then six weeks old. Around the end of the break, her husband called to tell me that his wife had started to bleed so profusely that she had to go to hospital. It turned out that a haematoma had formed on her cervix. This was the source of the bleeding. We know that haematoma does not arise by chance; it must have been caused by some strong physical influence. My patient's mother immediately came to mind. Obviously it was no coincidence. When I managed to get in touch with my patient, I asked her to continue bonding analysis because the haematoma probably had a psychological source and this was the only way we could resolve it. However, she was afraid to overstep her gynaecologist's orders and spent two more weeks in her own bed. The break was then six weeks long in all – the entire length of the critical period. She still had the haematoma when we finally met again and it bled from time to time. During the first session after the break, when she connected with her womb, the image of a needle appeared. At that point, a multitude of data gathered from her analysis pointed to the possibility that she had been an unwanted child and her mother tried to abort her in fantasy or concretely. Nevertheless, I told her that the needle may represent her mother who had tried to abort her and is now trying to do the same to her child. It was not enough, however, to intervene only on the unconscious level – we had to do something with the haematoma. She began to massage it with her mental hand to quicken the healing process. The haematoma started to retreat and, as I remember, the bleeding stopped completely.

She woke up that weekend, to soaked bedding. An examination performed on Monday showed that almost all the amniotic fluid was gone. The heart frequency of the foetus was under the critical limit. Medicinally speaking, nothing could be done. During our next session, fused with the caul, she felt its rupture. We began to mentally thicken the caul. The needle appeared again, but it bounced off the thickened membrane. The leakage of the amniotic fluid stopped thanks to the mental repair efforts, but we did not have time to compensate for the lost amniotic fluid. The baby died.

My patient later mentioned that on the day of the onset of the haematoma, as well as when the amniotic fluid started to leak, her relationship with her mother became a subject of conversation. The tragic case, according to my hypothesis, was brought about due to the effects of the already-mentioned intrauterine maternal representation.

Despite this woeful event, our opportunities of primary prevention have no doubt grown. *Just as it is possible to heal psychosomatic diseases such as ulcus (stomach ulcers) or colitis ulcerosa (inflammatory bowel disease), to mention only two examples, with psychotherapy, so bonding analysis becomes more and more useful in the restoration of biological functions in vivo, in the efforts to save babies' lives, and to improve their quality of life.*

We truly have come much further than our initial intentions and the goals we then set. Babies born from bonding analysis are started on a different developmental course. Their opportunities in life are different, as well as the quality of their life. They sleep little during the day. They are born with their complete and whole selves. They do not dream of returning to their mothers' bodies. They are immersed in the reality surrounding them with their full capacity. They observe, explore and think. When they do, they stop moving altogether. They focus their gaze at a single point, drawing their eyebrows together, wrinkling their forehead. When they are finished with concentration, they go back to movement. There it is, in the corner of their mouths, a coy smile. They know full well where they came from and where they are headed.

8 Intrauterine encounters

Csilla Cseri: "You could see from his eyes that he wanted to know what the world had in store for him"

My first child, my son, was born by Caesarean section. This took a toll on me. I would have loved so much if Csani had come into the world naturally! I heard that whoever gave birth by Caesarean would quite probably have their second child helped into the world in a similar way. At the same time, every bit of me was opposed to the idea. It was in those days that I heard of the technique of connection between baby and mother, and I looked for Dr Raffai. I thought that this might give the opportunity for my second child, who was on their way at the time, to be born naturally.

I managed to connect relatively quickly with my baby; it came to be on the third session. It was always very strange. This was a similar state to dreaming; this is how the pictures came. By the way, the progress of the session is such that when the pictures come, there is a choice to either turn what I see and hear into words right away, or to describe the whole of what happened between the two of us at the end of the session. For me personally, it was simpler to tell right away. The messages came to me as a cartoon during our connection. I know that this is not the same for all of us, because different mothers told me distinct experiences. Therefore, in my "movie," my womb appeared as a small apartment. It had windows, chandeliers were hanging on the inside, from which my baby could hang and swing.

I sensed once, even though he did not say anything, that he was hungry. I asked him whether I had understood correctly and he affirmed it. Right then, tiny people came wearing chequered pants and brought food on platters. I saw it as a completely concrete cartoon scene.

In the last week of analysis, we had to say our goodbyes. There is a precise method as to how. Meanwhile, birth had to be explained to him. Even though he cried in the first session, he accepted in the second one that we must part. You could see from his eyes that he wanted to know what the world had in store for him. We were standing, facing each other, in an elevator. I would have loved to stay that way, but he was glancing outside and longing for what I had been telling him about for three months.

DOI: 10.4324/9781003331865-8

During my first birth – even though my pregnancy had passed in joyous expectation – I lived through each pain wanting it to be over and done with, because I could not bear it. With Lili, I listened to music every evening, "Come to me" by Vangelis, and I was able to become one with the pain, that is how I waited for her. The pains were bearable and the whole thing passed very quickly. When she was born, she did not cry out. She did not really cry at all. If she was hungry, she yowled a bit, like a kitten. She was a peaceful, calm baby. And her eyes! She observed the world with a wise, piercing gaze.

Lili was six months old when she started crying in the evenings. I called Dr Raffai, because I did not understand what this change was. He explained that this usually occurs later with babies, but a bit earlier in those who take part in the analysis. She therefore believes what she imagines. So if I go out of the room, she thinks that I do not even exist anymore. This has to be explained to her. Then one evening and the next, while nursing her, I told her that I sleep in the other room and that I was still with her; nothing bad could happen to her. From the third day onward, she did not cry. We could therefore continue communication after birth, now vocally, because the channel that formed between us remained.

I have a lot of memories if I return to the moments after birth. Of course, it is difficult to recall the old ones since then, but I vividly remember those gazes. She could look so happy and even-minded. I believe that this can be accredited to the analysis. It is hard to compare my children on the basis of bonding analysis by the way. I did not go to analysis with my son, my second child is a girl and I already connected with Lili … and I do not know how she would have developed without the analysis. However, she developed faster compared to my son both emotionally and physically and did everything much sooner. Most of all, the joy that could be read from her eyes struck me. She could even tell what she needed, what she wanted. She was joyful, harmonic and balanced. She did not look around as if she did not know who we were or where we were.

Since then, I think she has changed a lot. She is starting to grow out of herself, and is sometimes afraid of putting herself out there. She was quite small, could only sit, when she noticed the sound of dogs, listened to them, even when she could not see them. She turned to them with such close attention and curiosity. By now she is afraid, as small children usually are at this age, like "oh no, a doggie," and she snuggles up to my leg. I am still the safe haven. She is uneasy around cars and unknown kids from time to time. Therefore, what used to have an effect on her in my belly does not anymore. So back then, I felt like I could pass everything on to her and now she is affected quite a lot by her environment. By the way, she can process them absolutely fine. She was born as an Aries, so her being able to go up against anything may stem from this. She is not that much of a cowardly soul. She confronts everything she has to.

I could always look at my first child, my son, in a way that I was happy that he had been born and that I had duties. He had to be fed, bathed, his diaper changed and I felt a lot of love for him, because I had expected him very much. With Lili, however, I feel as though a part of my body had been taken out, and she lives, feels and thinks the same way as I do. This may be because she is also a girl. Our paths are beginning to split by now. I believe that a lot of things I feel we share came from this. I felt that, for nine months, our connection was stronger than those who do not attend analysis. So she might have lived through my emotions more deeply, and I perhaps hers, but these are not things that can be put into words. It's more likely that there is some faith and even some inspiration in the fact that we are the same.

This strong and close connection provides more of a support than an inseparable bond. Therefore, I can much more easily imagine her leaving home than my son. I can accept it, because up until then, I will have given her everything I had to give. I am not worried about that. I rather feel that this closeness is good and this was a spiritual staple for her, which will act as a guide and I do not feel that I could not let her go for one second.

By now small, fine spiritual details are showing in our conversations, of course very vaguely and simply, but she is getting a feel on things such as whom we love and how we love them. I feel that in our family the crew is split in half. One half is dad and his son; the other half is mom and her daughter. This may come from my daughter getting mostly my genes ... Still, I feel that from those couple of months that we spent together during my pregnancy, a spiritual strength was formed that will remain forever. She may well not recall these concrete memories I have written down, because she will get this diary of her analysis and her birth, but nonetheless I feel we are the same kind of person. She has gut feelings and I believe that this comes from the analysis. She was with me and we have lived through experiences together. She has remained like this and does not approach things rationally, but through gut feeling.

I cannot wait to give her the diary I wrote during the bonding analysis. I am curious what she will think about it, how she will take it. Here it is ... this, for instance, is about when I prepared her before birth for the separation – this was not easy – as well as the outside world.

"For three months now, the analysis sessions have been arranged in a way that I would have to tell what happened since the last session and what sort of tension the experiences I lived through – whether positive or negative – set off in me. Afterwards, the doctor says fixed sentences for me to close my eyes, settle in a comfortable position, get settled into it, for me to find my uterus with my inner sensors, caress it, become one with it, and rely on the feelings that happen between you and me. Afterwards, usually after a few minutes, the images come, each one more beautiful than the last.

In the 36th week of pregnancy, the sessions change to the extent that I have to tell you three things:

1. Soon, you will come out from there and be born.
2. This is not happening because you became unnecessary.
3. Nor is it because you did something wrong.

This was a bit difficult the first time, because it is a different thing talking about thoughts and pictures to a person who is basically a stranger to me and talking to you in my own vernacular with him listening. In the end, it happened, and it was good, during the session, I silently cried with happiness.

In the following session, the task changed so I had to let you know the three important things. I was not to say them out loud but with my inner voice. I needed only to talk about the effect and the pictures that appeared in my mind.

For several minutes, I could not really connect with you. My uterus appeared in front of me, with a wrinkly, ugly-faced baby inside, whom I rather quickly identified as the baby that lay next to Csani's room in the hospital and that was born with nerve damage.

In the next picture, a snake came out of my uterus, which again filled me with sheer fright.

Then the pictures came so rapidly one after the other that I cannot even recall them, but eventually, like a bird escaping from a cage, I started flying out to space, crossing every limit and boundary. The speed of my flight suddenly slowed down, when I came upon millions of sparkling stars in the dark sky.

And you, dearest, were waiting there, floating in space. I told you the three must-knows from within, to which you reacted sadly. You reached out your two tiny hands to me, as if you did not want to get torn apart from me. With my heart filled to the brink with love, I not only flew to your hands, but since you were small, I took you into my palm, as a heaving little bird.

And as I consolingly said the three important things, my two closed palms became a white flower's chalice, in which you, a little seed, lay.

Your task was that once the petals opened, you had to fly up into the air (be born). However, you were just grasping the bottom of the chalice, shaking.

I reached a mirror towards you and showed you:

> Look how beautiful and perfect you are (you have not done anything wrong) you are just a small seed now, but the whole wonder of blooming lives inside you! Take a look; from your two tiny legs the stem will form, on your butt and head, the small snow white flower petals are already visible. Do not be afraid of leaving the chalice!

Upon that, you carefully showed your little head, looked around and I conjured a beautiful field for you, right in the centre of outer space. The sun was shining brightly and the field was full of flowers, such as ourselves, the birds were chirping and above each flower a bee was buzzing, and from the flowers tiny babies came flying out one after the other, in flower petal hats and petal panties (you are not unnecessary, that is the order of things with everybody). Every baby sat on a bee, and they flew back and forth joyfully, with great laughter.

You therefore mustered courage as well, tried it and flew around gladly on your bee. Meanwhile, we have arrived at the final five minutes of the session, where I have to say my farewell to you, my sweet little girl.

The field disappeared from around us. You happily flew back to the big flower's peace-giving chalice and the flower became a palm once more (because we were just practising birth).

I could not say my farewell to you in outer space, even though we met there. I gently closed my palms, I flew back to earth, to a field like the one we saw up there, and once I arrived, I opened my palms. And you, like a little bird, flew away towards the Sun."

Györgyi Szántó: "I felt that this kid has always been here and that we knew each other"

I had already been buying baby and maternity magazines a year and a half before Zsófi was conceived. We were looking forward to having her a lot. Then in one of the magazines, I once saw a drawing that caught my eye: it depicted a pregnant woman, with a baby in her belly and they were speaking to each other on the phone. Next to the drawing was Jenő Raffai's article. It was then that I acknowledged how interesting it was that one can actually get in touch with their baby. Then, finally, I got pregnant, but initially I was … so even though we really looked forward to having her, I was not an entirely joyful mother-to-be at all. I had been with my husband for eight years, so it was a planned baby. That is, they were babies, since it started as a twin pregnancy. I got into a horrible state. Rhapsodic moods were coming and going, one time I was very happy then suddenly I broke down crying. My gynaecologist told me that these mood swings may come on due to increased hormone generation in my system during twin pregnancy. It really wore me out. Then it occurred to me that Dr Raffai may be able to help me, because this was unbearable. After the feeling of euphoric, perfect happiness, I could not do anything with the other extreme. I felt that it did not have a place here.

I looked up his phone number and checked in. We arranged an appointment and immediately agreed what this all meant and what I may or may not expect. I went to the first session two weeks after that. Only I got there with just one baby. One of the foetuses had died. I read a book on twin pregnancy, in which it turned out that around 50% of pregnancies start off as twin pregnancy, but it is not noticed. It was not noticed at all way back. Now with twin pregnancies, one of the foetuses usually dies off by around the tenth week for some reason. It was in my fifth week of pregnancy that I first went to an ultrasound, where I found out that there were two of them. I probably should not have rushed that ultrasound, because … well, it wore me out. It began with me going to Raffai and we then started the bonding analysis; everything changed. From then on, I was the happiest mother-to-be in the world.

I was three months pregnant when we first met. The mood swings were still present. Of course, it was terrible for my family as well and even more terrible for me. They saw how much I was suffering, even though I really wanted to be happy, but it did not always work out. I did not think that Raffai would instantly turn me into a happy mother-to-be, but based on the article, I thought that bonding analysis as a thing itself may help. We talked about this as well and I told him honestly what my problems were.

By then, I was 30 years old, I had been working for 12 years and I loved my job. I worked in a hotel, I had been a hotel receptionist since I was 19, but due to my twin pregnancy, I had to quit my job when two months pregnant. This must have contributed to my condition, because I did not plan things like that at all, that I would quit everything and that my entire life would change so suddenly.

When Dr Raffai told me what this method basically entails, I thought I understood, but back then I did not know after all. How should I put this, I expected some sort of miracle that – I am going to word this oddly – my child would speak to me, in an inner voice, after a few sessions, and say "hi mommy, I love you." Not as concrete of course, but close. So she would talk to me in the way one talks to themselves, in their inner voice. Some people might have it happen that way, but there was nothing of the sort with us. We did not communicate with words at all.

On each occasion there was an introductory part, getting tuned into my womb, where the exact same sentences are spoken each time. Dr Raffai utters these and I have to repeat them sentence by sentence. On the first occasion, I lay there, we uttered the phrases, and I waited for it as though it were a magic spell, thinking "hey, now the kid is sure to say something." But she did not. I do not know where I got this idea from. I went home and thought that I must be doing something wrong. Then I realized something. Actually what am I thinking? That my three-month-old foetus will just converse with me?! No, this is not going to be right. Next time, I tried to really, seriously concentrate on what was in the phrases. I therefore caressed my womb, turned towards my baby and tried to convince both of us to concentrate on each other. I strongly concentrated … I tried to sense it … so much so that it happened! And then, somehow, I felt like such an idiot on that bed, because it was a feeling like when joy just fills you up! And on that bed, I grinned so much that I could not close my mouth. From that point on, it got better and better. Raffai always encouraged me, saying that I was doing well, and from this whole thing, I felt so special and fantastic that, I do not even know, those who have kids, or who have been pregnant, know what I am talking about. I felt as if my baby and I, the two of us, had been in a completely secluded world …

And I believe that we really were special. I have a basis for comparison. I went to prenatal fitness classes and met a lot of other mothers-to-be, my friends were giving birth one after the other. So, I heard from several mothers-to-be that they cannot talk to their kids because they feel so odd. In the first three months, before I started going to bonding analysis, I just said things like "hi baby," and the like. I had no concept of these deep psychological processes. I certainly did not say anything about my feelings to the baby, since I thought she could not understand anyway. However, once bonding analysis began, I realized "hold on! Not how it works!" Because it is not at all true that they do not understand. In fact it really gets to them.

I am not saying that it came in a single stroke, but after two to three sessions my emotional problems were resolved. I had zero problems – my husband praises Raffai ever since.

It must be known that I am not the progenitrix type. There are women who already communicate with their babies when they are little foetuses, as if it comes to them naturally, and when the child is born, they do things as if it goes without saying. I am not like that. Not at all. I am a vibrant, hasty personality, being busy sometimes here, sometimes there, and I am not that calm, safety granting, true matron type. For instance, I never really led the household, nor did I know how to cook, even though I finished a college of catering and hospitality, and I could have learned it. Then I started cooking, stirring meals in the pots, and meanwhile I was singing to her, because I felt that I really was a mother right then and there. But really, I had changed from the inside, spiritually.

Another thing led me to feel how much this worked: everything happened much sooner, earlier than what is usual with babies. And this is not merely my imagination. Theoretically, a pregnant woman should feel foetal movements around the 20th week. Well, I felt her moving during the 15th. Interestingly, it first happened at Raffai's office, where I felt that hello! She did not kick; instead I felt a soft, butterfly wing-like motion, this was it! During the 16th week, it was definitely her, and by then it was more intense, and this happened there as well, on that bed, while I was talking to her. I went seven or eight times a month for five months, so not a few times, and during this period, there was only one time when she did not move. Every time when I was going up the stairs or in the elevator, I felt that she was waking from her sleep. Once I lay there, she let me know that she was there, listening, in that instant. She was constantly moving and reacting.

I had an odd experience with her. I really like crowds, bustle, but at that time, I simply could not stand people. When we were in places with a lot of people, that really irritated me. For instance, there was something of a commotion in the supermarket around me and I had already collected half of what I wanted to get, but suddenly I just put down the basket and took off. Therefore, she was the one who felt uncomfortable there for some reason, but I felt as if I had to leave. So, we were intertwined.

I had another equally bad experience, which I discussed with her afterwards. We went to a party and I really wanted to enjoy myself. I was in the fourth month more or less, but this must have been really uncomfortable for the baby, because I got such an ill feeling that I told my husband for us to go home immediately. Then I talked about this party to the baby during bonding analysis, that I did not feel well there and that I got a feeling that she did not either. So she let me know that she did not want to go to places like that with me anymore and please could I spare her from them. But she did not say it with words … it is so difficult talking about this, because one cannot even word it to themselves properly, because these are not concrete things. Yes, perhaps that is why so many speak of this as humbug, because it is intangible! Many have laughed at me for it, even my closest friends who know me. Then after a point, I realized that I need not tell anyone about this. If anyone was calling, looking for me, my mother simply said that Györgyi was busy. We did not talk about this, that is all. People did not comprehend it. Luckily my mother did and she was a complete partner in this. I did not have to explain myself to everyone. So, it really is a very intangible thing – that is a fact. One may feel a lot of similar things without bonding analysis. But for one thing, I am not that type, I could not have experienced it by myself nor will we ever know what would have happened had I not gone to analysis.

It was at about the third or fourth session with Dr Raffai when I had a strange feeling … the unlimited joy came once more and I started thinking about completely womanly, girly things: flowers and colours came out, pink pictures … Hang on! Maybe the baby is telling me that she is a girl. Then I grew uncertain. Ah, perhaps I am seeing these images solely because I really want, or secretly hope for, it to be a girl. But she kept sending me similarly girly things. By then, I knew she was a girl. My friends were asking me what if it turned out to be a boy. I must admit that I replied a bit condescendingly: "How could it be boy, once it is a girl?!" Of course, I did not add that she clearly communicated this to me. Then during the ultrasound, once I was in a state where the gender could be determined, they told me that "mommy, it is a girl." I was not at all surprised but I was fantastically happy.

There were some concrete things that I later recognized to have bought or thought because of her influence, for example, the colour yellow. I have never had yellow outfits since I was born. I am not going to say that I hate it, more that I do not particularly like it. I was four and a half, maybe five, months pregnant when we renewed our apartment. I asked her once during analysis whether she would like to talk about the colour of her room then and there. I tried to mediate colours to her, or think of objects with different colours, so I started with pink and went through the colours, then different shades of yellow arose, I do not know where from, because I really do not like yellow. This was one of our discussions. Then we went to a clothing wholesale to buy baby clothes, where I individually picked off this and that, and took them home. I saw then that I had picked a bunch of yellow clothes as well. There were one or two other colours, but I realized that "good heavens, this kid will be all yellow!" Yes, I may not have randomly picked those. The first dress she ever wore in her life was yellow. I thought that she deserved to wear this colour, if she already liked it.

I had another odd feeling. So, I saw a picture of a baby with long, dark hair in a magazine. The girl lay in a white dress, a month old at most, and I looked at her all the time. There are a thousand babies in all the magazines, all of them beautiful, but that one always caught my eye. I even showed her my husband, "look how adorable this kid is!" He liked her too, he did say that she had a bit of a big nose, but she was still very cute. She was my favourite. When Zsófi was born, and I saw her, she was the spitting image of the girl I had seen in the photo, only mine was a bit prettier. I do not know where I got the idea from that she would have hair at all, but for me the baby in the picture was the BABY. This was another small sign, that she was so alike in the end.

Another interesting thought, which she communicated to me as it turned out, came in the usual situation, I was lying on the bed and the pictures were coming, I was swimming in a lake, a newborn was swimming next to me and she appeared as the baby in the picture … basically it might be that I just wished for her to be like that, no, that is silly, it is rather the other way around: she was like that, and that is why I noticed her in that photo. So we were swimming around, even though I am not much of a "champion" in that, but these swimming images came ever so often, so I realized she liked water. Then, I was consciously speaking to her and sending similar images. I showed her how we swim. Then, I brought her father into the images too, so that she could get to know him. I brought the fact that the three of us were there into these messages and thoughts, and how great that was. I always got such a good feeling and I was happy! Then, after her birth, when she was not even three months old, we went baby swimming. It turned out that she enjoyed it very much. About 12 of us started out in the group and there were numerous groups, meanwhile a lot missed out, groups were merged and then only the two of us stayed. Usually, parents get all enthusiastic that they are going to take the kid, who shrieks once or twice, does not feel well, and it turns out that it is pointless. Zsófi on the other hand cried only once during the eight months in the pool, even then only because she was terribly hungry. So, she loves the water, and … she sent this to me well ahead, too.

We talked numerous times with Dr Raffai about how difficult births are caused by psychological hardships and I believe that subconscious, unconscious and conscious anxieties are behind the scenes of that. So, all sorts of conscious worries, for instance "good God, how painful that is going to be," "it is going to be awful," "what if I am not going to be a good mother." These worries prevent separation. We discussed how she would be born in four sessions and how the whole thing would go. Meanwhile, I kept telling her at home that we were really looking forward to having her and how good it would be for us to be together. I tried to radiate these thoughts towards her. During all of this, I did not even notice how my fear of giving birth had completely faded. Rather I was curiously anticipating this experience, which is sure to have stuck on her too.

I always told Raffai that my baby would come sooner, which he accepted doubtfully, because these babies are not usually born early. But in the end, she actually did arrive sooner. Essentially, we both communicated it to one another, either I said it to her, or she to me, I do not know, but we were prepared for this. I was certain that she would be born before 24 June. And so it was. By the way, I was born earlier as well, I weighed 2.70 kg and she weighed 2.73 kg, but she had an Apgar score of 9/10, so she was completely mature and developed, even though she came sooner, she was not a preterm.

I must add that I started to think about which part of the day I should give birth in approximately a month before I went into labour. Of course, this is not as if one exactly decides, but I said to myself that it would be best in the morning. Let the day start with that because you get tired when evening comes. My husband often got home late. I was awake from half past eight until midnight and by then I would be dead tired. I would not want to give birth then. Well, I sat up in bed in the morning of 20 June and my waters broke. That was the incident to which I awoke. In my opinion, this was not random either, she tried to help me with that: "I am going to let mom sleep, then I will get going." Earlier, I was so afraid of giving birth, I even told my husband: "of course, because you do not have to." Before my pregnancy, several occasions during our relationship, when having a kid was mentioned, how should I put it, I pitied myself, that I had to give birth. Even in the first three months, before I started visiting Raffai, I had thoughts such as "oh God, I have to give birth, if only it would be Caesarean!" Then this gradually changed. I specifically remember: I was sitting on the couch in the living room when I realized that I was feeling something else. I looked at my husband and said: guess what, I am not afraid of giving birth! Afterwards, I gave voice to what I thought. I thought that I should be rather envied, because this was going to be an incredible thing. I discussed with the kid as well that what we were going to live through was going to be fantastic. Then, after beginning in the morning, a few hours later, there you are, she was born. They tell me that I am really lucky that it happened this way, even though it is also true that something hurt terribly initially. Then, the midwife told me that I had the awful pains because I had widened to four inches in 40 minutes. So that is why it was so intense for me. Afterwards, I comforted myself that of course it was intense, me being that sort of buzzing, just as our relationship was intense. That was the right way. By the way, half an hour after Zsófi's birth, I was saying to my husband that I would go in for another round! I said that it was horribly painful, but the actual pushing part was a piece of cake, it came after three pushes and it was a fantastic experience. By then I did not feel pain, just that this was something miraculous. I would have gone back to do it a couple more times. I am sure that my wanting to see her so badly contributed as well! I concentrated on "just let me see her," and not the "oh, what am I doing exactly." I did not care for that then.

It really was the best day of my life. Even though I had talked about giving birth with a lot of women, I had never heard about anything similar from anyone. Everyone accentuated the pain and suffering from the whole thing, and how much they had achieved. True, we heard the same from our grandmothers, that it is very difficult – this is definitely inherited by us, this is how they indoctrinate us. To this day, I feel that I was not the only one who gave birth, it was the two of us: she was there exactly as I was and she helped me exactly as I helped her. If she had not taken part in it so helpfully, I would still be lying there.

Even though these psychological processes were so ungraspable and these questions had remained relatively distant for me until my pregnancy, it is important for one to believe that bodily things are controlled by psychological things to some extent, not all, but certainly for giving birth. Consciousness can halt things. I decided that I wanted this to be over quickly. And it was a success. The entire delivery room was astounded that she had just come in an hour ago. Then again, the noises I made during the birth! They must have assumed that this hysterical chick would be suffering here for 20 hours. An hour after that, we got out of there and they placed Zsófi on me with the navel cord and all, and she just looked, blinked, she did not cry out but just looked at me, and she was so wise, as if she knew everything. As she lay in my arms, I felt that this is how it had always been, I had always known her and it was such a strange feeling. Of course, you are here! I could not even sleep in the hospital, two hours at most during those four days. We just lay there and looked at each other.

It was very strange and it can also be seen on a photo how she lay on her side in the swaddling-clothes. She turned two hours after she had been born. The nurse came and enlightened me that that is not how you cover a baby. I asked if she seriously thought I had purposefully laid her on her side on the sheets. And they just stared. I do not even think they believed that the kid turned by herself. But that is how it was. So this is not a usual thing and it is typical for her to be much more developed in movement, as well as above average physically, emotionally and mentally. She turned, crawled and sat up two or three months before the others. I am not sure if that is a good thing, but that is how she is. She turned 11 months yesterday, but she had already started speaking at nine and a half months. She does not, of course, say sentences, but uses concrete words for concrete things. She is not babbling, just points at something and says what that is. I do not think that this is the norm for a kid her age either. It is such a great feeling, that whenever we meet someone, they all see how emotionally balanced she is! She is probably more skilled, creative and different than most because she did not have to worry about finding the voice and the connection with me, because it was pre-existent. A lot of mothers say it is difficult to get tuned in with your child after birth. We did not know that. I felt that this kid had always been here. I knew her and we knew each other.

When people came to visit us, everyone found it odd, they even asked: well, does this baby ever cry? If she had a problem, she was hungry or her diaper had to be changed, or was just bored, then she groaned a bit, gave a cute growling sound! Of course, I was immediately there and we did what we had to. The typical baby crying, the distorted face, red head and closed eyes were unknown to us. We did not give reason to it, as soon as she gave a sign, she got what she needed. I trusted her and thought it necessary for her to know to trust me. Therefore, I do not have the right to leave her crying for half an hour. Then came people with a forewarning, "you are spoiling this child terribly, you will see that she will constantly be clinging onto you." Yes, we spoil her. By now, since she has stood up and crawled around, this happened before she was seven months old, she does not require me to be with her 20 hours a day. She is wonderfully off on her own. Although in my opinion there are fewer kids who were in their mothers' laps in the first two months more than she was. She did not like to be alone and she slept half an hour twice a day, sometimes three times. It was astonishing, as a newborn of only a few days, that it was all the sleep she needed and the rest of the time, she just paid attention, then of course entertainment and novelties had to be provided. She would not just stare at the ceiling or the bars of her bed, we constantly carried her around, she was in our laps, and we thought that was natural.

From that first moment, we treated Zsófi like a partner. We discussed everything with her as if she were an adult and she would also understand. We got her signals and we felt that this worked, and from this we became calmer and more certain. My friend told me that Zsófi is more like my second child because of how I handled her, the way I changed her diaper and bathed her from the first moment on. I perfectly trusted my feelings. This must be due to me knowing that what I do is good, since we felt from the beginning that we are one. Therefore, she connected naturally to our lives and my teeming pace. I am almost unable to spend two days in a row at home. I already feel a lacking of something, that life is just whoosh while I sit around. So from a really early age, when she was two months old, she started coming with me. I scooped her up and we were on our way. It works for us. She loves looking at unfamiliar faces, getting to know everyone; she is friendly, not afraid. Meanwhile, I am adapting to her as well, it could not be otherwise, because she is such a full personality that she has specific notions and voices them too.

It was a daddy birth. It helped a lot that my husband was there. This is so interesting, because afterwards, when Zsófi was born and we went home, I was looking at him so much! Even though this was not that fresh, flaring love, still I looked at my husband as I did in early times, with some new-found realization and I felt some great flaring. I was grateful to him for Zsófi; also, the birth – if such a thing can be said after so many years – welded us together even more. Once again we did again something together and that was fantastic.

Andrea Fejérvári: "You get to know yourself better as well"

The most important part is that Panka was not a planned child, and my partner was not prepared for this. I read Raffai's book titled *I am conceived, therefore I am* (Raffai 1998b) and at the very beginning of my pregnancy, I thought that the child should sense it as little as possible that my partner was not looking forward to having her. Later, I thought that this phase was important in our lives. In reality, this book made me realize that this was the grand uniting power.

It was in the third month that I went to bonding analysis. Well, initially it was not easy at all to get in touch. It is not that you decide and then – whoop! – you are connected. Then, interestingly enough, it was quite good when I felt and knew for certain that Panka was going to be a girl. I was absolutely certain of it! The other fantastic experience was that once I got through to her, she did anything I asked. There were exercises when you had to move the kid around, for instance, for them to fit their head into the pelvis minor, and these she always managed to do. Therefore, my first birth was very easy. I gave birth to Panka in four hours, because she fit her head so masterfully during the exercises.

I tried communicating with her at home as well and it is an incredible feeling. One would not even think they can sense something of their child. So I told her everything, I even talked to her while I drove the car. I told her that it was snowing. Not in the way I talk now of course, but rather with my inner voice. She reacted to nearly everything. I told her about the snowfall when we were in Austria and I also told her what the mountains were like. It was shocking, because I actually felt like she was reacting.

Then when she was born, it was clear that everything got to her. For instance, the music I listened to was familiar for her. I listened to Mozart's *Requiem* quite often with her and she recognized it after her birth. She recognized Raffai's voice as well. The good doctor usually visits the children, once they are born after the bonding analysis. So he came to us and you could see it on Panka that she recognized him! She turned to him immediately and gave an adult-like, astonished look. She had such an astonished, recognizing look on her face! She was so cute!

Panka is a very intelligent little girl and she is fairly extraverted, therefore open, and forges relationships easily. She is going to be three soon, so she will be off to kindergarten before long. The first period was very easy with her as well. Oh, yes! I prepared, almost "trained" the kid for night sleep during analysis as well and the daily rhythm was self-explanatory to me. Both kids slept through the night from an early age. I tried telling them in my belly when I was getting ready for bed, that this is the time when people sleep and both of them really understood. Panka's waking up was prolonged, I almost felt sorry shaking her, but I knew that night feeding is very important during the first period. Kata, the second, is ten months old now and everything is just as simple with her. She is more low-key and I knew that when she was in my belly. She is a completely different character from Panka; she is a bit more introverted. She likes to communicate, but she is somehow not as open towards strangers. Panka is much more extraverted. Perhaps Kata opened up to me less during the analysis as well, for instance, she did not let me know of her gender, as Panka did. She was more closed. Panka basically told me that she was a girl. She was kitten-like, moving like a little girl. And suddenly an image appeared, I cannot grasp it; it flashed in front of me, that she was a girl. I did not even check on ultrasound whether or not she was a girl. I was so sure that we did not even consider boy names. I was less assured with Kata.

In the end, as I think back to the intrauterine connections, recognizing how much a child can comprehend and sense was quite dramatic. I listened to a particular Liza Minelli song a lot. It is about a mother leaving her children, but she is singing that I am leaving, but your father will be there with you, and whenever I was listening to that song, the kid always reacted. Then once I felt that she was frightened, as if she were anxious about it. From that point on, I never put it on again. I was thinking about how odd it was, since I was listening to the song in English and I did not tell her what it was about. I think that the feelings that the song induced in me had flown through and got to the kid. The feeling it induced in me, passed on into her emotional world.

When we were preparing the child for birth, well, thinking back in retrospect, it happened with some difficulty. Truth be told, from the whole four hours of giving birth, two hours went just into pushing. I know that this goes so easily for others and that is why I think the separation did in fact go roughly for me. Even though I tried to prepare her for it. Interestingly, it went better with Kata; she was born in under an hour and was out on the third push. I think I prepared either her or myself more consciously for the separation. Perhaps you get to know yourself better during these analyses and that also helps. You comprehend better, especially after the first kid, what your mistakes were. In my opinion, I was overly attached to this state and this clutching originates from a deep feeling that it is where the kid belongs, so she should be kept there. Of course, these all play out in the unconscious, but eventually everything surfaces. In reality, you are always searching for yourself and you are always changing. What is certain is that the analysis did not only help the relationship, it also helped me get in the clear about a few things about myself. I was an overdue baby by two weeks. Perhaps this was another reason why separation was so hard. So even though Panka came in time, these memories were repeated in some form.

When Kata was born, I was prepared for the jealousy, but there was none of the big tension that I had heard of from others. With a lot of kids, it plays out as one hitting the other, trying to harm them physically. Panka was intelligent enough to be incredibly withheld with Kata. Instead, some form of anger came out towards us, but that is not even a problem, since these should not be repressed. We did not have sibling rivalry, I was lucky enough to evade that and I did not have to constantly be on edge. By now, she can bother Kata as well and they play wonderfully.

My partner was there for both births. By the way, even though he was initially distant from the idea of bonding analysis, he did not oppose it, but accepted it. He is less of a believer in such things, but he respected my thinking or worldview and supported me so much so that he even came in for the births, which had been very much unlike him up to that point. It is interesting how he could not initially identify with the whole thing, but then in turn it benefitted our relationship, because he took part in both births. And he was very proud of me, and of what a great thing I had accomplished.

Judit Gombocz: "As if I were hearing it with my non-existent third ear, feeling it in my heart and soul"

The milieu was strange at first. One goes into an apartment, into a little room, and there they somehow change the world – back then this seemed a bit unimaginable. A friend of mine gave me the book called *I am conceived, therefore I am*. I was very curious about how a tight connection can be formed between mother and foetus. Then, during mid-pregnancy, I got to Raffai after the fourth month, so relatively late. The first session was an introductory discussion. My friend had been to Raffai a while back, therefore I was convinced and had no doubt that something would come out of it. Then … well, it started off with such difficulty! Raffai told me at the beginning never to expect that he would solve the whole thing, this would be my job. Still, I remember trying to rely on him a great deal, so I absolutely expected his help. In light of what I have just said, establishing the connection did not happen at the beginning and we could not get in touch with Álmos. Ever since then, if I am reading a related article in some newspaper or magazine, these usually refer to something extra and incomprehensible for the mere mortal happening and the incredible simplicity of establishing a concrete connection side is emphasized most of all. If only the reader knew that it is not the case; it in fact takes very serious inner work! These articles are too story-like, too attention-hogging. Therefore, they do not convey what this is all about, that a very tough will is needed for it.

I regularly tried doing it at home. Among other things, this led to me trying the method to see how it really works. I believed that this would be great for the both of us and I knew that I would really need it, since my profession is an excessively stressful one! I am a lawyer, oftentimes I think that this job really is not cut out for women and after having had to work through my entire pregnancy, I was terrified that Álmos would sense that. I was simply unable to switch off. I couldn't not bring things home, which is what led me to Raffai, because I wanted to "be done with" the remorse. So, I woke up with this thing and went to bed with it, before I started seeing Raffai. This was a kind of stress that I was not sure Álmos could endure, since it was difficult even for me … and I had an enormous help in that, because I finally sensed through Álmos's responses that he could endure it and that we could power through it together.

Once we finally got connected, that was it … I broke down crying … even if I think of it now, I get so emotional! I think I cried back then because the whole thing was unimaginable, that we could get in touch. I had different types of sensations than what I read in the magazine and newspaper articles about this method. Masses of emotions … warmth filled me up … a comforting, blissful feeling, simply incredible. By the way, he played hide and seek quite often, even when we became connected for the first time and oftentimes he would be unwilling to communicate. There were occasions when we established a connection, but … even when the connection formed, communication did not have a continuous flow. There were times when this went really well and others when it did not go as well.

At home, I managed to establish a longer, more stable connection once or twice by the end of the pregnancy. We had bad weather as it was winter. I was afraid of getting into the car by then and I knew that there was no other way around it. I had to do it myself. It worked, but not in the way it had worked with Raffai. I do not know, perhaps that place has a spirit of its own. This is an apartment block, a tiny room with many books. The noises of the house could be heard as well; meanwhile he had his twins. They lived their lives beside him and yet in that little room, one could … interestingly enough, tune everything out. I lay on the bed and stepped into another world, a different dimension. It would not have come together without Raffai, I am sure if this; his radiant personality was needed for it.

Our relationship was constantly about me telling all sorts of things to Álmos. I practically told him about our entire family, whom he was going to meet, I told him our entire lives well ahead. I involved him in matters concerning work as well, what sort of day he should expect now, in order to prepare him. When we were talking like this, I actually felt that he understood … his movement … so the way he moved around … On some occasion he was almost hopping around, he would reply, react unmistakably. He had a rhythm … by the way; I always felt that he knew where we were going at that moment. Of course, I was telling him in the car that we were headed to Raffai's. He loved being there. These replies … so these … first off blood rushes to your head, you feel that some message has arrived, I cannot explain in detail how I felt. This is a physical sensation as well. It would be far-fetched to say that I was hearing voices, because I was not, this was rather as if I were hearing it with my non-existent third ear, feeling it in my heart and soul. This is not an exact thing, you sense that either this is positive, or … yes, I got it! So for me it usually came as a yes or no answer. I formed my own questions in a way that I could expect either an affirmative or a negative answer and I knew for certain that he would reply. Although it happened that there was no reaction. So the connection was established, but we could not talk. This was mostly in the period when we were preparing for the separation and he completely rejected that. We had a connection, but he would simply be unwilling to talk about it – I definitely sensed this.

I tried to find in myself whether these were his answers, or my phantasmagorias. For I knew that it could be my imagination playing games; that in itself is not excluded. His answers come into my consciousness as well and I tried to separate and differentiate between the two of them. In that specific state, when you are tuned into it, I felt that these were definitely his reactions. For if I would not have been certain, I would have probably forced it. I am a bit down to earth so I have "demanded" from Raffai that we clarify whether or not I felt his reactions, or vice versa, that I wanted to hear my own fantasies. In the beginning, I could not really differentiate between the two, but then in a moment something clicked and from that point on I was sure that these were Álmos's reactions.

Truth be told, I did this in quite a selfish way against Raffai. It is probably a professional expectation for doctors that one would tell what is happening – for them to be able to help and for me to continuously put what Álmos is feeling and doing into words – and I kept the messages to myself a lot, because they could not be put into words and more often than not, I felt like I could not pass the time by communicating outwards. This happens as one is lying there, trying to get themselves into this inexplicable state and either they succeed, or they do not. But once it came together, I was so overjoyed that I feared that if I started explaining my emotions – and thus not concentrate on Álmos, then everything would fade away and who knows if it would happen again … Then I hinted at wishing to stay silent, if he did not mind, to let me do it this way instead. I was absolutely sure of it, he thought so as well that the goal of this first and foremost is not my feedback, but what happens between me and my kid.

I longed for Álmos to show himself so much! Even though I saw something before me, I told Raffai as well, that perhaps it was him, but I was not sure, I rather felt that there was a picture living in me of what he would be like. He said that is alright, you do not have to get stuck on getting an exact sense of it. By the way, he turned out to be like the picture that appeared every once in a while … or something similar.

The beginning of the entire process is quite interesting. You arrive, lie down on a bed, then we speak the tune-in text: Raffai out loud, me quietly to myself. It happened a number of times that I asked him to repeat what he said, then again and again. Because you get into this slowly, but you can easily fall out of it. Success therefore depends on the state of mind in which you go there. Once I had to ask him four or five times to repeat what he said. So this meant that this is not just a mere text, for one does not request any text that they know five times.

Towards the end of my pregnancy, a serious issue arose. Several weeks ahead of the expected date of birth, I had uterine contractions and the risk of a premature birth was imminent. I was terribly anxious. I had a great obstetrician, we understood each other, but obviously he focused on the organ-based part of the issue and prescribed me some sort of medicine. Well, I thought, if I have to take some medicine then there is something very wrong! Analysis helped in this as well. Step by step, I realized that this would not be a premature birth – let us leave that medicine aside! This had to be discussed as well. But first, I had to pick up contact not with Álmos, but with my uterus. So when Raffai first told me what I had to do, I answered let us give it a try, but I did not have high hopes for it. It is one thing to talk with your kid living in your belly, but an organ is something else! How could I?! Well … it is a very strange thing. During that time, Álmos got barely any time because this anxiety had to be dissolved. The whole thing was very odd, since my uterus had to be personified, and I had to ask it to calm down and relax. In the end, the whole thing came together and it worked out. But I worked quite hard for this as well, so one should not imagine for a second that we started off and in the next minute it went swimmingly … I remember that there was a point where I completely lost faith in myself and then it ended up coming together because I really did want it that much. Remorse also played a big role in it, that if Álmos should have any troubles, it would be my fault. "See, Judit Gombocz, this is your life's most important goal, you waited for long years and now you mess it up!" Something like that was inside me. That one hour every session was far from enough, so afterwards, once I got home, I had to continue by throwing myself down, putting my legs up, and trying to relax … but it was never as intense as it was at Raffai's. Usually, there, how should I put it, I had emotional fits. I am a romantic type anyway.

These things went differently for me than they usually did for others. The time of birth was a cardinal point as well. How does one discuss this, when Álmos in turn – as it turned out during the clarification of the panic around the premature birth – did not want to be separated, or come out. But I knew that he was determined to stay inside and I overcarried him accordingly. As I began to let him know in detail, telling him as part of the method that he would soon have to separate, he really opposed the idea. I probably clung to him as well, I liked being pregnant, I liked the whole state. My own pre-existent fears might have played a role in this as well. I probably got stuck, or came to the world very slowly during my birth. My phobia of tunnels and narrow spaces in general may originate in this. I absolutely refuse to crawl into caves or holes. I might have projected this onto my giving birth and onto Álmos. But we managed to evade it. We got into the clear and dissolved the tension, even though this is still an existing, powerful anxiety of mine. I went to give birth in full peace, anticipation and calmness of mind. By then, I had been talking to Álmos for days, so the birth would not have to be artificially initiated. I had to go in on a Saturday and my doctor planned to initiate the birth on Monday morning. Álmos did not wait that out, for he was born on Sunday night. Eventually, he came around. The other thing – I am saying this quite honestly – was most probably my weakness. Raffai sensed this as well and said when he visited us afterwards that I let go of him with great difficulty as well. I am a devoted type. Therefore, it was hard for me to close all of this down and I obviously conveyed this to Álmos.

I cannot say that it was an easy birth, although I do not know for sure what a difficult one is like. What I do know is that when he came out, you would not have been able to tell that he was worn out by it, even though it did not last a short time. I discussed these with him well ahead, the widening as well, even though this part of the story did not come together as effectively, of course due to bodily traits as well. It may have been much more difficult if we had not thought it through, or had not bothered with the course of the birth at all, but then again, I do not have a basis of comparison.

As he came out of my belly, he was feeding the next minute, meanwhile I had no experience whatsoever and I did not even know how this whole thing was going to be, still it started off by itself, entirely naturally. Another especially peculiar thing, he did not lose an ounce after being born, even though according to hospital statistics this would have been natural. He already gained weight in the hospital. Kids usually grow thin a bit during those few days in hospital, while they get used to existing on the outside and he powered through this so beautifully as well.

In addition, the way that Álmos moved or the way he discovered the world for himself, the way he tagged along to people, in company ... we started going to playgrounds early on, when he was one year old and he managed to fit in immediately. He is such a social child, absolutely communicative, and this can be observed in specific situations. His abilities developed so rapidly as well. By the way, there are dated photos and videos of this. At three or four weeks of age he lay on his belly and gazed at the toys hanging on his bed with his head held high, at four months he crawled like a champion, on all fours, as it should be, he stood at six months of age and walked at ten. He did not toddle, he straight on walked. Usually, when you see a child walking you instinctively reach out for them, God forbid he fell! But he took off after paying attention to how others were doing it – and imitating the pattern, started walking himself. He started talking when he was a year-and-a-half-year-old, and at two his speech was like that of a three-year-old child, so he talked with the quality, choice of words and confidence of child a year older than himself. When he was a bit older than two, he knew 30 songs and nursery rhymes. He often corrects me as well. From these capabilities of his, it was clear that he had an indisputable advantage, something had happened to him. But even stranger, the way he acts with other kids ... the scenes. There were social situations when people said that there must be something in Álmos, some extra emotion, or some sort of sensitivity, which usually cannot be found at that age. The way he treats other kids, how he feels sorry for those for whom we should feel sorry, how he helps a lot. He solves problems easily. It is odd how the kid overcomes obstacles on his own, as if he knew this from somewhere.

It was certain to me that it was not just prejudice, because I even heard strangers in awe that my barely two-month-old or six-month-old son could do such and such things. These are hugely different from the average. The other moms saw how different Álmos was from other children. This made me happy and proud of him because we are ordinary folk with nothing special about us. Then why would he be so extraordinary? If there were more of his level in our family, it would be natural that he would be gifted as well. Of course, all the other kids are cute, adorable and smart too. These "add-on" traits, are the product of our connection before he was born, I am sure of it. I am convinced that all the time we spent on the rocking chair played a very important part as well as all the things we did during pregnancy that Raffai advised us to do.

It was as if he knew he was going to have "difficult" parents. I had to go back to work when he was one and he adapted very swiftly. I had to leave home about once or twice a week. Luckily my line of work has the advantage of working at home and I only have to go out sometimes. At the same time, I was quite concerned about what this might inflict on the child! Once he himself let me go. When he was two and already spoke clearly in simple sentences, he said: It is alright mom, you can go, I will wait!

When we were planning and I was expecting him, I felt the pressure of having a child relatively late – I am 37 now. When you start working after university, you cannot just quit. Now of course some will say: "You have got to make sacrifices and give up things." But I would have liked to stay and I wanted to keep it that way for the long term, since I had neither the time nor the energy to start it all over again. I had to think it through thoroughly.

He lived in me as "Álmos" from a very early stage and it was an interesting state of being together. It still sounds rather strange to me that some mothers eight or nine months in still do not know what to call their child. But that is all right, everybody is different. He was a part of our family during pregnancy, long before he was born, ever since I had started the analysis with Raffai. I managed to introduce him to my family, also my parents, everywhere, in such a way that we all felt that he is there. I could almost "hold" him in my arms, at Christmas, even though he was not expected until March.

When I could project this feeling towards my husband, and he understood, he could also talk to the baby and we sang together "In the depth of the forest." That song is what we always sang to him. Álmos can sing this song with a perfect pitch and I am sure that he had already known it when he was born. It was possible to calm him down with this song as it worked most of the time.

His father gave it his best shot, talked to him and sang to him, but I do not think the same type of inner bond was established between them. However, Álmos's dad says that when he held him right after birth, while I was attended to, he felt something amazing. He probably would not say it if it were not truly there, for he is a very rational man. He declines everything that is not tangible. He is an engineer, so all of this stuff sounds unreal to him. Many times he remarked when the baby did something amazing that it was because of Raffai.

I want to be pregnant again, not only for the child, even though that is the point, of course, but, being a bit selfish, for the whole experience and sensation of it all. My friends are also considering more children. It is interesting that these "old girls," my peers want to give birth again. So this is how it goes these days. But what I see with them is that they want it all to be over and done with as soon as possible. I want it to last, even if I look like a cow. Let it be! So what?

We just stopped breastfeeding, on his second birthday. I will be honest: I was afraid of it. If we are so used to it, how can we end it so suddenly? My friend told me that the only way we can ease into it is if we go to the countryside or if I put something on my breasts that does not taste good to him. But then, to my surprise, it was so easy! It happened the way we had talked about it: I told him "Álmos, they will not give milk after your birthday; you are a big boy now." He replied: "OK mom." Just like that, no hassle. He accepted it. He quite liked breastfeeding, though. He conquers obstacles very easily; I just tend to overreact and worry. Then he in a most natural way moves on. I often wonder where this kid came from. I do not know, but I feel like he came from somewhere. It is like he has a past.

Mónika Szoboszlai: "I want to unveil what it is to be"

I was visiting a friend in Pécs around March. I asked her for a book to have something to read on the way home. She gave me Jenő Raffai's book *I Am Conceived, Therefore I Am*. My friend had already had her baby at that point. My partner and I were planning our wedding for May, and thought that we wanted a baby right afterwards. I read the book on the train, and was already sure at that point that I would get in touch with György Hidas or Raffai.

Eszter was conceived in June. I found Professor Hidas after a lengthy inquiry, and started visiting him following the 20th week. I wanted, since this is about me too, to get past my own difficulties quickly, so as to focus on the baby right away. I knew that I had an issue or two that could affect the baby as well, since I am a fairly conscious person motivated to introspection, and that these would be good to resolve. I was very scared of giving birth. I had long had this anxiety, but the desire for a child was much stronger than the fear of labour. My mother always told me how terrible it is, how painful, and I have a low tolerance for pain, and this instilled an awful sense of dread in me. This was one of the reasons that made me want the bonding, and the other … I had self-esteem issues now and again, and the role of a mother raises a closely related question: am I enough, am I suitable to be a mother, and the like. I am suitable, of course, but this uncertainty popped up in me sometimes, and that is why I wanted to address this. We had relatively little time for this, however, since the connection was very slow to form.

Imagine the classical analytic situation. I am lying on the couch at chief physician Dr Hidas's place, and I am supposed to loosen up completely, body and mind, and this was the task: relax. Perhaps I am too rational, I keep myself under constant control, and, well, it took a very long time for me simply not to constantly be checking myself. It took several sessions for me to turn off the control.

Meanwhile, I was continuously looking for the connection with her at home, too. I placed my hand on my belly, and when, according to the instructions of Hidas, I was trying to send love towards her, then I tried with my entire being, and with my hand too, and the little one curled up against my palm. The first time I felt this it was such an incredible feeling!

The first moment of connection at Dr Hidas's, the encounter, is an indescribable experience. It is the experience of fulfilment, or when one is praying and gets in touch with God, when one's entire being is floating, and when only the truly perfect and significant things exist, I do not even know, we do not have words for it, how we could express what a transcendental connection means, that which sweeps everything away. Moreover, the whole thing is expressed in bodily sensations as well. I was lying there in complete calmness, loosened up, and I got into such a state of arousal that my cheeks were blushing and my entire body was signalling the connection. It is so strange, it cannot be described or told, but Hidas, he saw it in me, that something was happening.

When I found her, when I sensed Eszter like that, it still was not clear for a while whether I am hearing or thinking my thoughts or if they are really coming from her, because a dialogue developed between us. It was mixed up for a long time, and György Hidas always said that it is not a problem, just say it, it is not a problem if it is not coming from Eszter, this will develop later. It was mixed up in me until the end, and it should have been distilled, but we could not go down the path the way I wanted to.

So, at that point I experienced it as being perfect just like that, since the bonding, the dialogue took shape. We were in constant dialogue. I was always telling her, which she probably felt too, that I am awaiting her, that I really love her, and that a life began which, for now, we are spending like this, symbiotically, but she can always count on me even after she is born. In essence we prepared for the life that continued with her coming out of my belly. We only left out the details of the event itself, the birth, although it would have been good to get to that as well, because of my fears … Well, oftentimes it was hard to separate her experiences and mine.

Something interesting happened once. When I was in this relaxed state, I managed to enter my womb, and saw myself in the foetal position … and at first I did not know … that I was in my own mother's womb, I am seeing the amniotic fluid, seeing my hand as I raise it, seeing my umbilical cord. I could not distinguish whether I went in to Eszter, and I was there, or if this was my own, old experience. Looking back now, I know that it was my own, old memory. Later, I could go into it in such a way that I did not feel things like that, but saw her, Eszter. I could not discern her little face exactly, and I did not know what her physical appearance was like, but somehow I felt her hand, I could clearly sense as she drew it in front of her face a few times.

When we were talking, I sensed an excited movement inside my belly, she is usually calm, but when we picked up the connection like this, she let me know through movement that all is well, and calmed down at that point, cuddled up against my hand, and settled into a waiting position. I felt that she was open and paying attention. And when the free associations came, when I was almost dreaming, well, then I felt a movement from her that was as irritated as a protest. Afterwards I could not separate whether I was thinking this, or she was saying it. I asked her to repeat herself, if she was the one saying it. It was interesting, since this happened at a stage when I had set aside my all-controlling and regulating self, and in this incredibly open, receptive state I let things just happen, rather than be directed by me. At this point, however, I felt that if this really is her telling me this, then I have to be sure of it. And then she repeated herself. This was not like our usual conversations, but like an internal thought. And I translated this global feeling for myself into her not wanting to come out, because she felt like it would not be a good thing, she was afraid of this life. Whereas we really were so prepared! So she sent something really negative my way. But, interestingly, I asked her whether she was healthy, and she told me she was. I was not worried about that for a second, because she was so clear in communicating it that I was sure that everything was alright with her. But she gave me a sense of something being amiss.

Once or twice, she sent the message she made me feel that something was not right. And I remember, that is when I told Hidas, that I do not know whether this is my fear, that something is not right, or if Eszter is telling me that something is off, and towards the end I sensed several times that she did not want to be born, she did not want to come out of there. After that I placed a huge emphasis on convincing her that things would be good for her out here, that she had to come out of there, that we were so excited to see her, and that so much love would surround her! That all that was happening was that she would be in a separate body, but other than that nothing would change. Only after a long time will we actually part. After this she did not give such a negative signal again.

My blood pressure got very high at the beginning of the ninth month, and I had to spend the last three weeks in the hospital. On account of this we never got to the point of discussing the process of birth. I tried to make up for this in the hospital, and to be ready not to have a Caesarean section, although high blood pressure projects this possibility, so in these cases a Caesarean becomes likely. The readings that showed up! Then I told her a bunch of times how the birth will go, and as she and I had already agreed that there would not be a Caesarean section, it did not come to be. Although they almost took me into the operating room a number of times during the birth, since my blood pressure was 190/160, but after all we managed it the natural way. All in all, it was fairly easy and quick, she was born in three and a half hours weighing 3,650 grams. I felt Eszter before and during, where she was lying, where she was, how she was doing.

Then there was a real big complication around breastfeeding. I am very partial to breastfeeding, and I already said in the hospital that they cannot give her any kind of formula, but I did not account for the difficulty I had in getting started with breastfeeding. I was measuring a total of 10 grams, and poor Eszter was completely starved. The paediatrician told me that alright, he respects my efforts, but it will not work if this is all the milk there is, and that I would have to give formula as well. So that when we came home, she got a bottle of it a day. But then our GP came and said that I should forget the formula, that the baby was big enough, and it is not an issue if she loses some weight. Then I was breastfeeding 10–12 times a day, all day basically, and finally my milk started flowing properly. But until then the both of us were suffering and struggling. It was horrible when I took her off my breast and she cried. Only 10 grams, or 20! My God, I cannot feed my own daughter! I decided that I would talk to the doctor after all, and that he would surely say to give her formula now, because this cannot go on like this. It had almost been four weeks, and she still had not regained her birth weight. And yet the doctor kept encouraging us to keep trying a bit more, not to give her formula. Then it got going a little more. Everything is alright now. I am talking about the breastfeeding thing in such detail because it was lurking in me during pregnancy too, that I really wanted to breastfeed, and I hoped, I was nervous, whether it would go well, so I wanted to pay attention to this, as if I had sensed that something would happen.

As much as the breastfeeding did not go well, I should have fallen into a deep depression and, I think, we are doing as well as we are in spite of everything because we had another channel to understand each other. We carried it on from our story, that we had already found each other in there. And Dr Hidas just accompanied the process, and let our bonding develop in its own dynamics, he let us find the connecting points towards each other, he did not try to indicate paths to it, he just helped this state of relaxation form. So he was a crutch, a secure foundation for us.

Eszter and I really found harmony. Even when I was on the bus, I was talking to her in my mind, so we really understand each other, and we are really attuned to each other. But this did not happen with my uterus for a long time. György Hidas always emphasized that a lot, that I should reach my uterus. I was surprised at first. What do we want with my uterus? And it is no accident that this was not in my conscious mind, since I deflected everything that had to do with my uterus. Among other things, I was glad to be pregnant because I did not have to menstruate. I suffered through that each time, and I was mad at my uterus, so much so that I viewed it as my enemy. By the time it became conscious that this is how I relate to it, I faced that this is unfortunate, since I was going to give birth and I should cooperate with it after all. We made attempts for me to get in touch with it, and I could not do it for a long time. A session passed, then two, but I did not feel it, did not see it, no image, no sound.

Of course, it happened in the end, and how it happened is very interesting. But something happened in this lengthy search, this concentration, a big thing. So it is as if my psyche prepared this encounter with my uterus. This happened by an image ... generally, I always saw crystals. And then something "crystalized," of course, from the crystals, something took shape, and I tried to understand it, so I saw ... in the image, that I want to unveil what it is to be. I did not reach it at first ... my hand was always going ... I was reaching for it ... and all of a sudden I pulled it away, and for just a moment there was my womb! After this I went home feeling that well, next time I will make it happen. I tried again next time, but it did not work after all. And at that point I remembered Eszter, that now, when I was relaxed and really got in contact with her, I would ask her to help me find my uterus. Perhaps this was the most astonishing experience for me that she was feeling around my womb from the inside with her tiny hands and legs. And I felt, I finally felt that it was my womb! There, outside of where she was feeling around and kicking. I could not do it alone, and she helped me. At this point we really had some sort of bonding to work together, to bring Eszter into the world.

We had a quite good conversation with Eszter for the duration of the pregnancy, and we felt both the positive and the negative. It is so strange, that a mother can feel the fear of her child to such an extent, even though the child is not even outside yet, but still inside. I was watching a movie at one point, maybe it was *The Purple Violin*, or something like that, it had modern violin pieces in it, I for one enjoyed it, but Eszter did not. She was wiggling around so much that I felt her saying "mommy, get out of here, this is awful." On the other hand, she really loved Mozart, and there were a few other kinds of music that she liked from what I listened to.

All in all, she is a very calm baby, and this was evident especially in the first two weeks, when both the mommies and the babies are still confused. Now that she is more communicative, I can see that she wants to express so many things that she is attentive to everything. She found her little hand very quickly, she was not even two months old when she discovered it. She is playing around with her legs too. As she is sitting in a baby seat, she sees her feet and moves them around. Of course, I do not know exactly what another baby might be like, but I am reading books that talk about childhood development. These talk about the big median, and compared to that she is more mature and developed, especially mentally, in the way she looks at me, in the way she expresses herself. I think she can cry in a differentiated way, she "talks," so she plays with her voice, and she started babbling early on, and all of these show that she did not begin developing here, after birth, but inside, in my belly.

My husband initially saw this bonding analysis as a bourgeois gimmick. "Alright, fine," he said, "so be it, do what you want." When I got in from bonding analysis, he always asked "Well, what happened?" and when I told him something, and I saw that endless scepticism in his face, I did not even keep going, because I felt that he thought it was silly. And then, as my belly grew, sometimes he would lean over and start speaking to Eszter, "Hi, here is daddy." At that point I told him see, I have essentially been doing the same thing, just for a longer while. He revealed that the whole thing was hard for him so far, but now that she is more "visible," it is a little different.

When Eszter was born, we spent an hour-and-a-half to two hours in the room, and he immediately held Eszter in his hands, because I was still so weak that I could not even hold her. Later my husband told me that he had already seen at that point how intelligent her gaze was, and how calm a baby she was. And then at home, he was melting as he was looking at her. He confessed that now he feels that our little girl is like this because I went to this bonding analysis. And he is convinced of this, because he sees that the kid is already a total personality, which could not have developed so quickly after birth, but was like this from the start. She is able to feel, think, just like us, she just does not have the tools to express herself, and I had to find these channels. Now he completely accepts that this is a real thing. And he feels that in that very moment, when he first saw her, he suddenly realized everything.

Judit Pásztor: "When his head popped out, he immediately opened his eyes and looked around curiously"

I have a four-and-a-half-year-old big boy, he is in kindergarten, the whole thing began in fact with him. My situation is quite special, since both of my children were home births. When the preparation for the home birth began with Dr Ágnes Geréb, it came up that about 10% of home births end in the hospital, primarily for psychological reasons. Many cannot give birth to the baby because anxious, unconscious content comes to the surface. At times like this the innermost conviction gets actualized, according to which the mom cannot do this by herself, needs help, and therefore the birth has to continue in the hospital. This is what I was trying to avoid. At about the same time as my interest in home birth was forming, I read Dr Raffai's book. I found it completely by accident at a bookstore, and recognized right away that I needed this method too.

I basically have a phobia of hospitals. This is probably fed by the fact that my mother almost died during my birth, and she told me as much, without making a big deal of it, she did not wail, she just said it plain and simple, and this knowledge lived deep within me. This did not happen because I came to the world in a particularly difficult way, but they simply did not pay enough attention to her, and she almost bled out. This could be its basis. So I knew the story, and we were not even planning for the kids with my partner, I had not even heard of home births, but already the hair stood on my neck when I thought of a hospital. I felt that, if there is ever a kid, then I will not give birth in the hospital. It was after these thoughts being articulated inside me that I first heard the name Ágnes Geréb, well, I knew right away that this is meant for me. I was eight weeks pregnant, and that is when I got to Dr Raffai.

Interestingly, there was a similar session with Ágnes Geréb during the preparation, as was with Dr Raffai. This happened in a loose, relaxed state as well, when I tried to pay attention to the baby, his thoughts, and convey to him what good things were waiting here in life. So this was very similar, but naturally it matters quite a bit whether one does this once or regularly, for months on end.

It was very difficult in the beginning, because I had a lot of internal strife. I was paying a lot of attention to myself, and I was surely right in feeling that I could not give birth at home. So the situation was rather contradictory. I was tearing myself up over this: I do not want to go to the hospital, but I do not have the courage to give birth at home. Ádám was a very difficult birth, I was in labour for 24 hours, and it probably would not have worked if I did not go all the way, because … well, I had had an abortion quite young, at 18, and it was also on account of this that I thought this case would cause trouble, I could feel it. Ági Geréb said after the birth that women who have had abortions usually cannot give birth at home, because they cannot establish the inner harmony, the acceptance towards their child, that is necessary for a birthing process without disturbance or intervention. I only learned this after the fact, but felt it instinctually at first, that this might be an issue. Ági said that there have been counterexamples, and that I had the typical healed, post-abortive birth. A horribly long pushing phase; I was pushing for three hours. Since then, I have heard of women who had it even longer, so my first birth really was an exciting day of my life.

The attunement was difficult, because the situation was very strange: a complete stranger, I practically fell into his office off the street based on a book, and I do not make friends easily, and it was difficult at first on account of this. Then things started taking shape over time, after two or three sessions I could let myself go, since this is the point of the whole thing, for you to really be able to turn inwards and pay attention.

Ádám, he is a very interesting baby, and the most wonderful part of this bonding analysis thing is that we get to know our children before they are born. I knew exactly what they were going to be like. Ádám was already a gentle wallflower in my belly, withdrawn, a little sensitive, but at the same time temperamental, and this interesting duality is present in my husband too, he has a similar nature. Ádám, when he did not like something, would kick, and he did this until he got what he wanted. There were times when I woke up early in the morning to him poking me, and I would start singing to him. He loved singing, and would start kicking again as soon as I stopped.

Jutka never kicked, she was always smiley, jovial. Back then I said to Dr Raffai that she is like a little Buddha, because she was smiling with such satisfaction, and I really knew that she was like this, even in my belly. She is just as smiley today. I saw images more frequently and clearer with Jutka, and saw her better too. Ádám, I recall, did not come forward with such visual clarity.

It was really interesting that when I was concentrating on the child, oftentimes my own experiences came up, when I was the foetus, so my own prenatal memories. I lived through … well, it might sound incredibly laughable, but I relived the moment of my conception. At the time, I did not want to believe that this really was that. But the good doctor said that there is nothing extraordinary in this. The feeling came upon me with such a scary, elemental force that it was unbelievable that such a thing could exist, when the zygote gets embedded … actually these all started with being calm, now we turn inward, and I would feel the child first, who either signalled or did not signal, I felt that she was either sending a message at the moment, or did not happen to be sending anything. So I always concentrated on her first, and then moments later I felt within, that I was inside something. This conception was an amazing experience! And it was so unexpected, it was not even an image, because the embedding visually … no, these were feelings. But very strong, intense feelings, I do not even know what to compare it to, a shocking recognition that struck like lightning into my consciousness. These were then concrete feelings and definitive. So the recognition struck me, I knew right then that this was it … but from where, even in retrospect I cannot quite comprehend. It felt like when you arrive from complete uncertainty to the perfect place, to the Garden of Eden … and you reach home … and you feel the love and acceptance. It filled out the entire universe, the whole thing was practically a flash. It was miraculous, it is really hard to express it with words. I experienced this with her, with Jutka. So this was one of the definitive experiences of my life, and there have been a few like it since.

I always started from my womb and the child, and that is why I think I probably had a lot of strife with myself, because the concentrating inward usually ended in this, the baby did not even signal, so it is likely that I had a lot of unresolved, unprocessed internal issues.

I was a half-expected child: my mother was expecting me, my father was not. They are together to this day. My dad did not want me, and I still have a contradictory relationship with him today, of course he ended up accepting me, but now we have conflicts once more. My relationship with my mother, thank dear God, is really good. So she really was expecting me from the moment of my conception. I have a brother too, who is three years younger.

The internal things, those were always accompanied by really good feelings. So the conception experience, and I remember something else, when I was already a foetus, I saw … this was really interesting, because I felt the amniotic fluid, and I was moving my hand around in it. This was just a flash too, and I knew for certain that it was me, not my baby, who was inside me. When these internal things came up, I always felt really good.

My birth was probably a rather big trauma for me, because at that time I simply felt that I did not want to … and that was bad … and a quite debilitating, constraining feeling came up, that I felt in every inch, a vice was gripping my head, I could not move my arms, oh, it was really bad … and it was long too, not a flash, it lasted for minutes, and it took time for it to completely stop. These came up in the first period, so when I was pregnant with Ádám, these memories came up with him. Obviously, I was struggling with this because I did not really know what to expect from giving birth, so that is why my own negative experiences were stronger. It was horrible, and it came up not just once but a number of times, and it lasted minutes. Basically, after the first two–three sessions, when I had loosened up, these old experiences came up one after the other.

When I was reexperiencing my own internal events, the child never moved, and I always felt him paying close attention to me. He did not move a muscle until things played out inside me and the whole thing was over. But it happened a few times that the experience got broken up by his signal, but it was really uncomfortable when he interfered. When the event itself got broken off, it was a birthing event. I think it was too much for him, he could not bear it, because I was experiencing this with so much anxiety … it was horrible, this sounds quite strange, that I am just lying on a couch, and feeling like hell, feeling concrete physical pains, and I think that these feelings were too intense for him. But oftentimes he watched the whole thing, and gave me a sign afterwards … it is so interesting, I was feeling a sense of consolation from him. Somehow, partly from his movement, it was a caressing motion, and on the plane of feelings, thoughts. So we had an exchange of thought between ourselves. He was already a decisive personality in there, and could express himself very forcefully, so when he was gentle and kind, it felt so good, I really needed that then.

Communication worked for me primarily through thoughts and feelings. Sometimes I saw images too, but this was very rare, and even then it was not movie-like, it was from the internal world, either related to them, or my own experiences articulated in sentences.

Ádám was a very sensitive little thing, he was very afraid of noises. One time, underneath the window where the analysis was happening, someone was yelling really badly at their child, so much so that we heard it, and presumably he heard it too. We were in a quite advanced stage, and he got really scared. It was always quite clear when he got scared, he got really tense, he almost froze. This was quite memorable, and I calmed him down in my thoughts, do not worry, no one will treat you like this, you are being expected with love, and no one will yell with you.

He really liked it when I rocked him with my breathing. So I was trying to breathe into my stomach, and this always had a good effect on him, I felt him enjoying it so much, and he would calm right down.

With Jutka, I was not afraid of giving birth, at that point I was not going to the analysis because of that, but I thought that the poor thing, the second kid, would anyway miss out on a lot of good things that the first one got, so I might as well make sure she gets this, this one hour of relaxation a week and a calm conversation. It is also true that I was trying at home every day, it did not happen quite so deeply, but I always relaxed for 20 or 30 minutes, I put on some nice classical music, and tried to get really close to her, and we listened to it together. These were two-person, happy celebrations. During your daily life you do not really have time for this, to turn inward, but then it was just the two of us and we were enjoying each other. It was incredibly great with both kids, when I felt that they were sending and giving love, as if they were radiating it towards me.

I got in touch with Jutka more easily, but there were difficulties there too. My blood test at the 16th week was not phenomenal, and they told me to go to a genetic screening and ultrasound. This caused a good bit of tension and anxiety in me. Even though you might feel like your child is healthy, because I think you can sense that. I had asked Ádám and I asked her too, but when you are face to face with medical results like that, then they try to calm you down, everything is alright, but go to the genetic ultrasound ... and at the genetic ultrasound they recommended amniocentesis, and I had had an abortion earlier. I do not even wish that on my enemy, I will never again ... I do not care, I will give birth to this child, whatever might happen, I am not going anywhere! This period was so heavy with tension, that she turned inward quite a lot. When it just matured in me, that whatever happens I will have this child, my mother told me that I cannot make this decision alone. I cannot do this to my husband, exclude him. So at that point I convinced myself, alright, let us go. But then my husband said no, let us not go, because he knows that the child is healthy. This was a long, strenuous period, and during the whole thing Jutka really turned inward. I could feel that she was offended, she was hurt. She showed this by turning her little face inward, not outward and forward, and curled up and pulled herself down all the way to the bottom of my belly. Apart from it not feeling great physically, it was even worse emotionally. The analysis helped so much, and we slowly climbed out of it.

With Jutka, I got a sense that she was a girl, it came visually: I saw pink. I am not the type to dress the kid in pink fluff, but when I went into my womb, and it was pink inside, I could feel it somehow. With Ádám, I knew from his behaviour, so clearly from his signals, kicks, demanding nature – well, he could have been a girl for all that, but I still really strongly felt that he was a boy. I was 19 weeks pregnant with Ádám when I first went to analysis, and I was already sure by then that he was a boy.

With Jutka it was a little earlier than that, because by the time this AFP examination came around, I was already going to analysis. Basically, it was through that that I managed to ask her to forgive me for having all sorts of bad thoughts about her in my head, and then she came out from where she was curled up, and from there on this situation passed. There were signs that the whole thing had resolved itself. Of course, I am not saying that after this I never felt anxious, it did happen a few times after that, but this general, fundamental disposition, I thankfully got rid of. Still, afterwards it happened a few times that it flashed in: well, what if? I swore that if by chance there will be another one, then leave me out of these blood tests.

I really want another child, but it is unlikely to happen. I got started with family planning wanting four, but my husband has some health issues, and because of that we feel that it would be irresponsible to have more children, we will see, at the same time he will not let me sell the baby stuff. I really liked being pregnant, it was an amazing period, even though I was throwing up in the beginning. It is a fantastic feeling, as this tiny creature is growing in your belly, and takes over all my thoughts, emotions, and reacts to everything.

Jutka's birth was lightning fast. It was so fast, that the doctor barely even got there. If she had been five minutes late, then my mom would have had to help. I was already pushing when she arrived. But that too only because my mom convinced me to call the doctor. I did not want to let her know at first, because I thought why the hell should she hurry over, for nothing. It simply did not hurt, I had none of the pains I had had with Ádám. With him I had pains that made me feel like I was going to die.

I do not think there was any trouble with either child. When we were trading thoughts about birth with Ádám before the fact, he was not afraid of his birth at all, unfortunately I was feeling anxious, and he was the one to give me strength, he was the calm one out of the two of us.

Now, looking back, his birth was the more pleasant experience because he was born almost smiling, and I almost croaked, but it was not a traumatic experience for him at all. The way he was born his little head popped out at the first push, and his body came with the next one. When his head popped out, he immediately opened his eyes and looked around curiously. My husband saw his face – he says it was indescribable. It still hurts that I could not see it. He was almost smiling and looking curiously. And this was so beautiful, and so calm. He did not cry. He was born in the morning, and of course we had to give the poor thing a bath by the evening. The vernix was completely stuck to his butt, and we had to wash it off, and he really did not like that. That was the first time he cried, but he did not give a peep all day before that.

Jutka, on the other hand, cried. I did not have the anxiety anymore, I think, I was more determined. I do not know why she was crying; I can imagine it is because she came so suddenly, and we were not expecting this speed. We did not have time to properly prepare. She was born at half-past-eight in the evening, we had not even turned the lights off. Even though we really were preparing for her, I was in labour since the morning, I was making a simple lunch, we went on a little walk, cleaned up, prepared Ádám, because my mother-in-law was going to take him. Every 20 minutes the small signals were coming, but then the last part was so fast for her, I think that is what put her off.

I think that the effect of analysis could be felt on the plane of an inner spiritual connection. Jutka was a much calmer baby. Ádám was more troublesome when he was little, he was very clingy, and honestly, I think this can be led back to that too – I am going to return to the analysis a bit again – I had something happen while I was expecting Ádám. This was among my most disturbing experiences. So I lost a baby a long time ago, and I had to say goodbye to that little one, and try to forgive myself too. This was happening right then, I was focusing on my womb, healing the place from where the baby was aborted, and in a moment I felt a pain on the other side of my womb too. I knew at that moment that I had lost two babies. Back then I thought that when I had my abortion, it was a twin pregnancy. It turned out after the birth, that this did not happen. Ádám had a twin, and this foetus died at a very early stage. I explain his need for security with that, it is certain that this took a toll on him, I just did not know it yet at the time. In the first three months, he was constantly feeding, 20 hours a day – that was insane. So it definitely was a big inner trauma for him.

I started going to analysis with Jutka around the 16th or 17th week, and it came up towards the end of that pregnancy, that I lost Ádám's sibling. I thought that I was remembering my previous pregnancy, so the one where Ádám was in my belly, and it somehow struck me how much he suffered from this, and he needs to be consoled, and calmed down and the feeling came suddenly, unexpectedly. At the same time the question came up in me, why this one, why the twin had to die... they were awful feelings once more ... I felt heat, and a burning, as though my body was on fire, and at the same time because of this horrible heat I shrank and hardened. So I was feeling exactly what happened then and there. After the feeling passed, I realized what this could be. This happened when I still did not know I was pregnant, I had no idea, and I was in a sauna. And it came to me, that is why the other baby died. Of course, you cannot go to the sauna, they say, that awful heat is no good. If only I had known!

Ádám is very developed verbally, he was speaking in sentences at a year and a half, and he has a scary good memory. His long-term memory is especially good. When he was two and a half, we went down to the sea, he is four and a half now, and he is still talking about it. When are we going again, because that was so good, when he was collecting pine cones. When he was three they said – we were going to a skills development playhouse – that he is ready for school. It is incredible, so he excels from this perspective. Of course, there are areas where he would not perform as well.

Jutka is an entirely different sort. With her we often listened to music while we were relaxing, and she might be so musical because of that. So she is not as developed verbally, although she is starting to converse now too. In turn, she recognizably sings different tunes. She is most likely to be musically gifted. She is some sort of an emotional trap, a little smilester, she laughs so much, she butters you up, her ability to form relationships is really good.

I was at my second ultrasound with Ádám, that is a really good time because the machine can capture the baby, it is still small but already has everything, and when they put the device on my belly you could see the top of the baby's head, and when he felt that something was there, he looked up, and you could see his whole little face, and it was sensational.

Ádám was almost three years old, we had Jutka by then too, when he approached me with a strange line: "Mommy, I am going to tell you something funny. Put me in your belly!" "Why?" I asked, shocked. "Because it is good and warm in there, and the food is tasty." Then he added: "tasty food, a soft warm pillow." I will admit, I was somewhat amazed. I could only guess that some image must have popped up in him, so he must remember something from his life in the womb, how good it was.

Angelika Seres: "… I found myself in a vast
space, there, the baby appeared"

It must have been two or three years ago when I read in a newspaper that two Hungarian psychoanalysts had made a sensational discovery: a connection between a mother and her foetus can be developed, with which actual communication may be established with the baby, well before birth. It was clear that if we were planning a baby and things went according to plan, how wonderful that would be for me. It was not a foreign thing for me, because I used mind control methods and also relaxed at home. We did similar exercises on pregnancy fitness. I therefore knew that a lot can be achieved in such a state. I thought that if there were some scam in it, I would feel it either way, since I know what it may give based on my experiences.

I gave a shot at relaxation on my own. I did not go to a course. I rather did it based on books, which was when I realized that relaxation means entering into an infinitely good and calm state, as if you were dreaming while awake and the whole thing has a very pleasant atmosphere. While I was still attending university in Gödöllő, I often practised this on the train to Pest as well. I could enter quite quickly into this state, which both relaxed and refreshed me. I relax nowadays too. So, when I know that Panka will wake up shortly, I do not fall asleep but rather I rest 15, 20 minutes and that pushes me over the deadlock in a physical sense as well. She is three months old by the way.

Once I knew that there was a baby there, fate brought me to Prof. Hidas. I was still working back then, going to pregnancy fitness two or three times a week and, luckily, I managed to arrange an afternoon appointment with him. I was quite excited at first as to whether or not a connection would really happen. Of course, the surroundings were foreign and I had to learn to relax there as well. Interestingly, if I went straight after pregnancy fitness, with 10–15 minutes of relaxation beforehand, I could enter into that state much more swiftly, since I was physically exhausted. From that point, relaxation came as a definite pleasure. Later on, my surroundings became familiar as well. We could lower the blinds if I wanted to, but it was not always necessary. I often wanted there to be light. I went in springtime and the sky was such a gorgeous blue! And when one's eyes are closed, you will not see what is around you either way.

All sorts of experiences came and we tried to decipher with the help of Prof. Hidas what it was that I went through. There was a myriad of pictures. I articulated relaxation in myself as one being able to control events to some extent in these conscious dreams. I felt somewhat like that. There was a lot of travelling in between these. It was all an experience and picture of complete singularity.

The session began with us trying to establish a connection with the womb, so that it would grant us entrance to the foetus. At first, I could only get in with great difficulty, as I recall the first time I attempted going in, a fruit appeared in front of me, a plum, and the closer I got to it, the bigger the plum seemed and I felt smaller and smaller. There was the plum, but I had no clue what to do with it, and then the good doctor said that I should try and get in. It had an interesting shape, with a longitudinal indent. I went around it but could not find an opening. But the doctor urged me to keep on, keep on looking – and eventually, I entered the plum at its stem where it hangs from the tree. It felt as though I were squeezing into something. Meanwhile, Hidas was telling me that I enter the womb like so. A great space greeted me inside. At first, I did not find anything. A space I could not define, for instance, it was not a room with corners. I saw a vast darkness. And then, suddenly, it was quite peculiar, as if statues such as those that support the ceiling in old buildings appeared and reached above me. Then I looked around, where is the baby then, where is it? Hidas immediately told me not to worry, that it would come. And indeed she appeared, leaning out from the wall, but I merely saw as far as her nose. I never saw her mouth, but then she looked at me and I knew it was her. The good doctor also noticed that I turned red. He therefore told me that he could see we got it, for there is a physiological tracking of this as well, in which we establish the connection. This was the first meeting.

On the second occasion, I thought oh well, the plum must come again, but no plum came. Instead, a myriad of glass balls came. They were quite colourful, at first I saw them as some sort of clockwork ... but as I went closer, I saw these balls ... which somehow rolled like cogwheels. It was as if they caught me in a current ... it was horribly frightening. I said, good God, I am nearing my death over here. Then, the good doctor calmed me down saying that I should not be afraid and that I would not die. Still, it was such a feeling ... a space so tight, into which I could not fit. Then, these cogwheel balls picked me up and I somehow adapted to their movement and I rolled in on top of them. I was inside again. And again, she showed herself as far as her nose. Then I became small and she became so big. But I never saw her gaze. I never actually saw it, only a great sensation took hold of me.

Every time I saw her, for example, the images suddenly changed. For example, I suddenly found myself in a park and a child was screeching for me to go over there. But hang on ... someone was crying a lot at one stage and she calmed me down, so that I would not be afraid. It is not a problem if a baby cries. Strangers came along as well and asked why this child was crying; could I not treat her well? So I was reprimanded ... Ah yes, a little boy came up to me, held my hand, and said everything is alright, babies cry. I did not know who that little boy in shorts was. Later, when I went closer, he got bigger, it was the boy with whom I spent my vacations in Mátraháza when I was a kid ... his dad worked at a petrol station in Hódmezővásárhely. So, this boy appeared. Back then I liked him, oh well, I must have been seven, eight years old. And we used to play a lot. At that time, we met up every once in a while, we kept in touch. It was peculiar for that little boy to appear.

Usually, the events and images drifted along, something impulsive always came. Once it was a shoelace ... in the final phase a shoelace appeared, which

I had to pull, a brown shoelace. I cannot remember what happened after that. But the plum really persisted. I had to climb through lots of berries sometimes. It was like a bunch of grapes and I climbed through that bunch. In the end, we had a lot of downhill sliding scenes. On one of these occasions, I was pushing her, like two people going down a slide. I pushed her from the inside, to go on, go on, slide more. Do not get stuck. I think that this was before the talks on preparing for birth.

Initially, it was always a blond boy that appeared, for I believed that I would have boys, even though the ultrasound and others confirmed as well that it would be a girl. And I was so pleased about it, for at the bottom of my heart, I had always hoped to have at least one girl, if we were planning to have two babies anyway. But during this state of relaxation her sex never revealed. Therefore, I was searching, maybe just maybe, but it never happened.

In the beginning, I dreamt a lot about my mom, in her youth. She was sporting her hair in a fashionable, 1970s fashion, with cute clothes and bathing suits. I cannot remember her as such, but perhaps those images manifested in me based on old photos. She was chatting to another woman. I met her a few times and she was so odd with that big red hairdo. She was sitting on a bridge in a fiery red bathing suit once, and then I knew … there was something … not even a disagreement, rather a concern, that she was watching over a child who was either mine, or not mine … how is this again? And then, the good doctor told me it was mine.

By the end of the bonding analysis, a lot of dreams came which included sliding downhill, bob tracks and immense spaces at the beginning. Therefore, whenever I passed a narrow place or hallway, I found myself in a vast space; there, the baby appeared. In the median phase, mostly aquatic experiences came. Once, it was as if we were at sea. We were just lying on a mattress, when I felt my body fluctuating. Then, as though the mattress were being pulled around by my head … this is still a persistent experience, and as such, I start spinning spirally with the mattress. Then we arrive in a vertical pose and I fear that the mattress will drift away, however it does not leave us, it stays, then a sudden slump into the depths, but the mattress stays all along … after that, we enter into a very tranquil state, the mattress is no longer there … however, Panka appears. I fell into her company.

I dreamt that I was in water, under the surface of the sea, seeing the plants and glimmer of water, a multitude of times. This was a nice event as well, quite calming. Oftentimes colour effects appeared, dark and light dominated occasionally, so contrasts or colours came on densely, all sorts: green, blue, yellow, red. I travelled a lot; there was a rollercoaster for instance. This sensation materialized several times. We start to travel. Then we gain speed, only to start sliding downwards and meander. In the end, some great light appears. Initially I did not understand; I solely felt the vast darkness. Then all of a sudden, I arrived into the light. Meanwhile, the professor was always questioning me, what do I feel, is it a pleasant sensation. I said yes, I am not cold; I am in a good place. As we deciphered them, we came to realize that perhaps I was reliving my own birth. I had positive feelings, so I was born into tranquil surroundings.

Then there were relaxations, when Prof. Hidas told me to send images. It was then that the peach trees were in bloom. Later on, I sent lily of the valley and lilac as well. After that, I sent photographs, for instance, of my husband and grandfather. Somehow, their photos came to mind at once, for me to show Panka. By then, I had shown her so much. We were in the apartment. We ate in the dining area in the living room; in the end I even changed her diaper. And I remember how hard it was when the good doctor told me to say my farewell, because the time was up. And I usually left her either in her cradle or on the changing board, so that she could be changed next time. Peculiarly, these functional to-dos did not come to me at all, rather just experiences, that hey, I see the baby, and we play, travel, later on these caring things such as feeding or changing times come to the fore.

Panka was reasonably active all along. She sometimes banged. It was very odd that she was able to bang. At times, I looked for and waited to find a connection with her on a completely different plain. I always left quite embittered when I could not meet her. It was a great sorrow. It happened a few times that I could not really communicate with her, that I held her in my lap with her head in my right palm. So that is what I imagined during relaxation.

Curiously, it is as if my musical taste changed during this as well. For instance, I was not an admirer of Mozart, but I listened to that as well as other classical music CDs. There was music that just annoyed me. I was not fond of watching TV either, from the second trimester onward. The radio actually bothered me as well. I could not stand TV to the extent that I was downright mad when my partner turned it on. Therefore, we did not watch a lot of shows back then. There is wonderful music to go alongside relaxation, *Kitaro* for example – I liked that and similar things. It was really strange that I listened to more classical music independently of the fact that it was a common recommendation of professionals and one can read a lot about it in newspapers as well. It instinctively felt pleasant; it let me settle. So I could do my thing, if that sort of music was playing. It was equally strange that *Enigma* drove me up the wall – this music is of a relaxing nature as well, it has set texts as well, the music itself is quite abstract – but back then I loved it. I felt it helped us to harmonize.

Besides listening to music, we occasionally danced too. We waltzed for example and I saw that she liked this movement. I could feel her mirth.

When I told her how birth happens, I felt a great silence, she was surprised. Then again as if she were waiting in silence, I did not feel that she was frightened, rather listening astounded. This part was quite beautiful too. When I was reciting the texts, preparing for birth as well, I felt such a responsibility in all of it. It was exalting, like a vow, when the professor read what I was supposed to tell her for the first time.

So, when these preparations were in progress, outer pictures appeared more often than not … so I was viewing myself from the outside. I could not feel my organs, I was somehow outside … and I saw her as well, as she was getting out. I felt that she was born, so during the relaxation, there were the three of us, meaning the father, her, and myself. Dad brought some strawberry chocolate for us. Otherwise, I did not eat any chocolate during my pregnancy. When this happened during relaxation, we broke it up, gave her some as well, and Panka was covered with chocolate from ear to ear. All three of us munched away. Once the relaxation was over, I simply had to have some strawberry chocolate and I finished the bar in one sitting. Afterwards as well, for days, I had to have it daily. And all this was because we sat there, the three of us and munched on chocolate.

Panka emitted a fantastic warmth and tranquillity from within. This calmed me down as well, for I was excited too, that good Lord I am having a kid, is she going to be healthy and I am going to be her mommy, but will we be able to take care of her, and will we suffice for her spiritually? So I had a bunch of qualms and she calmed me down completely until we got to the birth. Therefore, it was so natural that everything was in order and I felt that I would be a good mother.

I feel we had a good birth – for I imagine that it is how Anna feels, too. We went in at half past seven; she was born at a quarter to ten. She helped me a lot. It was interesting that once she was born, I did not bother with whether or not she was healthy. I thought it so natural that I was rather agitated to finally see her. As they placed her on my belly, that was such a magnificent feeling, heavenly, it cannot be articulated. That warmth that was so far inside is all of a sudden here and I find it on my belly, there, where she was inside me not so long ago.

Bonding analysis gave me such wonderful experiences, so, altogether I was delighted to have found this opportunity. It gave me so much confidence and I believe that is of great importance, especially with the first child, when the young mother is uncertain. She does not know whether or not she is prepared for it. These questions are certain to be answered there. Of course, it does not hurt for one to have a previous relaxation experience, for it facilitated establishing a connection for me.

Of course, I had to get used to her as well. She was like a seedling that had dropped down from the sky. I had to get to know her gaze and everything for it was so unbelievable that the baby had been born and that a new little person was here. I cannot tell what it would have been like if I had not gone to bonding analysis, but I felt we managed wonderfully to find the same wavelength. Naturally, I had it easy for myself, since she is a very even-minded baby.

I felt an infinite tranquillity even during her birth, and afterwards as well, as she lay on my stomach. Once she got out, she cried a bit. Then she was completely calm. They placed her on my breast and she started suckling right away. I asked the midwife, how could she be sucking now, when I do not even have milk, and she told me to believe that I do, and she showed me. There really is, that is the colostrum. And there was such peace. Then her father embraced her in his arms for a long time and Panka looked at him with huge eyes.

My partner anticipated her for a long time. I always told him what had happened during relaxation. He understood and completely accepted the feelings that surfaced within me. He was gladdened. We played a lot, the three of us. Once the baby was kicking a lot, my partner would tease my belly and she would kick there, where he last left his hand. It was such a good feeling that he got in touch with her and thus they played and conversed, even then.

Myrtill Várnai: "He basically exclaimed: I am not a girl!"

I was really looking forward to having this baby, for I am not too young. I was 35 when I gave birth. I had not planned to have a child, even though I knew I would love it, then due time came. Once it was here, all I could think of was how I wanted to provide them with everything I could give. I was already pregnant when I heard of the baby-mommy bonding. Perhaps on the radio, or maybe one of my clients mentioned it to me. I have been a psychologist for the past 13 years and I have been giving therapy for nine years. My partner is receptive towards such things; he is a social manager. He knew of Dr Raffai, and that he and György Hidas are professionals in this field. Shortly afterwards, I 'phoned Prof. Hidas. For one, I was interested in the method. Second, I thought this would be beneficial to the baby. Of course, I did not know much about it. When György Hidas greeted me, he said I had arrived at the best of times, for it is best to start in the fourth month.

This was not a challenge for me, for I had studied autogenic training and relaxation in my university years. I had not gone to analysis. Based on my experiences, this was a de facto establishment of a connection between mother and foetus through a method of relaxation, in a state of modified consciousness. So, a degree in psychoanalysis is most likely not needed. I believe that what is needed is a very deep, empathetic and accepting atmosphere. This the professor did marvellously.

Initially, it was strange for me to get connected to my womb. It would have been more natural to do so with the child. But with my womb?! I thought I may have done it differently, but back then, I had no real perception of what this is and how it goes. Then on the second occasion, this was not an issue.

In reality, I always got through the connecting with my womb part speedily and there I was with the baby, for I wished not to be connected to my womb, but my child, very much with the child.

I had a very peculiar connecting with him once, perhaps during the second or third session. I saw a colour and I understood that it was the aura. The first colour was pink, which is the expression of a love relationship in symbolism. Then the whole image shifted to blue. I did not know what blue meant in this case. I looked it up in a book in which the aura is discussed in detail and it turned out that the aura of the baby is what was visible – blue. I took it to Prof. Hidas as well and showed it: here it is; this is what I saw. So it was quite strange that this colour appeared.

It happened once, not during analysis, but always having "he will be a boy, he will be boy" in my mind can be attributed to it. Then it suddenly came to my mind – since I am a psychologist – that this was becoming such a principle in me, God forbid she is going to turn out as a girl – which is not an issue, of course not – but God forbid he will be a boyish girl due to that! Then, in that relaxed state, I imagined him in a pink dress, with blonde pig-tails, to which he responded with such a storm of movement, what a storm! He protested. Never, not before, nor afterwards – this happened when he was four-and-a-half months old, comparatively early – I never got such kicks as those. Really, he basically exclaimed: I am not a girl! This was quite surprising.

It was quite an interesting scene in itself, when we went to a heart rate examination, and then, well something amusing happened. They left me there, with my partner, and I do not really remember what happened, but we were in a state of bliss. And the baby had a terribly high heart rate sound. That was when I realized, Mother of God, I will be referred in here for the results! This is not going to work. Then I said, alright, listen up, I love you a lot, my little baby, but you will have to produce a normal heart rate, and it is true that we are in an elevated mood, but it would be nice to calm down. And for a moment, I shut my eyes and sent a big huge mental love package to him. Right after that, his heart rate dipped down to normal all of a sudden! It was nearly frightening. I asked for that sheet as well and I took it to Hidas. Those results must still be around somewhere. I marked where I told him to calm down and it visibly decreased so much that it was nearly dangerously low. Another part of the story is that I had shown to the doctor the part on the sheet where I had calmed him down. Then he smiled with a permissive look, he almost calmingly told me: alright, alright, alright. He did not refer me.

I constantly talked to him with my inner voice. I worked all through my pregnancy and I was glad when I was left alone with him. We always discussed things, I questioned, whether or not he was alright. There were these questions, what would you like now, do you want vitamins, or anything else, would you like to listen to a story, shall I put on some music? Things got mixed up from time to time and I did not exactly know, if it were my own thought what would be best for him, or if it were really his. And I even said, I do not know whether these are coming from me or the baby, it was difficult to differentiate. Meanwhile, perhaps I even analyzed the situation. I went through a lot of "oh yes" experiences in my initial therapies. Actually, from time to time, I would attend professionally as well, that oh my, what a good thing Hidas said right now, how precise! He did what he did marvellously, that I know for sure. So his analytical knowledge was important for me in this. He always knew the "what" and "when," when it came to things to say, he was so deep and humane, and I believe the elderly man's wisdom and experiences are in all of this, independent from views on the world. Therefore, he could accept my slightly differing views … or I do not precisely know what his is like … actually, it never came across. But he was absolutely open to anything that happened or anything I said.

In complete honesty, parallel to the bonding analysis such life events drew me in with my partner that periodically put off the state of relaxation. We did not want the kid to arrive at our current place back then. The fate of our apartment had to be discussed, should we renovate and sell it, and start looking for a new apartment, or should we come here. So, these dilemmas were powerful inside me. The topic often occupied my mind. This paired with a load of negative feelings. There were even concrete situations to which the baby reacted pleasantly.

I asked him once in the analysis, hey, how would you like Dávid as a name? And he said it works, that he liked it. I got a myriad of positive emotions from him. The truly good quality of the analysis was that the feeling of me loving him so much and his loving me often surfaced powerfully. We sensed the strength of the bond between us. This state returned a lot when I got connected with the baby.

There was a conflict regarding his birth, I had to struggle with the obstetrician for it was scheduled for the fifth of May. Then again, I had been to an astrologer and he had placed the date on another day. In reality, the doctor would have gladly initiated the birth after the fifth, so I was fighting for him to leave at least a week to it and for me to only have to report to intake then, provided that nothing would happen. I would have really liked to rely on fate. But I was also uncertain what would come to be. Therefore, we discussed with Dávid whether or not this was alright with him. I felt that even he did not like the early date. In the end, it started off on its own. The amniotic fluid began to drain on the eve of the 11th and I was called back for the morning of the 12th.

In the end, unfortunately, he was born by Caesarean. Although I have heard that these babies were born more simply. I cannot really tell what actually happened. There was something either on a physical or psychological level that caused it to happen as it did by Caesarean, or perhaps I had barriers, or Dávid did not want to be born this way. Something got stuck, or rather I was not widening. The fact that my muscles were very restricted related to this as well. So, I have done a lot of sports since I was a child, but for me to place my palms on the ground with straight legs, that was a no go.

There were difficulties after the birth as well. I do not know if the problem was in our relationship, but he did not want to feed. I think, and know as a fact, that when they brought him to me on the first day, he was already quite hungry – he was a big baby by the way – and he was so agitated that he did not have the patience to wait for my clumsiness with suckling. The nurses stood there so that they could help out. Poor Dávid was crying himself red, so they took him and fed him through a nursing bottle. And from that point on he preferred the rubber of the nursing bottle, since that milk got into his mouth with such ease, while on the breast he had to work for his keep. So he suckled for about three months, but he mainly preferred to be fed from a nursing bottle. But I will not exempt myself that easily. I do not know which part of this is my fault and which part is his. But I do not want to put the blame on him. The circumstances of his birth must have contributed: the Caesarean, the anaesthesia, the fact that they did not give him to me immediately as well as the fact that they gave him a nursing bottle because he was hungry. There must have been something that he did not like and he was rather stubborn. No worries, it all worked out like it did, at least he had a lovely head and he did not have to suffer through that whole thing.

Once there was no tight bond or necessity that you would feed, or not feed, so once this was not an issue, I felt relieved from then on and our relationship became magnificent. He turned three years old in the past month. It is definitely obvious that he is developing faster. He started speaking earlier and beautifully, with such vocabulary, that when I told him at two years old that we had got there, he answered yes, we have arrived. So he was already toying with synonymous expressions. He goes to an English kindergarten now, because we want to extend his intellect and development somehow. I once said to him once in simple English that the "bird is flying in the air," upon which he corrected me with "in the sky." I basically got used to him being like that, however, I am always a bit surprised that he already knows which of two synonymous words the correct one is.

There was a baby who was born almost at the same time as Dávid, about 30 minutes later, by Caesarean. Then for a year we spent a lot of time together. She was a little girl and girls usually develop sooner; they do everything earlier. Against all odds, Dávid was well ahead in every aspect. He is more skilled in everything, manipulation, speech, intellect, than the other kids his own age in the kindergarten, so he leads the entire group. He started going to kindergarten when he was two and by now he is in the middle year, at three years of age. What will come later? It does not matter. I do not know what will come. That will be a problem for later. We will have to resolve it then. The pedagogues keep saying that Dávid should go on. Alright then – I said – he will develop further then.

What is for certain is that we pay a great deal of attention to him and this openly affects his intellectual capabilities. The babysitter conversed with him in German from the start, and he spoke to her in German in the first instance, not in Hungarian. He learned the names of the animals first, for that greatly interested him. He was a year-and-a-half at that time. "Kücken" was the first one, the small chicken. We went to the US when he was one, he started talking there and by the age of a year-and-a-half, he was saying sentences such as: this coat belongs mother. He began using correct grammatical structure quite early on. He is an incredible observer, he remembers everything. We were going home yesterday through a neighbourhood that we do not really know. When the tram stopped at Kálvin square, he said that grandma lives not so far from here, and she does indeed live there, near Ráday Street. At two, he recited who he is, what his name was, his date of birth and home address. At two years of age, when he went to kindergarten, the teachers also acknowledged and mentioned how nicely, clearly and succinctly Dávid talks.

I told him once – but I never use this word by the way – come, let us put these linen pants on. Then, six months later, he requested the "linen pants."

The babysitter took him to Orfű on vacation a few times. He was a year-and-a-half old when they first went to a small zoo, where he saw a cute little rodent. He really liked this rusty-coloured creature, with small eyes and pointy ears. They told him that it was the meerkat. Then, when they were preparing for Orfű a year later, he asked if they were going to see the meerkat again. Kids usually do not recall things at such a young age.

Counting goes wonderfully as well. Initially, he always indulged in intellectual tasks, but now toys interest him more. He mainly plays with cars. He got a puzzle consisting of many pieces, meant for older kids, but he completes it in a flash.

He adores animals, especially fish. He has been looking at them in books from a very young age. We have an encyclopaedia about whales and dolphins with pictures and he can get really stuck into this. He knows nearly all of the species off by heart. There was an adorable scene when Dávid was just a year-and-a-half old. We were walking down the street when we stopped at the shop window of an aquarium. There was a myriad of beautiful fish in it, everything from sunfish to discus fish, and there he was, listing them. I could not drag him away from the window for the life of me, and of course we had to go into the store as well. There was an aquarium inside and he started to identify the species. He was so tiny that he could barely be seen. There was a tall counter in the store and the saleswoman was gazing round, who is there, who is talking – she did not see anyone. Then she came out from behind the counter and of course she merely saw a very tiny child, and she asked, who said what species of fish were in the aquarium? This kid, I replied. She nearly fainted, she would not believe it. I explained that we had these books at home, which are placed out there, and he recognizes the live fish based on the pictures.

He has a great nature, of course I cannot say for sure that this is because of the analysis, even though I do not know that, but he is a very pleasant child. Others say it as well. He can express his emotions so well, in such depth. He resonates to any problem, thinks it through, more so, he even settles the relationship between his parents. So he is very smart. And aside from this he can clown around of course. He is a joyful, easy-going child, like the rest. Then again, I believe analysis played a role in this as well.

Kinga Aradi: "Zita chose her own name"

I have got two kids, three-year-old Zita, and Szilvi, who is one and a half. I went to bonding analysis during both my pregnancies. Perhaps I did so first with Zita because I am not only open to new things, but I am also a little bit of a perfectionist, as much as possible. We were preparing only in thought for the first kid, and I was reading related articles, when I first heard about this new method on the radio, mother–foetus bonding analysis. At that moment, I knew I was going to try it.

It has to be said that I was pregnant once before, but the foetus died early. It really took a toll on me, when I found out. So, I was very nervous on account of this, for everything to go well, because until then I never thought that anything could go wrong. There was a lot of joy and anticipation in me, and we planned everything out. It was at the beginning, the foetus was eight or ten weeks old. They tried to comfort me, telling me that this can happen in a third of all cases. The fact that I was still working probably contributed to it, I had a stressful job, I was the head of marketing at a Dutch firm. I loved my job, but I had to work and travel a lot. That is exactly why I thought that nothing bad could happen, because I had never led a self-destructive lifestyle, but I just kept working, and that probably had something to do with it.

In the articles that I had read, the moms all said the best feeling was to know with certainty that their child was safe and sound; that was one of the reasons I went to Dr Raffai. There was also the fact that, with this method, your children will be more intelligent because one starts investing time and effort into taking care of them as early as possible.

It became very pressing when my second pregnancy, that is my first child, also had complications at the beginning. I got very scared that it could end that way again. The doctor immediately wrote me out of my job and prescribed 12 weeks of staying at home, lying in bed. Then my grounding gradually loosened up, I got better and could go back to work. This ended up being for the best, because I had to leave work so suddenly that I left them in a lot of trouble. So I went back for a few months, but not at a crazy pace, because they really understood at that point that I was expecting and I always left for home around 4 or 5 pm. They found my replacement during this time too, and I ended up handing my position over.

When starting the bonding analysis sessions, I was really nervous about not being able to get in touch with the baby, since I am not the relaxing, meditating type. I was afraid I would not succeed. Perhaps also because I am really a materialistic person, not in the philosophical sense but in the sense that I deal with numbers, business plans and rational things. Regrettably, I do not really have any affinity with art; although I like it and it really attracts me; I just cannot connect to it.

To my surprise, it worked out on the first occasion. The baby did not take shape, did not have a body yet, but there was a strange feeling when I stepped into my womb, that somebody was there. It was like a pond of tadpoles that scurry away when you reach out to them. I entered, and this somebody was surprised that someone else was there too, and suddenly disappeared.

I was not so lucky on the second occasion though. I could not make a connection. But the next time my daughter took on a shape, I did not see her face but she began to look like a baby, so I definitely sensed that this something was developing and growing, and tried to get a sense for what she wanted. Sometimes she decidedly came up to me, to be as close as possible. She loved caresses. I even told my husband how sensual she was, because touch was very important for her. This really is like this, even to this day. When she was still a little baby, she was always lying on this thick lambskin rug, and she still has this habit today.

We were in doubt for a long time about her sex, we could not figure out if it was going to be a he or a she. We had three names set out: a male, Soma, and two female ones, Zita and Janka, so I asked her: "Would you like Soma?" nothing, total silence. "How about Janka?" Still nothing. When I got to "Zita," instead of her usual signalling through a thought or feeling, she clearly started kicking. It was so surprising and direct that I did not want to believe and thought that it was an accident. So I asked again, to make sure that I really understood her well. I went through the list again, like I was testing her, and she repeated the same kicking motion. It was not only her thought I was feeling; she gave me a physical response for "Zita." That is the story of how she got her name: she chose it herself.

Unfortunately, there were some complications with Zita; she was in breech position. We tried to turn her around many times, maybe it was so because I have a long upper body; plenty of space to move, and she moved around a lot, mostly head towards me. I asked her many times at the bonding sessions to turn around, using my inner voice, and she did so. Then I could precisely feel it and also saw that her skull moved to another spot. This was in the early days of the praxis of Raffai and Hidas, and the preparation for birth and separation were not yet a concrete part of the bonding analysis programme. I went through this preparatory process with my second child. That being said, I tried my best to prepare Zita, to tell her about how birth will go, the life out here, the family and such.

The explanation for her delivery with Caesarean section is that apart from the fact that she did not turn she did not get into the birth canal either. Also, to add to that, her heartbeat sounded like it was fainting, they thought, because she moved a lot, she had become entangled in the umbilical cord. Once she had been born, they found no real reason for there to be complications, the umbilical cord was long enough, she was not entangled, the widening went well, so there was no physical reason for her not entering the birth canal. It may be an important factor that I myself was born in a breech position and my mother's sister, my aunt, too, and even her baby. But they did not perform a Caesarean section on my mother; even though she had twins, with me first in the breech position, when technology was not as developed as it is now. My twin sister came out the "right" way. There were no complications. My sister also gave birth naturally.

The peculiar way Zita was born might have some psychological reasons too: she is really emotionally attached to me. Even after she was born, I told her to go to sleep from the next room by sending thoughts to her, the same way I did during the analysis. I was sending thoughts from one room to the next: "hush hush, rest now," and I sang to her, and she calmed down like that nicely. Of course, this was very much at the beginning, I do not know how effective it would be if I tried it out now.

During some of the analytical sessions towards the end, she was occasionally sound asleep. I did not bother her, I felt like a mother watching over her sleeping child. I kept a diary while I was expecting. I wrote on the 38th week that she is calming me constantly, even though I keep telling her to turn the other way, she is just calming me. I remember, yes, she told me not to nag her constantly to turn around, and told me to trust her because she is an independent, free being. This was on the 39th week, literally this idea was in me – I did not come up with this, she told us to trust her. On 4 February, I asked her when she would be born. She said, any day now. At the next, our last session, she told me that the journey had begun. This was two days before her birth, and she was born on the 12th. I had no sense that I was going to give birth until my waters broke. I was supposed to give birth a week later.

Dr Raffai told me there has been a case where the mother managed to turn the baby around through bonding analysis while already in the delivery room. I could not do it though, I was much too nervous. It did not help either that my waters already broke, and my uterus latched onto her enough that she could not move easily, she had no space there. I do not think she could have turned around there even if I had connected with her. In the articles I read, the mothers always said delivering was made much easier because of the bonding. I was specifically afraid of the birth, so it was a disappointment that I had done all this and it did not work out. But I processed it. I do not have any bad feelings about it now.

She was a very good baby. She was already smiling in the hospital, she was so calm that everyone noticed her behaving differently than the others. This is true for Szilvi too. They breastfed a lot even at the beginning, about 90–120 grams. Even the night nurses noted that while the other babies cried, they would sleep through the night from the first minute and only woke up once to feed. They were both very developed, calm, happy and balanced, to this day. They started doing everything earlier. Both Zita and Szilvi stood up when they were five months old, started walking at nine, and developed speech at one and a half. We recorded these first few speeches on tape.

When they were born, they did not sleep much, not because they were restless but because they were so interested in their surroundings. Of course, I could spend more time with Zita, because she is the firstborn. I remember I always had to lift her out of her bed just so she could look around. I read somewhere that the human brain works best if vertically placed and not horizontally, and that was the reality with her.

There was no question with Szilvi whether we would go to bonding analysis. I had a complete problem free pregnancy with her, thank God. I started analysis at week 14, and I wrote in my diary how calm she was – I guess this was the feeling inside me. I remember I could connect with her instantly as well; it was all quite balanced. I always had a little remorse in me because I knew I could not spend as much time with her as I did with my firstborn. She is 20 months younger so the bigger girl was a year old when I got pregnant, so she was still little, and needed a lot of attention.

When Zita was asleep, I cooked and did all the things I needed to, so I had time for her and I needed and enjoyed this too. I just could not do that with the second one. I could not listen to as much music with her or sit with her in the rocking chair that long. When I was at an analytical session with Szilvi, I could not stop worrying over Zita, so if she was sick, I was anxious about why she was sick, whether she would bear me being away for an hour and a half, I was constantly worried. Oftentimes during bonding analysis, I thought of Zita, what could she be doing now. I am very conscientious, overly so, and I couldn't not think of her, could not relax. I had a constant feeling of guilt over this in the last six months, so almost until she was a year old. My bad feelings were resolved when people told me that the benefit of being the second child is learning from the older one. I had to accept how right they were. She learned how to use the potty quicker, how to eat by herself, because this is what she was seeing, and by a year old she would sit on the potty in her diapers and say "pssshhh," she peed and wiped her butt, flushed the toilet, all imitating her sister. She had to do everything just like the big one.

If she felt like we were not paying as much attention to her as she would like, she just signalled to us. So, this was in my belly, we were around the 23rd week, and she asked for her dad to talk to her. She clearly said this. My husband was more involved with the first one too, then we got used to how things were with the second one, and then the baby asked for it. Even in the womb, she knew that she had an older sister, this came up right at the beginning.

One time, a completely fantastic thing happened during analysis: she let me into her brain. Dr Raffai told me what a rare thing this was, and as I said I had never worked on this before, this was a different level of communication than earlier. I was not trying to make it happen, it came by itself. So I established connection with her and she let me see her thoughts. I cannot really explain it, but it was as though I managed to enter her brain ... I could feel what she felt and knew. This was not how communication went between us until then, this was on a different level. I noted it, that is when I discovered that foetuses have a collective consciousness. This is a consciousness that basically already contains knowledge. I started telling her things and explaining it as I did to the firstborn, but she almost stopped me and told me that she already knows all these things. It was shocking. As it is passed on through the genes, I cannot explain it, but she really knew where she was and what was going to happen to her. This was all week 15. I did not even think that this existed, this was not my intention, I did not even ask to get into her head, she let me in, she almost invited me in, she took me in. I am open to a lot of things, this is true, but I never studied psychology, these things have been far from me up to now. I am more sceptical, but definitely do not have blind faith.

We did not know her sex either, but I had sensed that she was completely different from Zita and I felt after her characteristic that she would be a boy. Zita was the smart, sharp one, and this one was the wise thinker, the know-it-all. When the big one started playing chess with her dad at age three, she was only a year old, and she was packing the pieces left and right, but she is lining them up now. I just recalled that yes, she told me she was going to play chess and ride a bicycle, and she really loves riding her bike. So I thought that she was a boy, and we even had two boy names: we had Soma and along came Zsombor, and it drove me insane that she did not react to these the way Zita did. I did not understand why, and when she was born, I realized she was a girl, so why would she want to be a Soma or Zsombor. So I was asking her in vain. But I felt her as a boy, and she is so tomboyish still, it is amazing. I call her the little terrorist.

There was one more really interesting, almost scary experience with her. I was going to the analysis in the afternoon, and had an ultrasound beforehand. Zita never really liked it, but Szilvi had no problem with it. When the examination began, I sensed that she was asleep, but feeling me. And she started waving. Even the doctor noticed it, and said that she was waving. I told Raffai, and he said it is possible that she waved intentionally and knew that I was there. Even though she did not know for sure that I saw her, she felt my presence. I figure she might have waived at other times too, when I did not see her, but she knew that she was being watched and signalled that she knew this too.

There was a completely strange thing after this, the foetal experience, it was shocking because we were already talking about birth, what it would be like … So, I experienced what it was like to be a foetus, to be in the womb, what it was like to be born. I felt the environment and the process, being born. There was no fight or struggle, it went smoothly. It felt like a caress. Like when you are submerged in water and cannot hear anything, just the murmuring of the water, and the birth canal softly pushed me out, no pain, no bad feeling. It was not spiritually painful either, it was not a big trauma, but the all-knowing, a big wisdom, no anxious anticipation like "oh, what will happen now, what do I need to do," but everything went naturally, according to its own laws – that is what I felt. It was fantastic, I remember, that I was completely euphoric afterwards.

I got these two feelings, so the big experience I got from Szilvi, and the choosing of the name with Zita was this elemental.

Later on, I was in a mood at one point, I do not know why anymore but I was sad, and I wrote that we were sad together. We did not talk; she just took my sadness and adopted it. This was like when two people lie next to each other and can feel the other's stirrings. I could not actively communicate with her and this shared feeling was great. That is another reason why I thought she would be a he; she was my supporting pillar, she would help me spiritually and with everything. I told Raffai many times over how smart she was, a thousand times smarter and wiser than I was. She was so curious! She asked me things, it is amazing, that were so scientific and deep that I could not answer them. The world was incredibly interesting for her.

We had our 26th analytical session on the 36th week. We were consciously preparing for separation. She accepted it mentally, but rejected it emotionally. She knew that she had to be born, but she was not mature enough for it. I told her: "You will not lose me with birth. Your options will broaden, because then we can talk not just like this, I can hold you in my arms, I can properly caress you, you will see your dad, and me too." At the second separation analysis – I noted – she was sad because of the separation. I think that this is a step, she has to give herself over to this mood, that she is sad, and later this attachment dissolves.

I managed to complete this process with her, and I remember, at that point I was asking not just her but my womb as well, when the birth was going to come, and even if I did not get a concrete answer there was a soothing feeling, that everything would be alright. I had to go into the hospital earlier, on account of my first birth, the Caesarean section. Her, of course, I wanted to give birth to naturally. I went into the hospital around half-past-two, and I was praying not to have to stay for long for nothing, because Zita was on my mind then too. She was born that evening, at half-past-ten. It went so smoothly that if I had not already been in the hospital, I might not have made it in. I almost had to hold her back, waiting for the doctor to arrive. As soon as the doctor came, I walked over on my own two feet to the table, I lay down, and she only came out on the second push because I did not have any practice as a birther, and I did not feel how strong I had to push. I pushed once just to try it, and they already saw her head. My doctor said to give it another, and she was out just like that.

My husband is an economist too, an absolutely realistic thinker. I do not usually talk to him about these deep psychological things. When I was pregnant with Zita, the firstborn, he said go, do it, because I see that this is good for you, but believe me that you are not feeling what the baby is, just what you want to feel. That thing is not communicating anything yet. Of course, I knew that this was not true. But I left it to him, I did not argue, because you cannot explain something like this. He only started believing in it when something really happened, and he accepted it when he really experienced it. After our daughter was born, and he saw how things turned out. With our second child, he initiated the whole thing, and asked me whether I was going to go. He is not the gushing type. This is the maximum he is capable of, acknowledging that he sees that this method really has a right to exist.

I hope he will ask me soon: you are going to go this time too, right? Because I would like a third.

Katalin Forró: "I felt she could hear and understand the things I told her and that they really did get to her"

This story is closely connected with the period before we were expecting. Before I got to Dr Hidas for bonding analysis, I went for four years to a self-awareness group. It was held by a psychiatrist, for our little group of six who had all known each other for years. We started the work based on our own concepts about getting to know ourselves to better navigate our lives. If I were to use bigger words, I would say the goal was to explore the unconscious a little, which is not an easy task, one could even say almost impossible, but we started looking around inside it. Starting with childhood experiences, then all sorts of things came forward there.

I first heard about bonding analysis from the leader of the group, who recommended the book by Jenő Raffai, *I am conceived, therefore I am.* This was at around the end of the fourth year, when we started to talk more and more about feeling ourselves more mature and started thinking about having kids and a family. I was 30 this year, although people usually think I am younger. I am younger in my ways of thinking too, I know, because this, among many other things, came up in that self-awareness group. I think I am mature enough to be a mother though, even though I act like a clown sometimes.

The book really influenced me, it was so beautiful. A member of the group got pregnant in the meantime and decided to get in front of the whole thing, and looked up György Hidas for analysis. I only got pregnant much later. This girl said wonderful things about her experiences, so I thought at the time that when this would become relevant to me, I will not miss out on the analysis. So I already had some psychological background insofar as I had worked with my unconscious before. Bonding analysis is built on this too, because when we are establishing the connection with the little foetus in our belly, we are practically getting in touch with our own unconscious too.

Even though I already had similar experiences, it went slowly for me. I read up on it on the internet, who experienced what through this method. There is a website of this baby-mother bonding where a lot of moms posted, women who participated in the programme and women who thought the whole thing to be snake oil–type nonsense, who think that no such thing exists, because you can only establish a connection with your child once it is born. I read, however, about moms who got very far in the analysis, who went to places I did not.

I had difficulty with getting in touch with my emotions properly even in this self-awareness group. A lot of things are stirring inside me, things not entirely processed from my life … this made it more difficult for a strong bond to form with Dorka. But I would like to go with her sibling too, who knows, maybe it will be easier if we go into it all together.

During the few months when I was going, although I never had very picturesque images, I did feel like I managed to get down to real depths and get close to the baby. But this did not happen at each session, not every time, and it really was just a few minutes sometimes, when I could get relaxed enough to really get in there to her.

I had been going for two months, when I was telling the baby, in thought, during a session what kind of room we wanted to set up for her. And I told her in detail, what we are going to put where, what kind of picture will be on the wall, and where her crib is going to be, although as a newborn she slept with us for months. Afterwards, I asked her to tell me about where she was living, how she felt in there. I wanted to know so we could later talk through this big change with her. And after a few minutes this really interesting feeling came up, all of a sudden there was no sight, no sound, but it was as though I were in a greyish-black, warm, large space, and I had a feeling that she practically pulled me into my womb. She took hold of my hand and drew me in to show me, because now she is telling me about it. This moment really stuck with me, that we are holding hands and really, we were holding each other's hand. It was a little cloudy, but it was definitely my womb. The feeling stayed for a few minutes, then it dissipated, and I returned to reality. This was a really, really powerful, memorable experience, one of my most important moments of connection with Dorka.

I often felt during the session that I was a foetus too. So when I relaxed and gave myself over, then images started coming up for me when I was in a large space, in a room or a hall, and I am curled up in a corner there, like a teeny-tiny creature in the big world. It was bad, and I felt that I had been left behind, and usually around this time I got a headache and I snapped out of it. It is possible that this was my own intrauterine experience.

I was an expected baby, I was born second, I have an older sister and we have a relatively small age difference between us. But I do have to say that I did not get the care from my parents that I felt like I would have needed, I am trying to have this lack mended by my husband, that love and attention and care. At the same time, I have a good relationship with my parents, there is no big drama. Somehow, we lived without any real warmth, although there was not any real "coldness" either. They dealt with things in their own way, and somehow what was important for me was not important for them. Mom, even now, when Dorka is crying tells me to leave her be, that she will cry herself to sleep. But I think that if she is crying it is because something is wrong, she is feeling bad because of something – why should we let her cry herself to sleep?! Certainly she would fall asleep from exhaustion at some point. But who is that good for?! And well … I think I was left not once, so to say, to cry myself to sleep. This is a horribly bad experience, and I could tell many more … but I do not want to talk about myself. But this probably is connected to my relationship with Dorka.

Sometimes I am shocked to see how my dad relates to Dorka too. He says, "oh, she is so small, he cannot do anything with her, only when she is already talking." My sister recently had her second child, they live in America, and my parents were out there visiting them. I asked my dad "well, what is the little one like," and he says "you know, I do not think much about these tiny ones, only when they get bigger." What? "I do not think much of them?!" Alright, so I have my own thoughts regarding my parents … so, unfortunately, they treated me like this during my childhood too. And, of course, it is well known that the first year or two are the most deterministic during the baby's life, that really follows you for the rest of your life.

On the one hand, these childhood experiences come up during analysis, on the other hand I can also see the rational grounds for how my mother relates to Dorka. So we simply do not trust them with her for an evening, to go off on a walk just the two of us, or anywhere. She should not treat her the way she treated me.

Dorka moved very little, or rather I sensed very little from her while she was in my belly. After birth it turned out that it was because the placenta was positioned in such a way in front that it absorbed all her stirrings. Every mom is glad for this of course, that her baby is kicking inside, and their relationship is more colourful because of that, but we had less of this type of messaging. I was really looking forward to the sessions with Hidas on account of this, because then I really felt like I was paying attention to her, and we were together. Other times I could only look inward and concentrate with a huge effort, that there is the baby, what is she even doing – I felt so little of her. I liked going to the ultrasound too because I could hear her heartbeat, and saw her moving around. She really did not kick a lot, and sometimes I got scared, "Jesus Christ, is my child even alive still?" Because days would go by without me feeling a stir. And since I was so excited for the encounter, I always really prepared emotionally for these one-hour occasions. I knew that that hour was just ours, no one would bother us. That was a really good feeling.

The connection was beautiful but rather quiet for me. I did not have these powerful visions, and there were not huge changes within me. For me it was always a quiet, internal, peaceful deepening of thought and feeling. When I got into this deep, relaxed state at the beginning of the session, I saw a yellowish-red light appear before my eyes. This regularly returned, as we started to relax. The whole thing started by me having to look inward, and then a few minutes later this yellowish light appeared, then I sensed colours coming in waves, then a white and yellow light was moving before my eyes. But I could not associate it with a concrete feeling or a concrete event. I always told Hidas just that too, that there is this colour here, or this vibration or this change, but nothing else came along with it.

The influences from my childhood are probably still alive in me, this accompanies me, that feeling was never in vogue in our family. This came up a number of times in the self-awareness group, and we tried to find the cause, what could have happened back then. This really is like this still, that mom and dad suppress their emotions continuously. They are rational types. But it is not about their being ashamed of their feelings, they simply do not acknowledge their internal worlds and their problems. There is no problem. We solve everything. They suppress things so well, and they do not even dare admit everything to themselves. And well, we grew up in this atmosphere, and we have a lot of suppressed emotions too.

One time there was an occasion in the self-awareness group where the leader gave me an interesting task. He said that I should close my eyes, and I keep telling myself I am not allowed to feel, and I keep repeating it as long as I can, maybe this would release some sort of emotion or memory. And when I started repeating this, I got so ill after a minute or two that I was almost choking, as though something was blocking my throat, I felt it in my throat, I could barely breathe. And I could not continue, I had to stop, because it was physically unbearable. So, sadly, we did not get very far, but it became clear that this "I am not allowed to feel" really left its mark on my life. But why not, and what am I not supposed to feel, did not really come up, and I do not know to this day. I thought it could be that this followed me regarding Dorka too, it is certain. I did not dare feel her in my belly either, so I did not dare to give myself over to my emotions. So, what the problem is in my life – even if unconsciously – I pass on to her like this, unfortunately.

It was the end of the most beautiful period, when we were preparing for the birth in the last two months. I cried a number of times, while Hidas was reading me the texts related to giving birth, and I passed them on to the baby, to prepare her for life outside of the womb. It was so touching. I felt she could hear and understand the things I told her and that they really did get to her. Of course, it is hard to assert this, because later, when she really was born, she did not fully accept what I had told her, and that made me lose my confidence.

We sang a lot to her and we spoke to her, while she was still in my belly. This is again thanks to Hidas, because with me going to him, every evening I told my husband these experiences, and almost every evening we made it a point to focus on Dorka. My husband loves to sing, and he sang little children's songs, starting with "kis kacsa fürdik," a lot of really beautiful songs, which are not necessarily even children's songs, but it can be for children too, János Bródy and Tolcsvay have a really sweet song or two, Peti sang these almost every evening. He sang it into my belly, to Dorka. We could observe her reacting to specific songs. Sometimes she would start kicking up a storm, sometimes she got completely quiet. We sensed her paying attention from inside, and really, it was as though she listened to the whole song. There were six or seven songs that we regularly repeated to her, and we could feel which one or two she loved more than the rest. It is interesting that now, after she was born, when she hears these songs from us, no matter how bad she is crying, or if there is something wrong, she immediately calms down. This really is incredible, but such a nice and beautiful thing, and if we sing her a song that did not have much of an effect on her in utero, she still reacts the same way, she does not give a damn.

It has a quite big significance that we went to Dr Hidas, because we have been engaging with Dorka from the moment we found out I was pregnant. She got constant attention, because we always let her know that we know she is here, that she is here with us, even when she was a little inch-long foetus in my belly, she was just as much a person as anyone else. If something was not good for her, we did not do it. For instance, I could not handle taking a shower, somehow I always felt like throwing up, and I figured that she did not like it. So, I solved it somehow. I took a bath or I showered with colder water, because I felt that it was too warm for her, she did not like that. These messages, signs we could already observe when she was a tiny foetus, and I really tried to make note of them.

Obviously, I could not do much sport the same way then. Although I heard about people doing exercise for eight months during pregnancy, and continuing without missing a beat. I could not do it, even though it was missing. One time during the summer, in the fifth or sixth month, we were playing volleyball with my husband on the beach. She really did not like that. I got sick not during, but afterwards, I felt such pains around my pelvis and groin, that I got scared. I decided afterwards that I would not do such intense movements with her. I did however go to a pregnancy exercise class, and I did not gain much weight during the pregnancy either. I could do everything else all the same, so I came and went with her. Although I did not work anymore, because as soon as I found out I was pregnant I left my job. I was working at the headquarters of a department store chain, I was an educational leader in the human resources department, which I really loved to do, so I would like to return at some point. But I am in no rush, because at this age the baby really needs just me, so I would like to stay with her at home as long as possible, and we are planning a sibling as well, within the next two years, I would like another one the sooner the better. I think it would be really good for them if they got to grow up together. My sister and I are a year and a half apart, and that was really great; we grew up in a great friendship and that is still so.

It is quite strange for me that there are moms who say how hard it was to give birth, so pertaining to their emotional state, because somebody really grew on them during those nine months in their belly so much so that they could not really separate from them and accept that there is no baby in their belly. I did not feel this at all, because I was so excited for the moment when she would come out and I could get to know who was living in there. Ever since then, I really enjoy that she is definitely here, she is tangible, she is kissable.

In the end Dorka was born with the umbilical cord wrapped around her head three times. Even though there is specifically a part where we are preparing for the birth and this gets an added emphasis, and we talk about only heading down the birth canal after putting the umbilical cord aside. So theoretically I explained this in great detail. I placed an added emphasis on this because I was born with it wrapped around my head, too, and I was supposedly a bluish-purple, so I came out low on oxygen. This happened a number of times in the family. My sister, even her firstborn came into the world that way. So I explained it to Dorka many times, in a lot of detail, on account of all that. Even still, it did not work out, maybe it came about in such a way during the birth that she could not do anything with it. Not only had the cord wrapped around her three times, there was a knot on it too. They showed me on the bed then and there, what it looked like. It was properly tied onto it. So she even had to crawl through the umbilical cord. This might be a familial tick of ours, or a genetic heritage. Later I asked around about the potential cause of this thing. I heard that today almost every other child is born like that, because the umbilical cord is different from how it used to be. More and more women have much longer cords, but this is not really a huge problem. They overly mystify this a little, because only a few cases occur where the child's life really is in danger because of this. I had a cord over a metre long with Dorka, of course she managed to tie herself up in that wonderfully.

Regardless of this, the birth was a fantastic experience. It went really well. I had most of my labour pains at home, and we really just went in for the very end. We spent maybe three hours altogether in the maternity ward. It went so smoothly, and when I was getting ready to push, I saw an image of Dorka sliding out. I concretely saw this. It appeared in front of me. The doctor congratulated me at the end. He said he rarely sees such a thing, that somebody can pay so much attention to the internal during birth. So, I spent those two or three hours there having no idea who was doing what, or what was happening around me. We talked through the whole thing beforehand, how I wanted everything to go, and my husband was there, so he was obviously in contact with the doctor and the midwife. I completely transformed; I was transfixed on the internal processes. It was an experience where if someone asked me, I would honestly say that I would give birth every other day, it was so beautiful.

She only breastfed for four months, she did not eat anything, we could not put anything in her mouth but my breast. I had milk, but not enough. The doctor said he saw enough milk being produced, but she did not put on as much weight by four months as she should have. He recommended formula as a supplement, but he said always to breastfeed first, to pump, and then give her the pumped milk after each breastfeeding as well and then, if she accepts it, to give her some formula. We did not want to give her a bottle, and stuff like that, so we bought a device at a specialized store that we could use to give her formula by pouring it into a container, which I would wear around my neck and lead through a thin tube to my breast. I will not say she did not notice, because these babies are not all that stupid, but she accepted it. She got all her food for six months like this, on my breast, and now she gets food from a sippy cup. We are giving her fruit now as well. But I would have been glad if we had managed only to breastfeed, the longer the better.

Dorka is a really open, really friendly baby. I see this as an effect of the bonding analysis, that she is so attentive to what is going on around her. Because I inspired her even in there to form a mental, emotional connection, and to pay attention to each other. She is more alert than a lot of other babies. There are a lot of babies her age in our vicinity, and they are nowhere close to where she is. We observed it with my husband, that they just sit around, they are staring blankly, and they are just sweet little babies that way. With Dorka, I have a sense that she is constantly attentive to her environment, and it is as if she understood everything. This is obviously my partiality too. Of course, every baby reacts to some extent, and they know how to fight for things they want. So they are clear on the effects they can have, but with Dorka I have a more pronounced feeling of this, and this is wholly due to the bonding analysis, that even then, as a foetus, she was paying attention outward, and she still has this skill.

If I had to put it into words, what our relationship is like, I could maybe say that it is as though she were not seven months old, but at least 12. I really feel like this, that we have known each other for a long time. Of course, this is understandable, because when I started going to analysis, something had already started there. Since then, the emotions come and go between us.

Adrienn Fenyvesi: "I had a strong feeling of being one with him"

I was already expecting when I learned about the method of bonding analysis online. I was paying attention to everything that had to do with pregnancy, or babies. I searched for a long time until I found Dr Raffai, but he was able to take me in after a month in the end. I started going to him in the fourth month. On another note, I worked with the baby until the end, I only stopped for the last two weeks of my pregnancy. Since I am in sales, I had to travel abroad a lot by plane, but when I got pregnant, I stopped with the travelling and switched to business correspondence.

In the analysis, at the beginning of the session Dr Raffai told me to try to get inside my body, and find my womb, and the baby within. I was looking inside myself, where these things might be, and then I felt a movement, like a hand, that is I caressed the inner wall of my womb with my hand, and all of a sudden somebody poked that hand. I could not believe it, that he was there, that it was him, but Raffai affirmed it, that yes, that is the baby. I could not see him at that point, it was just a feeling that completely lit me up. This happened during the first session, that we found the connection. It went easily. A colleague of mine was going to him too, and she needed many more sessions for this, and this – to be honest – made me feel a bit uncertain. I thought that the thoughts I was feeling were not even coming from the baby, they must be my own I am projecting. Raffai stopped me, told me to trust my feelings, because he sees and he is sure that they are coming from the baby.

Images were coming and going almost every session, we communicated by me projecting an image towards him, and an image came back to me in response. This initially brings just a vague feeling, that clarifies slowly, and the thought of the message gets articulated. After a while the entire process got a lot clearer for me, this is a feeling that – it might sound strange, but I cannot put it any other way – is like pulling a thought out from your head. I felt this when the baby asked me something. When I misunderstood something, a sort of unease started working over me, that this is not good, keep thinking, think, this is not what he means, and I kept concentrating until what he said gained a clear outline, and then a calmness washed over me.

It was unbelievable at first and really shocked me, what serious thoughts were keeping him occupied. So I learned in the beginning that he is afraid of being born, and I was surprised by another thing too, a basic question was forming in him: are the two of us one? This was the first serious thought. Raffai said that I immediately had to tell him that we were not. And right as I told him this, he was seized by a panic that he would be born. I felt then that it was better to avoid this topic, until he matured more.

An image came up a number of times, we were swimming, and this kept coming back, that we were in the water together. And we played a lot, he loved the mirror game. We were standing in front of each other, as though we were the other's mirror image, and if I raise my hand and place it here, then he will do the same, placing his little hand in front of my own. We were getting to know each other, and a conversation was going on between us. I felt that he would be very mobile – I knew this in advance. I would have been curious to know what he looked like, but his image never appeared clearly. Sometimes I saw a naked baby, sometimes a baby in clothes, but not his face.

It is interesting, how much he knew about his dad too, and he could even tell what he thought of me: the caresses, the babying, warmth, and he saw his dad as a dome, a protective shield – this is what his dad meant to him. When we were interpreting this message with Raffai, he said that he is feeling his dad's sphere of power, and that this is giving him a sense of security. When the baby thought that the two of us were one and belonged together, he and I formed a circle, and I was trying to draw his dad into it as well so that he could see, this is how we all belong together. He looked at it from his own perspective. Later I tried to expand the circle with other family members, but he was completely closed off to that. He did not want to acknowledge anyone else. Although he did ask whether there were other children in the family, but I got the sense that this was some sort of jealousy.

Before the birth, Raffai told me to tell the baby where he would be born. I showed him the large spaces, but somehow this was not too attractive for him. He was more interested in whether there would be a little nook, a warm nest, like the one he was in in my belly. I sensed that he wanted one like that here, too. And it really was like that, because he got a little crib that he loves so much! He has almost outgrown it, but he is still attached to it. He always loved sleeping in small spots like this. When we went to Prague, there was a regular sized crib in the hotel and we put him down to sleep there. He turned sideways in it during the night, because the nook is what gives him that sense of security.

It is as though he knows exactly the concepts of night and day. Although I never told him that you have to sleep at night, and we are awake during the day. It is interesting that he had an idea of this already in my belly. I asked him during a session whether he sensed the nights and the days. He said yes, and he showed me that he sits up during the day, and a pointy mountain appeared at that point, he was sitting on top of it and looking around. He experienced the night-time bit floating in that warm nest, all curled up   this floating was the night-time for him.

Sometimes I looked for the connection, sometimes he initiated. Sometimes we did not manage to meet at all, because he was asleep. And other times he completely cocooned up, and pulled away to the farthest corner, as though something was happening that he did not like, that scared him. Well, yes. Then I will tell this story too. It is a part of the whole story that when I started going to Raffai my mother had already been very severely ill, and I was in the seventh month when she died. When this happened, the baby did not move at all for two days. We talked about it during the next session, and I explained to him what happened. And he just curled up in the corner. I felt him hiding in the deepest nook of my womb. But I felt such an insulation during the next session too, as though the two of us really were a little island, and around us – like a sped-up film – events were cascading. I had tried to explain to him before, that this does not impact our relationship, that things will clear up, I was explaining to him that there is nothing wrong with him. Later on, slowly, he loosened back up.

My mom's death took a really big toll on me, and I had a lot of difficulty processing it, or rather the fact that the two of them could not meet. Two or three months separated them from it. It is a dual feeling, because my mother had cancer, and in the end she was using opioid painkillers just to bear it, so you would not wish to extend that at all, but at the same time it would have been good for them to meet, and this was really hard to accept. I had to have the talk with the baby, what all happened, and that the two of us had to say goodbye to her now. I think he was just drifting along with the events at that point, and he sensed that something very painful was happening right there.

I did not know whether he was a boy or a girl, because he did not comment on this. The ultrasound did not show it either, only towards the very end. When I tried to ask him about his sex, he was very secretive. I sensed that he did not reveal it because this would have meant that he had to be born by virtue of this as well. I also thought that maybe he did not want to tell because essentially it did not matter to us, and he thought that we would find out anyway when the time came. One time I was telling him before an ultrasound appointment to show me whether he was a boy or a girl. He responded by saying that he hated the ultrasound, because they were messing with his peace. So, he did not take it as observation but as harassment. I said, it feels good for me to see that you are developing well, and I think I lightened his negative feelings a little bit.

Raffai went on a month-long vacation, and the two of us had to relax all alone. That was very difficult, and did not work out that well. When it was just the two of us, the bodily connection never manifested between us. Although I saw him, we did not touch each other. I do not know what Raffai adds to it or what he knows, but it is certain that the hours when he was there were much better, and not just because he helped interpret the messages coming from Marci. Around the time when he came back, I had a negative experience too. This came up during the sessions I did by myself, but later on I told Raffai that I felt the baby grabbing me from the inside, as though I was feeling a strong clawing across clothing or skin, it almost hurt. We figured out that he was also missing the close contact that had been before, and that he was looking for my hand again, then found it – during this Raffai session – what he was missing.

This feeling of "we are one" was very strong in him. And the fact that he had not turned around meant that he was not yet ready to be born. During a session, this was the last one, it became clear that his bodily boundaries have not yet formed. Then Raffai said that this was a problem, because he has not yet managed to distinguish himself from me, and he explained where he starts, and where I was.

I was born naturally, it was completely average, nothing extreme, but it did not go too smoothly. During the bonding analysis this also came up, my experience of birth. I went through it the first time as though something was pressing on my stomach, it felt like I was drowning … something was pushing me upwards … pushing me … and I had this choking sort of feeling. When this came up, Raffai said right away that this was my own birth. In instances like this the emotions coming from the baby and one's own experience of birth get mixed up. This was anything but a good experience for me, it was a stressful, suffocating, panicky, bad feeling. This has to be let up to the surface, because it might block things during the birth, if they do not come forward. One time it got so bad that we had to stop the session.

In the end he was born a little bit ahead of time, unfortunately with a Caesarean section, because he would not turn around and in the meantime other problems came up as well. Raffai believed that we could turn him around, but it did not end up happening. We missed the last turning-around sessions too, because he was born ten days ahead of schedule. All throughout when I was asking him about the birth, he indicated that he was waiting for something, so he was not in charge of when he would be born. I know that there are some who almost have a vision of the concrete date, but he did not say anything. He was waiting for a sign.

During the 36th week, they noticed that the baby is underweight because the placenta had insufficient blood flow. They said that this baby would not develop any more, and had to be taken out as soon as possible. It was a terrible disappointment for me that he most likely would be born not the natural way but through a Caesarean section. I will admit, I was afraid of giving birth. Afterwards I thought that this may have been his choice. I did not feel responsible for his not turning around. So it clearly came up during the ultrasound that the placenta had really bad circulation, and they were worried that the baby would start to atrophy. I had to go to the doctor frequently, every other day. The sessions were mostly oriented towards this with Raffai, too. I had to focus on stimulating my womb's functioning. After a while the flow definitively started … so I was spurring it on, and we managed to start a positive change, I could feel a pulsating start back up. It turned out that he could gain another 100–200 grams. And I could carry Marci for much longer, for another three weeks, and he was born on the 39th week. So, for another three weeks he was growing and developing beautifully. In the meantime, I had to prepare him for his birth and Raffai asked me to tell him about both methods – because he would be born one way or the other.

He was born with a Caesarean section, but even so everything was very natural. My husband was outside the operating room, at the window, and they gave the baby to him first. Then they left the three of us there alone. Marci started breastfeeding right away, he knew exactly what he had to do and where he was. Of course, I had told him before that he would be born in a hospital, and that we will go home and be together as soon as possible after a few days. We had rooming-in for four days, he spent three of those nights in the newborn ward, so I got to rest better too. He knew that I was there at night, and he slept well. When I went in to breastfeed him, he was always sleeping peacefully in his little basket. On the fifth day they discharged us from the hospital, and during the drive home he was already looking around curiously.

My husband never believed in this whole thing. He said there is no need for this, but he let me do it. My family did not know about it either, that I was going to bonding analysis, because Tamás did not take this seriously either, and we did not make a big deal out of it. But when Marci was born, and he saw that the kid did not behave badly, knew precisely what was around him and was different from other babies, he began to believe in it, that maybe there is something to this after all. When we came home from the hospital, Marci was already like a three-month-old. He did not have a vacant expression for even a moment, he was looking around like he was deep in thought. At night I breastfed without Tamás even waking up. Last year, three little boys were born into the family a few months apart, one in April, one in October, one in November. So there is a basis for comparison. It is possible that the big difference between them will disappear in a little while, but for now it is very clear that Marci is by far the most friendly, open, and balanced. Although he wiggles around, he pays attention and plays all day, he is still a very calm baby.

Until he was two weeks old, he virtually just ate and slept, but during the afternoons he was awake for longer stretches of time, and he was rubbing his little hands and thinking. A baby usually starts playing with his hands around three or four months old, and yet he had already discovered them when we came home from the hospital. It is not even a good expression for this, that he discovered them, because the hand was already natural for him, not a novelty. They were saying that these babies do not sleep much during the day, and I really do see that he begrudges the time to sleep, because then he is missing out: why sleep, when there are so many interesting things around here? So during the day he naps just for short bits of time, three times 30 minutes. The only thing that bothered him during the early days was a tummy ache, but luckily this has passed.

So, Marci welcomed everything so naturally, and he fit into his surroundings so easily. He was never afraid of strangers, and even now, at a year old, he is friendly with everyone. He has grown to accept the family as well. So much so that we even allow ourselves to go to the movies sometimes. During that time grandma and grandpa watch him, and there has never been any trouble, they played around really nicely. It seems that he is no longer closed off from the other family members, as he did in my belly. He gets along with everyone.

Enikő Pianovszky: "After we made contact, he was jumping up and down for joy"

The one who is playing right here is Eliza, she just turned one, and there is a six-month-old belly-dweller too who I feel like is a boy, but we have not asked him yet. So, I am very curious, whether this big feeling will turn out to be right.

In any case, the very first moment of contact was very interesting with him. It was a lot easier than with Eliza, because I most likely developed this skill more. Even more so, the first conversation was almost spontaneous. When I was five weeks pregnant, I got really sick. I caught some influenza-like virus, and I already knew that I was not alone, we were so glad that we were expecting. Then all by myself – Raffai was not there – I got in contact with him, because I did not want the sickness to leave some sort of a mark. He was a tiny, feeble, very weak baby, and I told him that we need rest now, because mom is sick, and we have to weather this storm somehow. When I came out of my sickness, I felt a few days later – this was not the real, deep connection yet, it was more of just a feeling – that my baby was taking shape and was a healthy, strong, developed child. This sense came up by, I do not even know what I was doing, it was not the usual relaxed, laying down state, but … yet, I was dealing with Eliza, and I was thinking about my foetus, that there are two now, and I felt, as though he were whispering that "I am a healthy, big baby, I am filling out, everything is alright." This was so calming, it boosted my self-confidence, and I really was sure that there is no reason to worry.

With Eliza, I started going to Dr Raffai around the 20th week. The first session was a total bust, practically nothing happened, even though I really wanted it, and I kept asking myself what I was supposed to feel, when it would happen. Rather, there was something, an unpleasant feeling came up. I was feeling pressure on the top of my head, it was a little painful, and I thought that this was not all that good after all.

On the second occasion, I could not get in touch with the baby herself, but I did get to my womb. It was quite horrible. I was seeing horribly frightening images, visions, regarding my womb. A witch came in with sharp claws on her hands, and afterwards an excavator's head appeared. We figured out shortly afterwards what was causing these images to appear, and in the third session we managed to interpret this second experience. Similar ones kept coming up, with this belly-dweller too, the one I am carrying now, the negative uterine visions are coming again. So we explained it by my womb's most important function being to protect the foetus. This is a natural reaction, which comes from its protective role.

Next time, my womb let me in, and accepted that I would like to get in touch with my baby, and that it had nothing to be afraid of. Eliza was around 21–22 weeks old at that point. It was a very intense connection, and we got really worn out by the end of it. Eliza arrived from the sky on a parachute. I was having visions all throughout, images, moods, so I usually saw things like that. What really grabbed me was that we were playing a lot, running around, swinging, we saw a lake, the sea. She was the one who showed me all of this, she led me by the hand, showing what wonderful things there were in the world. Events were moving at a great speed, we were doing everything incredibly fast, so much so that I got really tired at one point and that was it, I could not bear it anymore. I asked her to take a little break, because I was unable to keep up. So we finally took a rest. Afterwards I felt like my limbs were made of lead. My womb got completely slack.

After this there was something quite interesting, I was driving to the countryside, I was going to work. Eliza gave such a flip in my belly that it was unbelievable! I felt that she was jumping up and down for joy, she was so excited that we had met, that we were finally on the same wavelength, that I understood her, that we could play so much with each other. It was so good to feel her jumping for joy in my belly after we got in touch!

Related to this, there is an important thing I have to tell you. You are very happy when your baby is moving around, but I often felt that she was not necessarily moving because she felt good, but because she was feeling some pain and was crying. I woke up to this with Eliza one night. She was crying. I had to calm her down. As to what happened, I do not know the cause, I do not remember exactly what it was. But I suspected it. During that time, I was already far along with the pregnancy, and in spite of this I was working a lot. My job came first, so I had very little time for Eliza and the family. I worked as a consultant, I am in the IT system development field, and I had to go to the countryside to hold educational sessions.

During the eighth month I was holding a two-week course on one of our systems. I was working very intensely from morning until evening every day, and I was terribly tired by the end of it. My work took over all my time and thoughts. It is no surprise that at the next bonding analysis session I saw horrible, dreadful images: a rather ugly and wrinkled old lady came forward, who wanted to hurt the baby, and Eliza was crying a lot. I calmed her down, that the wrinkly woman – more than likely – was me, we saw my distorted face. I had to tell her that she is the most important to me, and that even though I spent a lot of time doing other things, I really loved her. I had to send a lot of love and positive thoughts and feelings her way, so that she knows that it is not about me not wanting her anymore, that I had changed my mind. So I explained this to my baby by saying that there is an ugly old lady in everyone, we just cannot let her take control. This is a part of life too, but I should not have let this side of me show. We experienced such emotions during that analytic session that I myself ended up crying. She needed a lot of love at that time, and it was such a beautiful feeling when I managed to calm her down. I could explain to her the reason behind what she was seeing, and I felt the love and acceptance coming from her, and this was such a good feeling that I really did tear up.

I lived through my own birth during one of the analytic sessions. I experienced it as though I was being lifted out my comfortable, very soft and warm nook by a crane. It started as a simple, normal bonding, and then all of a sudden, I could not move … I was stuck in a rock of some sort … I am walled in … and then this pressure on the top of my head came up again. I did not understand what it was, I just knew that it was not my womb, and I am absolutely not turning towards the baby, but I just let it happen, and we will see what comes of it. So this crane image came up towards the end, and it was clear at that point that this was my own birth. I saw a bunch of white things around me, and I was waiting for someone to hold me. I was really, really missing that, because I felt myself completely exposed, and the desire was incredibly strong: somebody, finally, hold me! And then I felt this somebody finally lifting me up towards her, but this was not my mom, I knew it, that this was not mom, and there was only a white colour in front of me. I think it might have been one of the hospital workers. As I am talking to Raffai out loud, I keep seeing the visions, the images, the moods, the colours, and as I am talking there is an asynchronicity between the two, because your brain is working on what is behind it too.

I talked to my mother about it afterwards, about how my birth went exactly. She told me that she really suffered, she was in labour for a long time, the birth lasted a really long time. She ended up getting an intravenous infusion, oxytocin, to speed up the birth. And she – since my mom was very weak by the end of it – only ended up holding me by the second day, but I think the hospital back in those times would not let me be with her even then. So what came up for me again and again was the feeling of being abandoned, and when could I finally see her, when could I feel her skin.

I do not recall which week this was, but it probably came up because the thoughts around Eliza's birth were developing in me, and because my mother had mentioned to me before that my birth was very hard, and this probably got processed in my deeper thoughts that my God, what will happen to me, will I inherit this really difficult birth too. In the end it was very lucky that I saw and re-experienced what happened. Afterwards the thoughts of my birth did not concern me, and did not influence me either. I thought that my case was entirely different. This, I think, would not have happened without the bonding analysis, because it would not have come up and I would not have been able to process it.

It is shocking how much I got to know Eliza's personality in advance. Now, when I am reading back my notes, I am so surprised that, good God, I already saw and knew these things regarding her character. She is very conscious of herself, she has a strong will, she knows what she wants and she wants to make it happen. She led me to things, she initiated what we should play, what we should do. We played a lot during the bonding analysis, and she kept holding my hand and showing me what she wanted to do. The swing came up a lot. Eliza still loves to be on the swing, to spin around. The children's books really attracted her too that I read to her often.

There was a time when I went to the ultrasound right after analysis. I told her what this was all about. I told her this by showing her the ultrasound images, ones they made already, so that she could see what we saw from out here. I explained this to her so she would not get scared. I told her that we know that she is a very developed, beautiful baby and healthy, and that nothing is wrong, but we have to do these examinations and that they will not hurt, there is nothing to be afraid of. Interestingly, she did not sleep during the ultrasound but kept her eyes open the whole time. By the way, her eyes were open when she was born, too. So even during the examination it was as though she were paying attention to everything, and she was opening and closing her fingers, like she was waving. It was really sweet. She kept watching us the whole time, and I think she really knew what was happening.

I often wondered, when we were at the bonding analysis, and we were seeing, hearing, sensing, that practically no evidence supported what my baby really was doing at that moment. What I am feeling right now, for example, that he is coming up, that we are clapping together, or that I am holding his hand, I would be curious to see if an ultrasound would really pick up that the two hands are coming out front, or if he happens to be smiling at me. So is the emotion reflected in what is happening? Of course, there was no analysis like this, sadly, that was tracked by an ultrasound as well.

I heard from a mom that she had a feeling that her baby avoided the left side of her womb for some reason, he did not want to go there, because he was afraid of something, and it turned out at the birth that there was a few-week-old, dead foetus embedded in that part of the womb. So the feeling was justified; the evidence came out too, just much later.

Rereading my notes, another interesting thing came up looking back. We did not know, and we did not want to know the baby's gender. Eliza respected this too, she did not show me whether she was a boy or a girl. At the same time, a little girl would come forward very often during our bonding, the same curly haired blonde girl I saw in pictures of myself from my childhood, and I always made note of this and underlined it, "little girl." Although I thought that this does not have a concrete significance, because this could just be me when I was younger. We had difficulty choosing a name for her, and, at first, we only had one boy name. She would have been called Botond, and this name obviously conjures up an image of a really strong, massive child for me. So I was telling her that if she is a boy, she will be Botond, and then she showed me how strong she is, and to demonstrate it she started pulling a tree out of the ground. Eliza really did end up being massive and strong – and a girl.

The birth was not easy in the end. The labour was quite long, and when I was already well dilated, the amniotic sac was still intact. The doctor said that we had to breach it. Well, I cannot say that it was a good feeling, I was really worried that she would get scared. In the end I had to tell the baby that the sac would get poked with a sharp thing, but not to worry, she will not be touched, and while they were doing it I was calming her, that everything is alright. This was such a drastic external effect for my womb, however, that it completely stopped functioning. There were no labour pains that could have pushed Eliza out. So I got oxytocin, and the process sped up a little. When the pains strengthened, we managed to bring Eliza into the world. They immediately placed her on my breast, she did not cry at all, but immediately looked at me and was holding her head, She was complaining like that, by holding her head, telling me how bad it was for her to be in the birth canal for so long and how uncomfortable the position was by the time she managed to come out. I immediately understood what the problem was, and I managed to console her right away. I explained that this was necessary because my womb did not have the strength, and we had to breach the outer membrane. I told her, you know, this will pass soon, and all of this does not matter, because we love you all the same and you will see how good it will be out here in the world.

It was a dad-involved birth. After Eliza came out at last, then – as I said – I was the one to take her into my hands, but after this she was with Francis for a long time, he was bathing her, and also while they were walking me into my room he was holding her, he had the baby. Later the midwife told me how well the dad and baby got along, and it was interesting how deeply they were looking at each other. By the way, Eliza got the nickname "wise owl" in the hospital, because everyone noticed that even at a few days old she was continuously looking around, her eyes were always open.

As time goes on, her relationship with Francis keeps getting better. They need more time, of course, to get to know each other, because on the one hand I have a nine-month advantage, and on the other hand I am the one who is with her all day. But it is clear that these days Eliza is more attached to her dad. As she is getting bigger, the tight-knit bond that forms, unwillingly, between the mother and the baby, is starting to loosen, and her interest is much more so towards the external world now. Recently, when she was a year old, I completely stopped breastfeeding, but, essentially, I have been seeing for six months that she is gradually opening up towards the external world.

In spite of the bonding analysis, I had to learn how to be a mother. When the baby is still a belly-dweller, and is in my womb, then you completely identify with it, and you try to adjust your own character to the baby as well. But when the baby is born, it is after all an independent little baby next to me, who I have to get to know in different circumstances, unrelated to our past. The bonding in utero does not necessarily mean that I have won every battle and know everything. This has to be learned! At the same time, it was very useful to prepare for motherhood. You are a lot more attuned to your baby, you understand the cause of crying more easily, so it was great preparation. Not to mention the confidence and courage I gained, which makes me bear the difficult situations entirely differently.

It is different with the new baby insofar as I can get in touch a lot faster and more intensely, so it takes less time to get in there. Although at first the images related to Eliza came up for me from the experiences still living in me, since all of it was not that long ago, but I knew that this is not the real thing, not his own. Slowly these things clarified, and our own experiences started coming forth, with this second baby.

I am still seeing strange visions from my womb, but I know now what they mean, and I am able to handle them, so I can tame them right away. So, when I establish the connection, I often see that my womb is a thorny cactus, but when I caress it the thorns of the cactus retract, and it turns into a soft ball, with a smooth surface, and it lets me in. This scene came up a number of times, that I had to go through a gate and angry dogs ran out trying to bite me, but when they saw me, they recognized me and turned into docile, sweet little puppies.

At our last session I got into a very deep, relaxed state. Something happened that has never happened before, and it was incredibly strange. In this deep state, all of a sudden, I see something separate out from my body and start walking around the room. It stayed there during the analysis, and I knew that what stepped out of my body is part of my ego, maybe my soul, that was also me. Then it caressed my entire body, but without touching me, just like so, it floated its palm above me, and I felt an immense energy. My womb became hot and so did my baby, who was observing the events without moving. I experienced this by my kind self giving me this energy, so looking at it I saw myself, who came out from the depths, and was very glad to be able to surface. It was smiling at me, it did not say anything, did not talk at all, I just saw in its eyes that it was glad. It was a good feeling. When this scene played out, it went back to where it came from, from deep within. My baby and I were shocked, we were looking at each other in amazement at what had just happened. He really was looking at me askance, like what was all of this. I explained to him that a part of me that lives really deep within came up to the surface. This has never happened to me before, so yes, that is why they call it depth psychology.

Unfortunately, now, with the second baby, I cannot go to Raffai quite as often as I did with Eliza. But in spite of that these encounters are more intense, and I experience much more each session than I did with Eliza. I think I am more receptive, I can get into that state more easily, so these images come up sooner and there is more time for everything. The nature of this second baby is different, he seems much more mellow. He is less demanding than Eliza, and I think he will be much more flexible.

What was new and different than with Eliza is that back then I saw a bigger baby, more so an infant, and now I see a real foetus in my womb, and I can hold his little hand, and we clap, and he smiles. It is also strange that he tells me everything he is hearing and feeling, and he asks a lot of questions, he is very curious.

During the first bonding analysis, I did not listen to a lot of music with Eliza, but now there is a really good CD that Eliza really likes, and we regularly dance to it. I will be curious to see that, when this belly-dweller is born, how much will he recognize and appreciate this song – a little French chanson.

Nowadays my baby asked a lot about Eliza. He specifically asked me to tell him about her. It is natural that he is curious, since I am with her all day and he can hear her constantly. I told him what she is like, I showed him pictures of her, and told him I think they will get along well; they will really love each other. When my daughter was in my belly, the time came when she asked about her dad during the analysis, and I showed her that it was not just the two of us but three, because Francis was there too. And now that the current belly-dweller knows Eliza, I showed him that it was not just the three of us, because my partner is there too, so it is the four of us. Then Francis came up, and it was so good to see the family together: he was holding Eliza, I the little baby, and then we switched, he held the little one, I my daughter. This is how we will live.

Csilla Pethe-Tóth: "It was like we both stepped out of our body"

I knew she was there almost from the first moment on. I was really preparing for this baby. And she made herself known. It was very strange, she showed up in a dream of mine, before the test showed that I was pregnant. A beautiful, golden child, as though she were poured from gold, the figure of a child's statue appeared and radiated outward, a golden light was flowing out of her. Immediately, a few days after conception, she let me know that she was here.

I met Dr Raffai through my work, because, as a journalist, I was working on healthcare matters. He had a book come out, I read it, and even then, I thought that if I ever have a child then I will definitely look him up. I knew that there is an immediate connection between the mother and the baby in her womb, or that there can be one. But I would have liked to have someone to help this along, for it to happen as soon as possible, or make it more intense, or maybe I was looking for reassurance.

When the first medical results were in my hand, that yes, I am really expecting, I called Dr Raffai. It was interesting – the doctor later revealed that it is very rare for the first session to yield a really intense connection. It was always a relaxation technique that brought on the attunement. He told me to close my eyes, to concentrate on myself, on my womb, and to try to feel what was happening inside. I did not see a tangible, intrauterine child, like you do in a photograph or an ultrasound, but a much, much more obscure image. Or rather, what I saw was less material, not tied to the everyday world. At the same time, it is completely existent, what you are seeing, it is not at all what your beliefs are projecting into it. Because I did not believe, I knew that she was there, and doing whatever she saw fit in that moment. From the first moment on, it was very characteristic of her to be incredibly playful and curious, which is her basic nature to this day – Flóra is 23 months old now. She rolled around, she did flips, she was floating on top of the water almost every time. She hung onto the umbilical cord, she wriggled, she clowned around, she giggled a lot, she felt really good in there. She was behaving back then just how she does now, at almost two years of age. She had a great need for movement even in my womb. And then as she grew inside the womb, she was wiggling around a little less, she clearly had less space, and, in the meantime, she was turning more and more towards the external world, asking about the things going on outside.

It is not easy to talk about our conversations. This works kind of like when you hear an internal voice. It is not audible. I simply knew what she was saying. Somewhat like when you close your eyes and think of someone you know or love. If I close my eyes right now, and think of my grandmother, I can see her before me and I can "talk" to her, because I know her, I know what she is like, and what she thinks. Just like that, completely everyday things. It was the same with her, I was waiting for her, and she came to us. Precisely because of this it was not even a question for me whether I can talk to her or not.

Who started the connection tended to vary. It depended on the mood she happened to be in at the time. There were some very interesting "conversations" that are still vivid for me. We were in the fifth or sixth month, when the outside world really started to excite her. The analysis was happening at Dr Raffai's flat. The doctor's twins might have been a year old or so. Flóra was asking what it was like outside, whether this world is good or not. I told her that, when she comes out, she will see how beautiful the sky is, how beautifully the sun shines, how many colourful flowers there are, and she will really like it out here, I will be here, and so will her dad, differently than now, but we will be together. And at this point the doctor's children began crying outside. So Flóra – or Raisin at that point, as I did not know whether she was a boy or a girl – asked me: what gives with that? If they are crying, why is it so good outside, and why do I want to convince her of this, because since they are crying it is probably bad for them? She did not understand how this whole thing worked. At that point the doctor said to me – and I do not mean this as bragging at all – Csilla, this kid is really smart. By the way, babies in utero are probably more sensitive to the higher frequency of children's crying, and this somehow causes a bad feeling inside them. She did not like the sharp, shrill sound of the ambulance either. Whenever she heard it, I always felt that she put her hands to her ears. She practically plugged both her ears!

Since my belly was quite big, several people said that it might be two kids, and the ultrasound just did not pick it up. Then the doctor said to ask her about it. I asked her, and Flóra started laughing. She looked around, peeked in everywhere, and said: "Do not you see that I am all alone? Nobody else would fit in here!"

On another occasion, something completely extraordinary happened. So, I do not know whether I can say this with confidence, after all Dr Raffai confirmed that this happens, it just happens very rarely. I will try to describe what happened: it was like we both stepped out of our body … I am lying on the bed, and there is a big circle, or a sphere above me, and that is me, and there is a little sphere – that is her, and the two are slowly approaching each other … they touch and they almost melt into each other. Well, an experience like this… this was simply … it was miraculous. It is so good for your soul, I cannot even explain it.

According to the doctor, it is really good to rock in an armchair and listen to music together right from the start, because this develops the sense of balance and has other benefits as well. Flóra was born in June, I kept working until April, and there was a period, a day or two, when because of the big hustle I did not have the time for it, or more precisely it is not that I did not have the time, I did not make time for it. And when we started talking at the doctor's, she started complaining immediately. She welcomed me with "why do not we rock in the armchair anymore?" because she missed it so much.

There was an occasion when I could not explain something to her at all. I was going to analysis after work, towards the evening time. We were heading to Dr Raffai, but there was suddenly an unbelievable jam on Üllői way, and traffic was barely inching along. I was, like always, constantly talking to her. I told her that we had to call the doctor because we will not make it on account of the traffic jam. Then she asked me what a traffic jam was. I started explaining it to her, that it was a bunch of cars backed up, and we cannot make headway, only slowly, like we are going on foot, and the problem is that we will not make it on time. After we arrived, she kept pushing, "tell me finally what this traffic jam is." She just could not understand it, but I could not explain it to her any better. I told her, okay, let us drop this, this is the thing you will have to wait and see when you are born. Even now, when we are in a backed-up line of cars, I tell her: see, this is traffic jam.

I managed to talk to her like this for months after she was born, and this works even to this day. I will try to articulate what this state is like. You have to think about it like a quiet, deep, calm, relaxed state in her and in me too. This is when we can really talk to each other. I had a sense after her birth that she remembered what things were like in my belly. But today – since she is two years old – these feelings blurred a little. But I know what impact the intrauterine bonding had on her.

I could not believe, when they gave Flóra to us on the first day, how vivid her eyes were! All the newborns I have seen so far, they all looked into the world with a glazed-over stare. So they are not completely with us yet. I thought this was natural. But Flóra – and later Dr Raffai said as well that this is typical of the bonding analysis kids – was present from the start. I know that she felt good with us from the first minutes on, in this world. Her eyes, her voice, her movements tell of it. The nurses did not want to believe their eyes in the maternity ward, when our parents came into the hospital with my husband, and my partner spoke, my daughter immediately looked over to him. She clearly perked up at the sound of her father's voice. She was not even a day old. The nurses said this was impossible.

Part of my nine months was something that really took a toll on me. As you should, I went to the AFP examination in the 16th week. I did not think much of it, because I thought that nothing could be wrong with this. I was sitting in front of the computer at the newspaper editorial office when the phone rang, my gynaecologist was on the line. He said he had bad news, I have quite bad AFP numbers, and since I am in the intermediate age range there is a good chance that my child has Down's syndrome. He recommended taking an amniotic fluid sample to find out exactly what was happening. The blood froze in my veins. I asked whether there was not an alternative for this, but he said no, you can only ascertain this by taking an amniotic fluid sample. The journalist in me started up. I tried to get as much information as I could about the disease, and the examination as well. As my husband was researching on the web, I called all my doctor acquaintances, homeopaths, anyone who might have some experience with the subject. I listened to them, but I still did not dare decide, but at that point I was basically racing against time. It was likely that I would run out of time. The next stop was a geneticist. An old man welcomed me, looked at the AFP values, and asked his questions: how many rooms are in my place, what is my level of schooling, what is my husband's, how frequently are we intimate. After I answered, he declared that sadly, we have to sting here, and this kid has to be taken away, but I should come back to him and he would do another examination. I felt like I was going to die. I felt deep inside that something did not check out. We had set the date; I was supposed to go in to the hospital at 3 pm on Tuesday. Monday, however, one of my colleagues – I still think of her with gratitude to this day – called a gynaecologist friend of hers, who was willing to see me Tuesday morning. I said whatever happens, happens, I will go see this person. He said, madam, there is a thin ray of hope, I should go to women's clinic number one, there is a special ultrasound there. I should be examined there too, and in light of the results decide what I want. I talked to Dr Raffai as well. Of course, what could he say?! This is my decision. I went to this ultrasound, or rather the two of us went, Flóra and I. The examination found everything in order, but they told me to come back in a week or two. I decided that morning – and my husband supported me in this – that I was not going to go to the amniotic fluid test in the afternoon. This child was developing so calmly inside, and I do not feel that anything is wrong with her. I will not go to this test! There is an equal chance of something being wrong as there is of nothing being wrong, and I did not want to risk a miscarriage. My gynaecologist – it might be an exaggeration that he was making threats – was protesting, and did not want to take on the risk. He said that a colleague of his was dragged through the mud recently over a case like this. I, however, explained what I thought. I said, believe me doctor, I am an adult, I can decide what I want, I am willing to accept responsibility, and if he wanted, I would state as much in writing. They found everything in order at the check-up, by the way – when I was in the fifth month – but at that point it was a young geneticist who gave me a lecture, how irresponsible I was, and that this child should be taken away, and his ward this and his ward that. At that point I dared to say that I was his patient at best, not his ward. He took offence at that. I told him that I had decided: I do not want it, that is that, leave me alone! After this there was another check-up, a special heart-ultrasound examination, where they found everything in order as well. I calmed down. I will not say that this thought did not come up now and again. Afterwards we were talking about this with Dr Raffai, and he said that out of 100 women 99 would have done the amniotic fluid test. I, however, knew that this was a very harsh intervention. Even at the simplest examinations, at ultrasounds, she was escaping from the device, what would have happened if they stabbed into me too?

I really believed in myself, in the feeling with which I was experiencing her. She was always present during everyday life, at every moment. One time I felt as though she had looked into my plate from above my head, and horrified said "Jesus, what are you eating!" And then an old geneticist comes to me and asks – it was shocking, that is why I mention it – whether I knew when the baby first moved. I was taking a deep breath to respond that it was in December, she was three months old, when he waved "of course, how would you know that!" It was on the tip of my tongue; I was just too emotional to respond; the question is rather how would a 70-year-old man – however excellent a doctor he may be professionally – know what and how I felt?! So, not for nothing, I would not encourage anyone to go about it the way I did. Because I knew all throughout what I was doing, and I accepted it along with all the consequences: I do not need another one, I want this child!

And when she was born it was clear that it was her I wanted, she was the one who came to us. I used to say that this is exactly the kind of child I wanted. Although I learned a lot about her during the nine months, it surprises even us how skilled she is. She has had an incredible concentration from the start, which is a huge advantage at gathering information. This is paired with a great degree of curiosity, and because of this what she does not yet know she methodically explores. She makes causal connections. Last year, during our vacation, we were walking along in a lush, green garden, there were a bunch of plants, trees and fruits. All of a sudden, my one-year-old child stops and picks up a piece of fruit from the ground. She looked at it, she inspected it, and then she pointed up to the crown of the tree with her tiny finger and showed that this fell from there, it belongs there. She finds the connections even in things she does not yet know. It is shocking that at barely two years of age she is already counting. But she does not just list the words, she actually counts objects, for example peanuts. She was a year-and-a-half when she went on a walk with my mother. She was asked a bunch of different things, and Flóra answered everything. Then my mother had had enough and decided to ask her something she would definitely not know: "Tell me, little Flóra, which river flows in Budapest?" And my one-and-a-half-year-old answered, considering it obvious: "The Danube." These are unbelievable things. It is a fact that she gathers information lightning fast, and it is stored at such a depth within her it is almost scary. That is how she knows at two years old some 20 or 30 songs, or the first stanza of "Családi kör," or "Falu végén kurta kocsma" to the end. We never taught her these things in the classical sense of the word, but if something catches her eye, she will repeat it until she has it memorized. But it is also true that both while she was in my belly and afterwards, I treated her not as a silly little child, but as a partner. A new arrival, to whom I would explain how things work here.

She never liked sitting in the pushchair, she sat in it twice or so altogether. She could not bear sitting and staring out at the world. She could not hack that. So I carried her around in a baby carrier. I was constantly talking to her as we walked down the street. Of course, not to teach her, but just conversing with her, because I think that is much better for her than to just stare out of your head. We have to be careful, too, because she remembers everything. She already knows the colours from purple through light green to dark blue – children start learning colours at three years of age. And her drawing ability! She holds the pencil from the first moment on like an adult, as you should. And she talks like a flowing stream. The other day she did everything she could to get me to raise my voice. When this happened, she noted with a wide grin: "Mommy is really angry now."

I might feel like she is so developed because she is my first child, and I cannot compare her to anyone, but my sense is that she is ahead of other children. What I told you about her are facts, they are hard to contest. However, she is not just lexically advanced, but emotionally too. She has had a wide emotional range starting from her birth. She can be mildly glad, moderately, but so much so that her face is beaming, too. She has a lot of willpower, she is very enduring, and there is so much love in her that it cannot even be described. At the same time, she is mischievous to no end, and she clearly really loves the world into which she was born. She has a real personality at barely two years old. While, in my experience, the same does not go for well-developed children of a similar age. All of this, and the knowledge she brings with herself provides a good foundation for her to get along well on her own when the time comes, and to be happy in life. I think this is more important than for someone to build a huge career for oneself. So, she knows how one ought to react in a tense situation, or not to panic if she gets in trouble. This is much more important than any lexical knowledge, or anything else.

And how well is the bonding we formed in utero working? She had a high fever once, 40 degrees Celsius. She was 15 months old. She got traditional fever medication, and then a homeopathic one too, but her fever did not budge. Then came the idea of trying to communicate the old way. I concentrated on her really strongly, and tried to imagine what was happening inside her. And then it was as though I saw what parts of her body were in trouble: I saw little flames where the fever was raging. I told her that we had to work together once more. Here is a little bucket, grab it, I will hold it too, let us go for water and put out the flames! We went for water, we brought it in the bucket, and splash! we poured it on the flames. We were bringing it, pouring it, putting out the flames constantly. It lasted at least for half an hour. Of course, it was thanks to the fever medication as well, but I think that this helped too, and her fever slowly started to drop. She was as good as new the next day.

But she has a really good relationship with her father as well. Since the birth was long and ended with a smaller operation, she spent her first few hours as a newborn with her father, who still tells the story in disbelief that they had a two-hour long conversation. He was speaking to his daughter, and the little misfit, like she understood everything perfectly, was answering in her own language.

It does not really matter at what point in your life you decide to have children, the important part is how prepared you are for it emotionally, because – I think – a young woman can form an emotional connection this deep with her child as well, if she is mature enough for it. I gave birth at 34, and I am not at all sure that ten years earlier I would have approached this thing the same way. By the time it happened everything was behind me, so I gained a lot of experience through my work, I learned a lot, and having this knowledge things were easier. It is unbelievable how much it counts for, even if your knowledge is not all that deep, to have a wide array of topics you understand. If anything is wrong, you know which way to go.

It is really important for people to know their options, and to know where to turn to if something is wrong. In my experience, the large portion of expecting women suffers from such an immeasurable lack of knowledge it is almost frightening. They read a medical book, where they learn that yes, this is where the kid comes out, and there can be such and such complications. But childbirth is not medicine! So this is a part of life that even we, women who have given birth, and have gained an intense connection to our baby, only have a hunch about. And the doctors can only influence the flow, the process of birth, the biological functions, and help that along. Of course, there are moments where this is necessary. But the first nine months of life, and the decades that follow, are very rarely about that. Generally speaking, what is happening inside of us and in our child is much more important, and an outsider can never know this.

Klára Lipcsei: *"… I was inside, way inside, and outside I was tearing"*

Shortly after my husband and I got married, Panka was conceived. We did not plan her. She was a true lovechild. We did not expect it, for I was nearing the end of a training. My husband was preparing for a scholarship in Germany for several months. Therefore, the first few months were quite difficult, while I digested that I would have to go through this pregnancy by myself, and well, I was suffering a lot. However, my classmates helped a lot, I was attending mental health training and there was another woman from my group who was pregnant. The psychodrama I lived through there helped me keep my momentum and overcome this tension. My thesis supervisor at the time helped me a lot as well.

I remember, later on, we were so excited about Panka that we pictured exactly how we would want her to be. If my husband were at home, or we were in Germany together, we would think every evening about what attributes we would want her to have. I spoke to her. I told her to be as serene as one of the grandmothers, as intelligent as the other, and for her to inherit our good humour, maybe even a bit of our theatrical nature. At the beginning and towards the end of my pregnancy, I was with my husband all through the last two months. Therefore, we spent this time together. I perceived the birth as beautiful. It went relatively easily, naturally, without anaesthesia. The widening phase itself was difficult, but after that I pushed the kid out in half an hour. The moment in which she was born was beautiful. So the entire thing was beautiful and once we were among ourselves, we lived some lovely moments. I will never forget that as long as I live.

We got home and it was absolutely unimaginable that we had become a family. I decided that I would not write my thesis and that I would devote all of my time to the baby, because … I was somewhat remorseful, that I accepted her with difficulty at first. I therefore wanted to grant her everything. God forbid that she would feel she had come into this world unwanted. And the time we spent together was wonderful … Those three months. Because then … she passed away … she died a cot death. Yes … and I must say that that remorse did not pass until Márti was born. It was my fault … I could not free myself from it … this is why I had to return to the therapist, who helped me with the acceptance of pregnancy as well.

The weight was truly lifted from my shoulders and I felt relief only when the breathing monitor went off multiple times with our second child, Márti. And that is how the antecedents of this tragedy in my family came to light. My grandmother lost a child in 1942 – probably the same way, because of sudden cot death. But no one spoke of this, ever. I knew of it, but a part of the family only came to know that there once was an Andriska when my uncle's tombstone was being renovated after his death and the letters were being gilded again. That was when it turned out that there was an Andriska there who lived … we do not know for how long. According to my mother's memory, a very short time, two months perhaps. In fact, this problem surfaced again with our second child, the periodical respiratory arrest … the monitor did not only alert us once or twice but frequently, especially in the first two months. We went to regular check-ups with Márti to the Madarász Street hospital back then. Márti's results in the sleep examination were minimally below the average. She was just in the health zone, borderline. We use the device to this day. It grants safety. When it goes on alert, I immediately rush into the room and take the kid out. This helps in not letting her go to sleep with her forgetting to breathe. Even if she does not flinch at the sound of the machine, or she does not restart breathing when I pick her up, I knock her out of that deep, sleepy state, and she breathes once more. In more dire instances resuscitation … but luckily, we have not got to that. While we were in Madarász Street, a lot of parents said that if there were respiration problems, then it was straight to the hospital. Even though in such instances, you must not take them to a hospital, but call an ambulance right away!

Therefore, when it turned out that I carry something genetically, I was some-what calmed down. Besides this, my husband has a vegetative cardiac arrhyth-mia, which may contribute to this predisposition. By the way, he does sports. He is not really ill, but rather full of life. However, perhaps my small weakness and his small weakness add up … but there is no actual scientific explanation for this as of now. I also know that this has psychological sides. It was difficult to accept whether or not someone may live a full life in three months … yet Panka lived a full life. I took her all around to the most important places for me. It is so intriguing that we compressed so much into three months!

It is also odd that it never occurred to me to sing to Márti about demise. But to Panka it happened from the first moment on. There, that picture on the wall … that was taken when she was sitting on my knee, and I was singing, and Panka was happy, so I believe that I knew at the bottom of my soul that I was not getting her forever … rather she was there for some other reason … And she passed.

I went to therapy – let us put it this way, in the simplest form – and I know that it was worth it. So, I just lived without a care, and perhaps this is what I got from it, I was naively childish. The loss of this naivety pains me to this day, but at 30 years of age, perhaps it was about time. It certainly matured me spiritually. I went back to work, they hired me part time and I finally wrote my thesis. I finished it. I feel that I gained such experiences, those that make my work more authentic. I am much more sensitive to mothers' flutters and what pains there are. It sharpened immensely, who feels what, and perhaps this makes it easier to help … not even help, but accept and understand people. My relationship with my surroundings changed vastly as well. Things became clear in these times: who loves you, who is really besides you, the quality of relationships becomes visible. New friends come, and one would not even think of it, while the old ones become distant. The bond with those who were true friends becomes stronger.

As I said, we planned how things would be … and that is how Márti … no wait … Panka came to be. This is how we wanted her to be. And she was pretty, and I think perfect … she truly was how we wanted her to be. Perhaps she was too perfect … so it is not a coincidence that things happened as they did. For I feel to some extent that she did not belong here, on earth. She was mature, despite her age, ready for contact, and her eyes! They told me every-thing she wanted. So that was that for her … only for us … to understand, and accept, those of us who stayed …

In contrast to this, once we were expecting Márti, and would already have loved her … we left ourselves a small interval, but when we felt that we could, she came immediately. Then I became a bit frightened. But then this was a sign that she really wanted to arrive. Interestingly, I could not tell her what she should have been like, perhaps due to the bonding analysis. I always thought of her with great love and I let her be the way she wanted to be.

I finished up the therapeutic connection once I felt that I had arrived at a period of grief where I need not frequent meetings with a psychologist. When a lot of things gathered that were related to this, I went once in a while. This connection exists to this day. If I pick up the phone because I need to meet, then I will get an appointment within the next few days and we can talk.

I came to know about mother–foetus bonding analysis when I found out that Raffai would be giving a presentation in an advanced training for speech therapists. That was when his book was republished. By the way, I suspected that I was expectant at that time, but there were no biological signs yet. I con-vinced my husband that we should go. Raffai said some incredible things. He did not even speak of the book, instead, he told a myriad of personal experi-ences, which he had lived through with mothers-to-be, from establishing the connection and so forth. I knew then and there that I had to get connected with this baby, and the sooner the better. But it did not really work. So I tried … there was a baby in my belly and I knew nothing about who or what she was … and I was constantly calling her Panka … I could not call or expect her as a separate individual or personality. I was always circulating around Panka, thus even if I thought of her, in reality I was not thinking of the new kid, but of whom I had lost. Now, in retrospect, I believe that no matter when I was to expect this child, even after three or five years, I would still have had to suffer through the whole thing.

Then I met Prof. György Hidas and I was very glad I ended up with him. For me, his personality … he is such a good-hearted, kind person … his grey hair, his tenderness, his infinite calmness radiated purity and peace. And it was so good that one could find a safe haven there. They could release some of the burdens, knowing that they are more secure there, with him, and they have a chance to build and create.

It was a long procedure and took several months for me to find a connection with Márti. First, I had to be on good terms with my body. With Panka, I placed my hand on my belly and we started talking right away or I told her what I was thinking. This did not work with Márti. When I went to Hidas, I initially had to get connected with my uterus. It had to be tamed, so that it would let me in … I remember how I articulated to Hidas how the biggest experience for me was, at the beginning, finally understanding how the body is the temple of the spirit, as in the Bible. One cannot simply yell in, do this and do that. First, you must knock on the door. Then, I nearly felt all parts of my uterus … because you do not really know that there are things there, like the oviduct … and such … but I felt and experienced this as well. Sometimes, I saw it in colour, I recall colours perfectly, purple! I loved purple back then and I recall a claret-purple colour.

Then … I do not even know if I should say this … but I had a very interesting experience when my connection to Márti was finally being established. I was going insane, trying to get to her, but I could not. I was still occupied with my uterus and then it pulled here, pushed there. All sorts of sensations came, sometimes it warmed up; it even ached in places, so it was odd. And what it was mediating … I think there was a gate … I almost dare not tell … what I felt … So … I lived through the moment she was conceived. So, I was lying there … and when one is with their partner … my body felt that … So, this is very difficult to tell, articulate even, it was a strange situation in itself that someone was sitting next to me. I am not alone, yet it was so intimate that I do not think it wrong, that then and there the connection fertilized. After this, Márti let me in to herself.

I always anticipated something. And I never got what I anticipated. I think that during the entire analysis, I saw Márti maybe three or four times. Once was very early on. She was surrounded by utter darkness. I saw her as a foetus. She was pulling me, pulling a lot. Perhaps I was slower in establishing a connection, as well as slower in the entire process, compared to other mothers-to-be. She revealed herself very slowly. I recall that after that she pulled me in with such terrifying power, like in space, a depth, as if she wanted to suck me in, with all of my organs and energy. I broke into a sweat and got blotchy. So this had outer vegetative signs as well. I was making a tremendous effort to keep up with her and to endure because it happened that I could not follow this unimaginable amount of energy. I was left behind. Truth be told, it is not a pleasant feeling. Therefore, when this happened, I almost compulsively wanted to avoid that my clumsiness would get in the way of her wanting something, so that it would not depend on me: I am the obstruction to this meeting, because I cannot keep up with her.

Perhaps my grieving with Panka was still in it. I know that by the time I was going to Hidas, impulses relating to Panka got to me once again, which was a setback to my connection with Márti – I returned to the psychologist, with whom we discussed things and she put me in my place. I tried to separate the two: Márti's story belongs to Hidas and Panka's story belongs to someone else, and even though there are overlaps, which must be taken into consideration, I thought I could not take time away from Márti. The time I spend with Hidas is hers only, no matter what goes on around me.

Márti spoke to me once, only once. That was so painful … that I cannot … I cannot … I do not want to say it … Panka … it was related to her too … So … We did not communicate a lot verbally. When she was really pulling, there were times when we would completely become one. I felt a shell closing around us, and we were so unified that we completely merged. Everything around us ceased and so it was just the two of us.

Once, when I wanted to meet her, a door stood between us, a grey door, and the question was who should open it, because it did not open. The problem might have been that both of us were trying to open it, one from the outside, the other on the inside. And there we stood, in front of the door, and it would not, could not open. I could not hug her, nor could I become one with her, because there was a door there! And I tried: listen up, mommy will not open it, mommy will just stand and not do anything, open the door! But she did not have the strength. Then, I told her to let me, step aside, so that I could open it! She did not move. And both of us felt each other's presence. We both craved for it, still it would not open and something was still there. Several times the door constantly reappeared and I tried to open it during many sessions. Then, I figured it out: let us try together! But by the time this came to mind, that this would also have been possible! And the problem of the door was solved in an instant. It never appeared again. From that point on, it was resolved, completely lost its function. It became unnecessary.

By the way, Márti was quite energetic in my belly. Rather, I felt her being very headstrong. When she decided something, I was incapable of doing anything I wanted. We had to come to some agreement, for it to be good for her as well, for the both of us. So it was an endless struggle, whose will should prevail. This has stayed the same to this day. I would want something, she would want something and we would constantly have to come to agreements. But I believe that with a little loving, it can be caressed out of her not to be the way she is, not to be as … I have some female acquaintances who are like tanks … so I would not want her to be that way. One can only handle her with love for the above-mentioned reasons.

Then, beautiful colours came … I remember, starting with grey … initially, it was black and white, crystal clear, with a sharp outline, then came gold, when I saw everything in a gold, silvery shade inside, then came claret, orange … These were moods, feelings, which, I believe, the symbolism of colours mediated.

It was also very strange, I tried to get connected to Márti at home but it would not happen there. I always needed the environment, which surrounded me at Hidas's office. I rarely got as far as actually meeting her. After a while – I will be honest – I did not even seek it, only for us to be together. So, I placed my palm on my belly and we just existed … Either something happens or it does not. I gave up on wanting anything at home … Whatever she wanted to happen was going to happen.

Then I recall … these pulls were unbelievably powerful, when she ascended to my heart and she kept pushing and drilling herself like hell. She wanted to get as close to my heart as possible, at all costs. I think that this began in the final three months. She gradually came higher and higher, but at the same time, I felt resistance as well. Not from my own body, but from my uterus, that it would not allow it. This might have had a biological cause as well, a short umbilical cord, for what was happening hurt tremendously and I had to stop her. I simply had to.

Once when she came up here was a beautiful moment. She snuggled to my heart. There we were, together, completely one … colours surfaced … Then a lovely tingling feeling came over us … and felt that I too … I was inside and there was this thing that enfolded us. And suddenly, I saw a face … which I did not recognize … only later. By now, I know that I had not recognized her then, and that … it was not Márti's face! When it appeared, it reminded me of a gorgeous head shape, and traits, but I could not tell whom she resembled. When the feeling came that she was in my heart and I was inside as well. And then, I saw her. I merely saw a head, her face … and I could not tell whom I saw … Then it disappeared and afterwards appeared once more … only the head was lying sideways. This all happened during bonding analysis … so this I will never forget, that suddenly this came out of my entire being, that face … and then as if a body belonged to it as well, but this is of no importance, rather … it separated, and started moving away … it started moving away from me … and disappeared. Whenever I think of Panka, I cannot think of her in any way other than as she was then … That was when I let her go. The one I saw lying sideways, the one I did not recognize at first, was her. It was Panka, for when she died, that was how I found her, with her head turned sideways. When I picked her up from her crib, that is how I hugged her to my body, and I saw, so I knew that it was over and done with. Yes, over … and now I just needed to love her … then just like that, I placed her on my heart, and carried and carried her, until the ambulance came. And only then, when she left me, slowly gaining distance, only then could I let her go. To this day, if I think of her – I think of her a lot nowadays – this image appears, voluntarily, involuntarily, of her moving away. I remember as I lay and my tears were flowing like rain, I was inside, way inside, and outside I was tearing. Then, I felt and knew that this was the end of something. But still, no feeling of absence remained, only the pain of … perhaps when your daughter gets married, or I do not even know … Perhaps this is a good comparison, when she finally separates. And you finally have to give her away. By now, not even that bit is mine. Everything is in a different dimension.

In reality, this is why I wanted all of this, for in the beginning, I felt that I just kept burdening Márti, that this would not be any better, for so many, but so many things depressed and scared me. And she could not suffer because this had happened to us. And Márti was the one who helped me – I know this for certain. I think that after that, everything was about the two of us. This image had such value for me, such a weight was lifted off me and from then on, I only cared about Márti and dealt with her. I saw Márti perhaps once, maybe twice after that. She had a pretty head and curved lips. Her face was unlike any other. When she looked at me and I saw her, and suddenly she snuggled in my body ever so softly, as if I were her cradle.

Then, she had to be born ahead of time. I feel sorry that it was when the separating phase of the bonding analysis began. She always pressed to my heart in the last time period, and once she started moving up and down. I think we were very close then and she was preparing for her journey. She came a bit up; then went a bit down. We were playing a game of cat and mouse and this went on for hours.

I believed for a while that I had a boy in my belly, because it was completely different. I had lost a lot of weight at the beginning of my pregnancy and everyone was looking for the kid. I could even keep it secret for a while because we did not want to talk about it until Christmas, when I had passed the eighth week. But even then, nobody saw anything on me. Márti was tiny and we got an explanation for this later on. There was not a lot of amniotic fluid from the beginning and the umbilical cord was shorter as well. In the end, I did not give birth to her naturally. During the last ultrasound – I had just entered into the ninth month – the doctor said that she must be taken out urgently, because the amount of amniotic fluid had decreased dramatically, but back then they did not know how short the umbilical cord really was. It would not have reached the end of the birth canal.

Sadly, she was born the way she was. She was taken from me immediately and that was almost the end of me. Every day from that point, I believed that I would go crazy. My child had been taken away from me, there I was, alone in the ward. I constantly wanted to place my palm on my belly, as if we were together. But we were not together; she was in a different room, on a different floor! The worst thing for me was that they forced things onto her, things that she did not want, or maybe wanted otherwise, but it did not matter. Feeding time was from 12 pm to 1 pm, for instance, and that is when you had to feed in the emergency room whether you wanted to or not. That is where she ended up and they put her in an incubator. The doctor said that whoever ends up here could not be brought downstairs under any circumstances, even if they are in better shape, whatever … these mindless things! So, they wanted her to feed during that time period and me saying in vain that be so kind, my kid is relaxed at exactly that time and awake an hour later. I learned this during those eight months and that was exactly when I went to Hidas for analysis when she was awake. She would be sure to eat, if they do not force her now, half asleep. They did not allow anything to be adjusted to her rhythm. It was so sweet when I went to her. She fell onto me like a broken angel and just snuggled and snuggled. It was clear how bad it was for her and how good when I was there. She was so hopeless when they took her from me. We could not leave and they were not at all cooperative. I think that some of the nurses downright hated me. I realized that they got her used to the pacifier, too. For that, I felt offended in my maternity, but oh well, the mother was not around; boom goes the pacifier! That was the simplest for them. By the time we finally got home, I sought to get as close to her as possible. She always snuggled until she got into her foetal position, even when she was with my husband and placed her head on my heart. She was tiny, fragile, and basically pushed herself there, took up her foetal position and stayed there for hours. She could just stay like that between two feedings.

She was very alert after the birth so she did not sleep a lot and sought connections, contact, with her gaze. Márti is 11 months old now and I must say that there is no one who would pass her on the street without a word. Although I am not surprised that elderly men and women notice her. But these sporty, buff, young men stop as well … Alright, I must add that I do not consider myself a lady of this and that, fit for them, in the end, these men look at Márti with wide eyes and jaws dropped. Her development of movement is spectacular, she is fast, infinitely skilful and her sense of balance is just amazing. She is very independent, so she has kept this trait to this day. She has a concrete idea of things and she tries to convey that. What surprised me is her femininity, even now: she loves bags and is crazy for necklaces. This, while she was in my belly, I would not have thought. I still sing a lot to her, as we listened to a lot of music while she was still inside. It is completely odd, unique, her development of speech. I suddenly noticed that she was speaking as though she were singing. Not the way kids usually do. She has a cousin, who is three weeks younger than she is, who says baby, mommy. And Márti keeps lala-ing: lilili, lalala, and with this she tells everything, every emotion, and what she wants to say, she expresses with song. And once she speaks in completely unequivocal blocks, lilili, lalala – with this she tells everything, explicitly, because she lets us know if she is angry, mad, kind, surprised or curious, so a complete and wide palette of emotions appear. With these two scales, changing the pitch, tone and range, she expresses everything and adequately applies it to the scale of emotions. And to all of this of course, mimicry pairs as well, which is incredibly rich and diverse. The emotions induced from the scale and her facial expressions are in complete unison. She is very musical, sensitive to music and she pays attention, especially if she is listening to live music with instruments, whether it be a piano or any other instrument. The moment she hears it, she wants to do it herself.

Zsófi Müller: "… flight has a goal, but it is unknown what it is"

Originally, I did not go to György Hidas for a baby–mommy bonding analysis. I am a psychologist. I went to the analysis for the sake of my studies, paired with a motivation for self-knowledge. Completely unrelated to this, meanwhile, I became pregnant a few months later. I came to know of the baby already in the first week and this immediately surfaced in the analysis. So, we switched to the mother–foetus bonding analysis once we had already begun the process. Compared to what I had read and heard of the bonding and experiences of other mothers, I did not manage too spectacularly – if such a thing could even be said – for I of course do not think that this is a task that needs to be solved.

My approach always was that the baby is already an individual creature in the womb. Nowadays too, but especially when I was a few weeks pregnant, I wondered a lot how these things really are … since it is such an initial state, just a tiny embryo, but even by then, an independent life. From the 10th to 12th week on, they are human. They move and feel. And I respect it as a human being from that point on. I therefore do not believe that I am the mommy and life is developing within me – no. I interpret this as I am a human, so are they, and we must get to know each other and pay attention to one another.

I experienced this belief of mine even more so with my second child, when I sensed how different he is, how different each and every person is. Even in their foetal stage, they are all individual cases, personalities. As they say, each pregnancy is different and for that it is true with children as well, that they behave differently with their mothers.

Lili was the first one with whom I tried to get connected several times in the analytical setting, but there was some initial resistance, and I felt that it was rather coming from the child that she did not want to. For me, the connection between my child and me was very personal and intimate. It arose in me, perhaps because that is what the baby alluded to, that why would Hidas want to hear this. I even told him, that alright, I will subject myself to the rules of the analysis and I will tell everything, but I feel that the child is not obliged.

Initially, just as the study analysis began, experiences from my childhood and even from the womb came to the fore. I had to organize all of these, the two practically ran parallel. With the second kid, Félix, it was much easier from this standpoint, for I had already been over my own experiences. While I was going with Lili to analysis, I spoke with my mother. Lili is her first grandchild. I am her eldest daughter and we were arranging things in relation to the pregnancy. Then, she told me about a traumatic experience, with her pregnancy, so my foetal age, one which appeared to me in its entirety. So this specific complication in the pregnancy left a trace of resistance in me as well as a distant attitude towards doctors. I felt that this was present in Lili as well, which is why the bonding analysis started with such difficulty, for back then she saw Gyuri as a doctor as well, perhaps she sensed in me that he was a sort of doctor too.

On the first occasion I went to the gynaecologist, with whom I gave birth, and he saw me, he asked in awe how there could be a mother from this little girl – meaning me. I was not exactly tip-top in her eyes. And truth be told, I did not feel the weight at the time. Then, the baby–mommy bonding and analysis really taught me and led me towards the role of a mother and motherhood.

I rather spoke to them in images, when they were in my belly. Of course, I spoke to them in words as well, as anyone would, but I sent my deeper thoughts as images, for they communicated with me in the same way. I always experienced the bonding as if I were dreaming. I saw what she saw, I am convinced, what she dreamt. My first concrete connection with Lili was in a dream, flying in space. I called this vast darkness space, with white spots for stars; it was a blissful feeling. Thus came the dreams, and suddenly, a thought flashed into my dream: babies come from space. But it was all a dream. And in retrospect, once I deciphered it, the feeling that the baby dreamt of flying in space came to life in me. And in my dream, I saw hers, while I was thinking of what this could be, why she would dream such a thing. And I knew that this was some sort of universal feeling. But all of this I figured out afterwards, when I was dissecting the message there, on that couch, in analysis. And the conclusion: baby, space, flight – these are all her notions.

Interestingly, this returned with Félix as well, only this time some technical factors also appeared; it was sort of a sci-fi movie. So Lili's dream and what I dreamt of Lili's separated. Félix had a spaceship, or perhaps a mother ship, and the entire thing converged, the spaceship, space, flight in space, him and me. Later on, when I was deciphering this dream as well, and comparing the two, I realized that both were essentially experiences of flight. There were no objects in the first one, just space and stars, and some sort of sense of existence. Not the fact that I am *me*, but the sensation of existence, and afterwards, when I know that I *am*, then *I am myself*, and I think of how babies come from space, or how their souls somehow fly from space to an earthly existence. This is a transcendental experience – but in the interpretation of my adult consciousness. In my dream with Félix, there was a round, somewhat flattened big spaceship. This could eventually be interpreted as a symbol: it most likely symbolized a mother, or the uterus. The two of us are in that spaceship, but we do not see, we just know of the other's presence. This spaceship is flying in the darkness; the stars and motion are there all the same and we feel that our flight has a goal, but it is unknown what it is. Then and there, that meant nothing to us, only the flight itself was significant. I had a bigger role in this dream as well. I was in it more myself.

I am fairly sceptical and critical, even a little bit jealous of those who have said they could see or feel when the baby sucks on their thumb for instance, in their bellies. Such concrete images never appeared to me. On the other hand, it was crucial to feel the baby's movement in my belly. By the way, I felt it much sooner than usual with both kids. According to most people, the time of that is around the 20th week, but I felt Lili in her 15th to 16th week and

Félix in his 13th week. Naturally it was easier with Félix because I remembered the previous one. This was an essential thing for me. It undoubtedly meant to me the proof of their existence. When you see a test, from which it turns out you are pregnant, it has to be very detailed for you to really comprehend and believe it. Especially since western people do not really dare to believe their bodies, their instincts.

With Félix, I dreamt that he would be a boy. I felt it, yes, and said it as well. I did not see masculine looks, or a male organ, but from his being, I saw that he was somewhat more conscious; therefore, he had to be a boy. With Lili, I asked twice and then dreamt that she was a girl. I did not really want to believe it because I wanted a son as my first child. I dreamt it with my favourite painter, a quite horrendous guy, Giger, who painted a portrait of his lover. She was a girl from the east, with the name of Li. In the painting, there is a beautiful, eastern face, with eyes shut and a medallion on her neck with Li engraved in it. I dreamt of this painting twice. We had known for a long time, that if she were born a girl, she would be Lili. So this I knew, and also that my child would be a half-breed as well, actually quarter-breed, since Zoli's mother is Korean, his father is Hungarian, so he is a half-breed. Therefore, I dreamt of Li's portrait, but I did not want to believe what it truly meant. I thought I must have manipulated it somehow.

When I was pregnant, I was constantly watching nature documentaries about the sea. I wanted to see whales, fish and so on. It was so peculiar to see how I preferred whales during my pregnancy with Lili, while with Félix, killer whales were the unequivocal winners. When I watched it, he wriggled in my belly, moving around vividly. There is a film, called *Free Willy*. I watched it. I do not even remember how it went … oh yes … Lili and Zoli were asleep, and Félix watched the whole thing in my belly. He liked it a lot. It is also curious how we could not really find a name for him, which was when Willy came to mind. That ended up being his middle name, Vilmos, but we ended up using Félix.

I listened to a lot of music while I was pregnant. My opinion differs in this aspect because experts usually say that you should place a radio or speakers close to the belly, so that the baby can hear as well. But in my opinion, it gets to them if I do not place it there. At the time, I preferred listening to music on a Walkman, even though I do not usually do so. Music came through the headphones, so it first got to my ears through a different channel and the baby listened through me. Thus, not only the outer acoustic senses are at work, but also my processed experience gets to her as well. So if I wanted to listen to some nice music, I would grab the Walkman, and listen, and feel that it got to her. These songs are familiar to her to this day. Actually, we sing them to the younger child with the older one. They have the effects of lullabies. They really do calm them down. It was surprising even for me how sensitive they were towards music. If I were playing a sorrowful or emotional song on the flute, they would start tearing up. First it was Lili, she was very cute, she would just stare at me with wide eyes and slowly they would fade with tears. She would be completely overwhelmed by emotion. That was enough evidence for me.

Living together for nine months is great to prepare them for what they will be born into. I even showed Lili the environment in which she would be. I walked around the apartment, looking around, so that she could see where she would be living, while I was preparing everything. At the time, we were living in an apartment that had an enormous room, so we had a bedroom and a nursery all in one. Then, when she was born, we moved her cradle to where our bed used to be, so where I lay when she was still in my belly.

We have a dog, a poor old thing. Naturally, we locked him out of the room after Lili's birth, but while I was still expecting her, a strong bond formed between the two of them. Sometimes I could lie down for a rest in the afternoon. Then the dog would hop up onto my side and snuggle to my belly. These two would huddle together and relax happily. Our dog is sick with epilepsy. Lili felt it once and signalled that there was something wrong with the dog. I woke up to the child squirming anxiously in my belly. I got up and saw the dog, looking ill. So they were very close in relation, even though when this incident occurred, Lili was quite tiny, three–four months at most, in my belly.

By now, sadly, the poor thing had to be locked out completely, once Félix was born. The first weeks, months, he howled and sobbed through. And he is old, deaf and blind by now too. But if I leave the kid in the stroller outside, he will lie down beside it and guard it. Lili was out of it, since she cannot play with him either for he is old. Perhaps she is even mad a bit at him. Although she was nice now, she gave him one of her old, ragged balls.

When Lili was born, I truly experienced the uses of bonding analysis at her birth, in concrete practice too. It lasted a day, but it was not a bad experience and neither was it difficult. It went down much like my mother had given birth to me: it can be split into two 12-hour phases. In the first 12 hours I was at home, in the second phase, I went to the hospital. The thing that caused a bit of a problem was that towards the end, the process stopped for a few hours, I lay in the bathtub and did not feel ill at all, on the contrary, and the birth just stopped. Then, the doctor said that up until then he had leisurely assisted, but by now we must progress. He gave a deadline. If I did not gather myself by then, or did not do anything, then the infusion and accelerator would come, and then we would change from an alternative birth to a good doctor birth. So that was the situation, and I stopped then and there to wonder a bit. Then I came to my senses and asked the baby, come on, time to go. I knew fully what she needed to do because our relation was not ready for the pushing phase. Then, I mediated to her, that this would be the task, I told her in the form of an image, no speech. She turned, faced the right way, started going down the birth canal and managed to wriggle herself in enough for her to be pushed out naturally.

Afterwards, things turned depressing for me, giving birth was a tremendous trauma. I was so sad that she would no longer be in my belly. This surfaced weeks before the birth, in the analytical sessions as well, in my emotions. I needed at least three weeks to get harmonized with her. Her father was always with her. The main trauma was that it should have been the three of us … I give birth to the kid, and then Zoli is kicked out of the hospital since daddy should go home for a beer with friends. They took the kid away from me for inspection and placed me in a room. And I had to stay there. I felt so sorry for Zoli, there he was, standing at the door and then daddy should go home. But that is not the point of it at all! So I did experience it tragically. In the hospital, there was a sweet baby-loving nurse and a meaner type, and you were so help-less regarding whom you would end up with … In my experience, there are baby-friendly and mother-friendly hospitals in Hungary, but there is no baby- and mother-friendly hospital in one. I realized that I got sick from having to stay for the third and fourth day as well … I left a day early with Lili anyway, even though I was completely out of it on the third day, I got depressed. Later, I did not stay two full days with Félix. I was home on the second evening and the next morning. I knew I would get sick from the hospital.

So luckily Zoli held the child, they were very close for three weeks then. And I suddenly realized how madly in love I was with my child and the entire thing was blown away like dust. There was no such thing with Félix. The hospital was undergoing construction, so they left the two of us together. My child, whom I had given birth to at three in the afternoon, was not seen by a paediatrician until 11 the next day. There was great peace and happiness. I thought that if only Lili could have stayed with me, just like that!

When I was expecting Félix, Lili wanted a little sister and Zoli was also more of a girl supporter. In my family, three of us are girls, so it was natural for me to have a girl first. Then, on the 16th week, it turned out that there was something of an excess of amniotic fluid and because of that, I had to go back to ultrasound. Then, I asked for them to tell me whether it was a boy or a girl. The doctor showed us a picture, and my husband and I saw a little bump. What else could it be? replied the doctor – a fanny – this is the word he used. So it is a girl, everyone was overjoyed, me not so much, for me all that mattered was for the child to be healthy. So, we named him Molli. We were already seeing everything in pink and even called him that. But meanwhile I asked him and he said to me that he was a boy. When I went to the last ultrasound on the 38th week, they finally told me, that he had an unmistakable penis.

Félix was born a week early. He was even bigger than Lili. At Lili's birth, the doctor said that she could barely fit through, so it was quite decent of Félix to come out sooner. Now, this is interesting, let us discuss when he will be born. When Lili was three months old in my belly, I took a look at the calen-dar. She was scheduled for a Friday, and on Thursday, there was a full moon. I felt certain that she would be born a day sooner, almost as if it had been arranged. And that is when she was born. We knew with Lili, that I am the type that gets excited at a full moon, it tones me up, and I thought that I could not last another day. With Félix, I checked when the full moon would appear, but it fell right in the middle, two weeks here, two weeks there. I thought that this would pass without complications. I did not plan to give birth two weeks too soon, or over carry him. Then, on the last examination, which was on a Tuesday, we agreed that he should be born exactly a week from then, on Tuesday. But he made up his mind and was born the next day. It was good for both the doctor and myself.

Before I would have gone in to give birth, I had two goals: to avoid an episiotomy, and to go home as soon as possible. I succeeded in both. I simply had to stay in hospital two days for the social insurance.

When I was pregnant with the second child, Lili got used to our bed again and slept with us, all three together. She would snuggle up to my belly, and hug and kiss the little child. She would instruct us to lie with mommy and daddy on the two sides, her in the middle. I could not turn to my other side because the kids had to face towards each other and the parents enfolded them like so, forming a nest. Good grief the pain I went through! This nest motif appeared in her first drawings too. She drew a huge nest on the wall at home too. One of her first drawings was done when she was two. It was a doodle of a circle. I asked her, what is this? A planet, no, not even a planet – she answered, grabbed that terribly pointy pencil, rounded two eyes and a mouth. She then drew a stick man. No, it is a Martian, she said. I was not pregnant with Félix around that time. It started coming together how interesting this was as well, the nest, the child, and by then she was saying that she wanted a little brother, because our friends were having babies one after the other. This was a daily topic. Martian – so babies come from space. And the nest motifs multiplied too. She became a mom as well and that was when she picked out a teddy bear, which is still her favourite.

If I think it through now, the relationship of the two kids, and how Félix simply knew he had a sibling! While Lili was in my belly, Zoli had a role of his own, which Lili took on in some respect when I was expecting Félix. I always bathed at seven, when I was pregnant. Then Zoli came in and we talked about the baby, and also about giving birth. And now that Félix was in my belly, Lili took over this external role and maintained a constant connection with the baby. She caressed my belly, sprinkled water on it while I was taking a bath and waited for the baby to move for her. When he did not move, she would get mad and wait for his answer, since she had messaged him. Félix adores Lili just as much now, but he is somewhat reserved towards her. He is not a mere toy but an independent being and he tries to convey that to her within his own constraints. So, for instance, when Lili gives him a toy and would later want to take it, he does not let go, but just clings on. By the way, it is happening much earlier in his development that he does not give back compared to the average baby. This can be associated with age as well. The same thing happened while he was still in my belly and Lili wanted the baby to move. Naturally, 90% of the time, he did not move.

Their difference in character was already unveiled in my belly. Lili differs because she is a firstborn and when there is no sibling around, the parents are completely stuck to their kid. Lili is an actress. If someone wanted her to move, she expressly delivers. When the doctor examined me and she was a big baby in my belly, she started wiggling. I am certain that she knew Hidas as well, because I went regularly and that she recognized the gynaecologist doctor – from the tapping too. There was a slight medical issue with Lili, and during that time, I had to go to weekly examinations. There is some flaw in almost every pregnancy, and since I am prone to anxiety, truth be told, I was very worried. Then these cast a shadow on our relationship. Eventually, everything is beautiful, but I will not forget that. The doctor examined me a lot around that time. Lili recognized him and would purposefully wiggle as he wanted. Félix rather pulled away. It remains all the same. Lili immediately gets close to everyone, as I have told you, she is an actress. She gives a show and gladly speaks of Félix's birth too. She took me to the hospital and brought me dinner in the evening. She actually peeked in to see what was happening with the kid. She then came in everyday and also to take the baby home – with her grandparents of course. So she was always in the picture, almost like the main star.

Félix is more of a mommy type, shy. He adores his father too. But, for instance, if Zoli comes home after a long day and leans against me, Félix would smell the cigarettes and people on him and he would flinch. It would even take a few minutes for him to loosen up. He is much more timid, introverted, so not the actor character.

I probably related to the bonding analysis differently than most mothers. The entire thing is on a different level for me. I always tried to examine what was happening to me with a critical eye, thus with an eye seeking to improve things and do them better. For instance, my experiences show that it could be beneficial for new mothers to continue a bit, for the sake of a "shake-off" analysis or two. I recognized this from the fact that I had the chance to go back after the birth, because for me, the analysis continued either way. Therefore, to this day I maintain that it is not adequate to follow the bonding until birth, because once the baby is born, the two have to grow close again. Even though there is a pre-existing, tight bond and they have come to know each other, nonetheless it continues differently; there may even be a great disappointment, for while the baby is still in your belly, everything goes smoothly. Later on, the kid will cry and problems may arise, especially after your first birth, with an inexperienced mother.

Despite being sceptical and examining myself from the outside also for my profession's sake in the bonding analysis, I know for certain that it helped me a lot. The thought of working as a psychologist once the kids are older came to my mind. I would like to work in this field, with mothers-to-be, and the babies developing within them. So, I would gladly learn the method.

Tables

Creating positive emotions in the mother and father

Genre	Goal	Practice	Time
1. **Interaction**	Releases endorphins, strengthens mother–father bonding	As much time as possible	Prenatal period
2. **Massage**	Provides joy and relaxation, strengthens bonding, freshens circulation, prevents leg cramps	Step-by-step massage on all parts of the body	Half an hour, two–three times a week from the first trimester to birth
3. **Breathing**	Helps with relaxation and metabolism, proper oxygenation stimulates the growth and intelligence of the child	Breathing exercises	5 minutes every day from the first trimester to birth
4. **Relaxation**	Stops anxiety and stress, helps with pains and dissolves tension	Relaxation programmes	5 minutes every day from the first trimester to birth
5. **Visualization**	Lessens fear of birth and releases endorphins, strengthens prenatal bonding	Visualizing exercises	5 minutes every day from the first trimester to birth
6. **Stimulating the mother's sixth sense**	Releases endorphins, encourages the emotional and physical growth of the baby	Viewing pretty images, listening to classical music	5–10 minutes every day from the first trimester to birth

Creating a positive external environment

Genre	Goal	Practice	Time
1. **Prenatal auditory stimulation** • **tape/disc etc.**	• Stimulates brain cells and nerve fields • Helps growth of brain and intelligence	• The mother, her speaking voice and song • Classical music	• 15 minutes every night from week 20 • 15 minutes every evening from week 20
2. **Prenatal tactile stimulation** • **Feeling objects out connected with the sound of the material** • **Tapping games** • **Rhythmic tapping games combined with singing** • **Hot-and-cold water** • **Games involving water**	• Helps linguistic, physical and social growth • Helps love and bonding • Releases endorphins • Decreases aggressive behaviour • Provides emotional security • Strengthens bonding • Stimulates brain growth • Helps intelligence • Learning and adapting to changes in temperature	• Tape/disc etc. (sounds of nature, e.g., the sea, birds) • Light fingertip massage from the baby's head to toe • Lightly tapping the abdominal wall if the baby moves • Lightly, rhythmically tapping the behind of the child accompanied by singing • Placing a hot or cold bottle of water on the belly of the mother near the baby's back	• Whenever possible from week 20 on • 5 minutes every evening from week 20, 30–30 seconds from week 24, from week 28, 2 minutes every evening
3. **Prenatal visual stimulation**	• Stimulating the vestibular system • Stimulates visual brain cells • Helps motor functions to advance	• Gently water jetting the abdominal wall while bathing • Placing strong light on the low belly pointed at the baby's eyes, then moving it front–back and left–right	• 20 minutes every evening from week 20
4. **Prenatal vestibular stimulation** • **rocking chair**	• Stimulates vestibular nerve fields • Develops the motorium and balance, possesses a calming effect • Aids emotional and cognitive development	• Rocking back and forth, left to right in a rocking chair	

References

Arabin, B. (1994): *Videoband*. Sophia Ziekenhuis, Zwolle, Niederlande.

Bick, E. (1964): Notes on infant observation in psycho-analytic training. *International Journal of Psychoanalysis* 45: 558–566.

Birnholz, J., et al. (1978): Fetal movement patterns: A possible means of defining neurologic developmental milestones in utero. *American Journal of Roentgenology* 130: 537–540.

Blazy, H. (2001): *Mit dem Vater zu Dritten*. Vortrag gehalten auf dem vierten Nationalkongress der ungarischen Sektion der ISPPM. 6–8. Oktober 2001, Budapest.

Blomberg, S. (1980): Influence of maternal distress during pregnancy on postnatal development. *Acta Psychiatrica Scandinavia* 62: 405–416.

Borstad, M. (1988): Interszubjektivitás a dialektikus kapcsolatelmélet tükrében. *Pszichoterápia* 7/5: 349–363.

Brezinka, C., et al. (1994): Denial of pregnancy: Obstetrical aspect. *Journal of Psychosomatic Obstetrics and Gynecology* 15: 1–8.

Busnel, M.C., et al. (1998): What sounds reach fetuses: Biological and nonbiological modeling of the transmission of pure tones. *Developmental Psychobiology* 33: 203–219.

Bustan, M.N., Coker, A.L. (1994): Maternal attitude towards pregnancy and the risk of neonatal death. *American Journal of Public Health* 84: 411–414.

Chamberlain, D. (1996): Neue Forschungsergebnisse aus der Beobachtung vorgeburtlichen Verhaltens. In: L. Janus and S. Haibach (eds.): *Seeliches Erleben vor und während der Geburt*. Lingua Med Verlag, Neu-Isenburg: 23–37.

Chapman, J.S. (1975): The relation between auditory stimulation of short gestation infants and their gross motor limb activity during coitus. *Acta Obstetricia et Gynecologica Scandinavica* 65: 853–855.

Collins, S.K., Kuck, K. (1991): Music therapy in the neonatal intensive care unit. *Neonatal Network* 9: 23–26.

David, H.P., Dytrych, Z., Matejček, Z., Schüller, V. (1988): *Born unwanted*. Springer, New York; Avicenum, Prague.

Davis, M., Wallbridge, D. (1981): *Boundary and Space. An Introduction to the Work of D.W. Winnicott*. Brunner/Mazel, New York.

DeCasper, A.J. (1994): Fetal reactions to recurrent maternal speech. *Infant Behaviour and Development* 17: 159–164.

DeMause, L. (1974): The evolution of childhood. In: L. DeMause (ed.): *The History of Childhood*. Psychohistory Press, New York: 1–74.

DiPietro, J.A., et al. (1999): Effects of socioeconomic status and psychosocial stress on the development of the fetus. *Annals of the New York Academy of Sciences* 896: 356–358.

Emde, R.N. (1971): Neonatal smiling in REM states. IV. Premature study. *Child Development* 42: 1657–1661.

Fedor-Freybergh, P.G., Vogel, M.L. (eds.) (1988): *Prenatal and Perinatal Psychology and Medicine.* Parthenon, Casterton Hall.

Feldmár, A. (1997): *Tudatállapotok szivárványa.* Gigant Kiadó, Debrecen.

Ferenczi, S. (1913): A valóságérzék fejlődésfokai és patologikus visszatérésük. *Gyógyászat* (53) 46:794–797, 47: 815–817.

Ferenczi, S. (1939): Das unwillkommene Kind und sein Todestrieb. *Bausteine der Psychoanalyse.* III. Huber, Bern: 446–452.

Ferreira, A.J. (1960): The pregnant woman's emotional attitude and its reflection on the newborn. *American Journal of Orthopsychiatry* 30: 553–561.

Field, T. (1981): Infant arousal attention and affect during early interactions. *Advances in Infancy Research* 1: 57–100.

Field, T. (1987): Affective and interactive disturbances in infants. In: J.D. Osofsky (ed.): *Handbook of Infant Development.* Wiley, New York: 972–1005.

Field, T., et al. (1983): Discrimination and imitation of facial expression by term and preterm neonates. *Infant Behavior and Development* 6: 485–489.

Fodor, N. (1949): *The Search for the Beloved: A Clinical Investigation of the Trauma of Birth and Pre-natal Condition.* Hermitage Press, New York.

Freud, S. (1946): Das Unbewusste. *Gesammelte Werke X.* Imago, London: 264–303.

Freud, S. (1972): *Die Traumdeutung.* Studienausgabe. Band II. S. Fischer, Frankfurt am Main.

Gabrielsson, A. (1991): Experiencing music. *Canadian Music Educator* 33: 21–26.

Gatts, J.D., et al. (1994): A modified newborn intensive care unit environment may shorten hospital stay. *Journal of Perinatology* 14: 422–427.

Giannakoulopoulos, X., et al. (1994): Fetal plasma-cortisol and beta-endorphin response to intrauterine needling. *The Lancet* 344: 77–81.

Hansen, D., et al. (2000): Serious life events and congenital malformations: A national study with complete follow-up. *The Lancet* 356: 875–880.

Hau, T.F. (1973): Perinatale und pränatale Faktoren der Neurosenätiologie. In: Graber, G.H., Kruse, F. (eds.): *Vorgeburtliches Seelenleben.* Goldmann Medizin, München.

Hidas, Gy. (1999): *Kommunikációs utak az anya-magzat kapcsolatanalízisben.* Unpublished manuscript.

Hidas, Gy. (2000): *Az anya-magzat kapcsolatanalízis.* Paper presented at the Congress of the Hungarian Psychoanalytical Society, 27–28 October 2000, Budapest.

Hultman, C.M., et al. (1997): Prenatal and neonatal risk factors for schizophrenia. *The British Journal of Psychiatry* 170: 128–133.

Humphrey, T. (1978): Function of the nervous system during prenatal life. In: U. Stave (ed.): *Perinatal Physiology.* Plenum Medical, New York: 651–683.

Huttunen, M.O., Niskanen, P. (1978): Prenatal loss of father and psychiatric disorders. *Archives of General Psychiatry* 35: 429–431.

Janus, L., Häsing, H. (1994): *Ungewollte Kinder.* Rowohlt, Reinbek.

Leboyer, F. (1975): *Birth without Violence.* Rigby, Adelaide; Wildwood House, London.

Lou, H.C., et al. (1994): Prenatal stressors of human life affect fetal brain development. *Developmental Medicine and Child Neurology* 36: 826–832.

Mancuso, S. (2000): Pregnant women 'Inherit' some characteristics of their children. *Zenit. org News Agency.*

Matejček, Z., Dytrych, Z. (1994): Abgelehnte Schwangerschaft und ihre Folgen. In: Janus, L., Häsing, H. (eds.): Ungewollte Kinder. Rowohlt, Reinbek: 194–199.

McIntosh, L.J., et al. (1995): Perinatal outcome of broken marriage in the inner city. *Obstetrics and Gynecology* 85: 233–236.

McGue, M. (1977): The democracy of the genes. *Nature* 388: 417–418.

Mendizza, M. (1996): Lifelong patterns of fear and wholeness. Interview with Barbara Findeisen. *Touch the Future.* Nevada City, CA.

Milani-Comparetti, A. (1981): The neuro-physiologic and clinical implications of studies on fetal motor behaviour. *Seminars in Perinatology* 5: 183–189.

Mosser, C. (1989): *Effet physiologique des stimulations sonores chez le premature.* Dissertation. University of Paris XII.

Nimby, G.T., et al. (1999): Maternal distress and congenital malformations: Do mothers of malformed fetuses have more problems? *Journal of Psychiatric Research* 33: 291–301.

Olds, C. (1986): A sound start in life. *Pre- and Perinatal Psychology Journal* 1: 82–85.

Piontelli, A. (1992): *From Fetus to Child. An Observational and Psychoanalytic Study.* Routledge, London.

Portmann, A. (1969): *Biologische Fragmente zu einer Lehre vom Menschen.* Schwabe, Basel.

Prechtl, H. (1987): Wie entwickelt sich das Verhalten vor der Geburt? In Niemitz, C. (ed.): *Erbe und Umwelt: Zur Natur von Anlage und Selbstbestimmung des Menschen.* Suhrkamp, Frankfurt: 141–155.

Raffai, J. (1988): *Towards a New Psychotherapeutic Approach of Schizophrenia.* Presented at the WPA Symposium, Washington, DC.

Raffai, J. (1991): Auf dem Weg zur neuen somatopsychoanalytischen Therapie der Schizophrenie. In: L. Janus (ed.): *Erscheinungsweisen pränatalen und perinatalen Erlebens in den verschiedenen psychotherapeutischen Settings.* Textstudio Gross, Heidelberg.

Raffai, J. (1994–95): The prenatal roots of schizophrenia. *Psychodynamic Counselling* 1: 461–464.

Raffai, J. (1995a): Az intrauterin anyareprezentáns. *Pszichoterápia* 4/5: 343–349.

Raffai, J. (1995b): The psychoanalysis of somatic sensations. *International Journal of Prenatal and Perinatal Psychology and Medicine* 7: 39–42.

Raffai, J. (1996): Der intrauterine Mutterrepräsentant. *International Journal of Prenatal and Perinatal Psychology and Medicine* 8: 357–365.

Raffai, J. (1997): Mother-child bonding analysis in the prenatal realm. *International Journal of Prenatal and Perinatal Psychology and Medicine* 9: 407–415.

Raffai, J. (1998a): Mother-child bonding analysis: The strange events of a queer world. *International Journal of Prenatal and Perinatal Psychology and Medicine* 10: 163–173.

Raffai, J. (1998b): *Megfogantam, tehát vagyok. Párbeszéd a babával az anyaméhben.* Útmutató Kiadó, Budapest.

Rank, O. (1924): *Das Trauma der Geburt und seine Bedeutung für die Psychoanalyse.* Internationaler Psychoanalytischer Verlag, Leipzig, Wien, Zürich.

Reinold, E. (1971): Beobachtung fetaler Aktivität in der ersten Hälfte der Gravidität mit dem Ultraschall. *Pädiatrie und Pädologie* 6: 274–279.

Roe, K., Drivas, A. (1993): Planned conception and infant functioning at age three months. *American Journal of Orthopsychiatry* 63: 120–125.

Rottmann, G. (1974): Untersuchungen über Einstellungen zur Schwangerschaft und zur fötalen Entwicklung. In: Graber, G.H. (ed.): *Pränatale Psychologie.* Kindler, München: 68–87.

Sadger, J. (1941): Preliminary study of the psychic life of the fetus and the primary germ. *Psychoanalytic Review* 28: 327–358.

Salk, L. (1962): Mothers' heartbeat as an imprinting stimulus. *Transactions of the New York Academy of Sciences* 24: 753–763.

Sallenbach, W.B. (1993): The intelligent prenate: paradigms in prenatal learning and bonding. In: T. Blum (ed.): *Prenatal Perception, Learning and Bonding.* Leonardo Publishers, Berlin, Hong Kong, Seattle: 61–106.

Sontag, L. (1966): Implications of fetal behavior and environment for adult personalities. *Annals of the New York Academy of Sciences* 134: 782–786.

Stern, D. (1985): *The Interpersonal World of the Infant. A View from Psychoanalysis and Developmental Psychology.* Basic Books, New York.

Stott, D.H. (1963): How a disturbed pregnancy can harm the child. *New Scientist* 320: 13–17.

Tajani, E., Ianniruberto, A. (1990): The uncovering of fetal competence. In: M. Papini et al. (eds.): *Development, Handicap, Rehabilitation: Practice and Theory.* Elsevier, Amsterdam: 3–8.

Thoman, E.B., Ingersoll, E.W. (1993): Learning in premature infants. *Developmental Psychology* 29: 692–700.

Trehub, S.E. (1987): Infants' perception of musical patterns. *Perception and Psychophysics* 41: 635–641.

Truby, H.M. (1971): Prenatal and neonatal speech, "pre-speech", and an infantile-speech lexicon. *Word* 27: 57–101.

van der Bergh, B. (1990): The influence of maternal emotions during pregnancy on fetal and neonatal behavior. *Pre- and Perinatal Psychology Journal* 5: 119–130.

van der Bergh, B. (1992): Maternal emotions during pregnancy and fetal and neonatal behaviour. In: J.G. Nijhuis (ed.): *Fetal Behaviour: Developmental and Perinatal Aspects.* Oxford University Press, Oxford and New York: 157–178.

van der Bergh, B. (2001): *The Effect of Maternal Stress and Anxiety in Prenatal Life on Fetus and Child. An Overview of Research Findings.* Paper presented at the UNO Vienna Child Care Conference. Vienna

van Os, J., Selten, J.-P. (1998): Prenatal exposure to maternal stress and subsequent schizophrenia. *The British Journal of Psychiatry* 172: 324–326.

Vas, J. (2001): Interaktív pszichoneurobiológia (IPNB): szemléletváltás a humán kapcsolati dimenziók kutatásában. *Pszichoterápia* 10/5: 322–331.

Wilheim, J. (1995): *Unterwegs zur Geburt. Eine Brücke zwischen dem Biologischen und dem Psychischen.* Mattes Verlag, Heidelberg.

Zuckerman, B., et al. (1990): Maternal depressive symptoms during pregnancy, and newborn irritability. *Journal of Developmental and Behavioral Pediatrics* 11: 190–194.

Index

For Product Safety Concerns and Information please contact our EU
representative GPSR@taylorandfrancis.com
Taylor & Francis Verlag GmbH, Kaufingerstraße 24, 80331 München, Germany

www.ingramcontent.com/pod-product-compliance
Lightning Source LLC
Chambersburg PA
CBHW050655280326
41932CB00015B/2915